NEVER
SURRENDER

NEVER SURRENDER

A Soldier's Journey
to the Crossroads of
Faith and Freedom

LTG (Ret.) William G. Boykin

with Lynn Vincent

New York   Boston   Nashville

FaithWords
Hachette Book Group USA
237 Park Avenue
New York, NY 10017

Visit our Web site at www.faithwords.com.

Printed in the United States of America

First Edition: July 2008
10 9 8 7 6 5 4 3 2 1

FaithWords is a division of Hachette Book Group USA, Inc.
The FaithWords name and logo are trademarks of
Hachette Book Group USA, Inc.

Library of Congress Cataloging-in-Publication Data

Boykin, Jerry.
Never surrender : a soldier's journey to the crossroads of faith and
freedom / Jerry Boykin with Lynn Vincent. — 1st ed.
p. cm.
Includes bibliographical references.
ISBN-13: 978-0-446-58215-5
ISBN-10: 0-446-58215-8
1. Boykin, Jerry. 2. Generals—United States—
Biography. 3. United States. Army—Biography. 4. United
States—History, Military—20th century. 5. United States. Army.
Special Forces—Biography. 6. United States. Army. Delta Force—
Biography. 7. United States. Dept. of Defense—Officials and
employees—Biography. I. Vincent, Lynn. II. Title.
E840.5.B695A3 2008
355.0092—dc22
[B]
2007039791

To my family: Mom, April, Randy, Aaron,
Grant, and Mimi. And to my best pal, Ashley.
I love you all.

Special Forces Creed

I am an American Special Forces soldier. A professional!

I will do all that my nation requires of me.

I am a volunteer, knowing well the hazards of my profession. I serve with the memory of those who have gone before me: Roger's Rangers, Francis Marion, Mosby's Rangers, the first Special Service Forces and Ranger Battalions of World War II, the Airborne Ranger Companies of Korea.

I pledge to uphold the honor and integrity of all I am—in all I do.

I am a professional soldier. I will teach and fight wherever my nation requires. I will strive always, to excel in every art and artifice of war.

I know that I will be called upon to perform tasks in isolation, far from familiar faces and voices, with the help and guidance of my God.

I will keep my mind and body clean, alert and strong, for this is my debt to those who depend upon me.

I will not fail those with whom I serve.

I will not bring shame upon myself or the forces.

I will maintain myself, my arms, and my equipment in an immaculate state as befits a Special Forces soldier.

I will never surrender though I be the last. If I am taken, I pray that I may have the strength to spit upon my enemy. My goal is to succeed in any mission—and live to succeed again.

I am a member of my nation's chosen soldiery. God grant that I may not be found wanting, that I will not fail this sacred trust.

"De Opresso Liber."

Contents

NEVER
SURRENDER

AIR ASSAULT

Washington, D.C.
2003

1

WASHINGTON, D.C., IS A FICKLE BEAST—especially in February. In that month, the world's most powerful city can wrap itself in sheets of ice and dare folks to step outside. Or it can flirt a little, enticing with a false glimpse of spring. During the first week of February 2003, temperatures spiked into the fifties and I saw bureaucrats braving the Beltway in shirtsleeves when I arrived from Fort Bragg for an interview with Secretary of Defense Donald Rumsfeld.

I was a two-star Army general at the time—commander of the John F. Kennedy Special Warfare Center and School at Fort Bragg—and the Army had nominated me for a third star. Here's the way that works: Up through their second star, military officers advance in rank through promotion boards. But for any stars after that, the defense secretary has to submit a nomination to the President. Then the President has to endorse the nomination. *Then* the Senate has to confirm. That's one more hoop than a Supreme Court justice has to jump through.

And Rumsfeld added another hoop: anyone nominated for a third star had to come in and interview with him personally.

Which was why I made the trip to D.C. Rumsfeld was still in the media's good graces then, which meant he was in America's good graces. (The former, I would soon learn the hard way, is finely calibrated with the latter.) The Secretary had just overseen the U.S. military's crushing defeat of the Taliban, the group U.S. intelligence identified as the primary backer of Osama Bin Laden's September 11 attack. Now for some months, his attention had been tuned to a new target: Iraq. As Saddam Hussein pretended to cooperate with weapons inspections ordered by the United Nations Security Council, Rumsfeld, a former fighter pilot who served in Congress and under three presidents, sparred with the press over the Bush administration's case for war. In the midst of all that, I walked into the Pentagon, just a routine item on the defense secretary's daily calendar.

The world's largest office building, the Pentagon is built in five concentric rings. More than seventeen miles of corridors wind through the place, and I truly believe a person could wander for days and never find the office he was looking for. As I made my way to the inner sanctum, the powerful "E Ring" where the Secretary has his office, I remembered my first time there twenty-five years before. I had arrived just days after Iranian terrorists loyal to the radical cleric Ayatollah Khomeini seized the American embassy in Tehran. I was a young captain then, one of the first three officers to make the cut for America's brand-new, highly secret counterterrorism unit, Delta Force. I could recall hunkering down for days in a cipher-locked secret room off the E Ring, helping plan Delta's first mission—rescuing American hostages from Iran. I had done a Pentagon tour since then, but those tense, smoky sessions spent calculating against impossible odds were what flashed through my mind as I headed for Secretary Rumsfeld's office.

His senior military aide, Lieutenant General John Craddock, showed me into a large, dark-paneled executive space with a sweeping view of the Potomac and the Capitol complex beyond. Rumsfeld kept a large mahogany desk in his office, backed by a matching credenza. But there was no chair behind the desk. That's because he never sat down while he worked. Instead, he did correspondence and paperwork behind an elegant chart table, standing up.

"General Boykin!" said Rumsfeld, striding toward me in his customary fleece vest. He always took off his jacket in his office, but thought the air conditioning chilly and usually wore a fleece vest over his shirt and tie. "Thank you for coming in. Here, have a seat."

He and I sat at a small circular conference table, opposite the stretch conference table on the other side of the room. General Craddock sat down on a sofa nearby.

Rumsfeld flipped through my service record, which, because of my career in Special Operations and intelligence, was classified. "You have a very interesting record here," he said. "Spent a lot of years in Delta Force."

"Yes, sir," I said. "About thirteen." I had been a founding member of Delta Force, and later its commanding officer.

"You've spent most of your career in Special Operations?"

"Yes, sir. I did spend some time on the staff of the Joint Chiefs and some over at CIA, but most of my career has been in Special Ops."

With Delta, I oversaw both the rescue of CIA operative Kurt Muse from a Panamanian prison and the capture of Manuel Noriega, the brutal dictator who put him there. In Colombia, I helped hunt down the drug lord Pablo Escobar, a cruel and filthy-rich thug who terrorized a nation, personally ordering the deaths of more than a thousand people. The Secretary noted that I had also hunted war criminals in Bosnia, helped rescue hostage missionaries in Sudan, and tracked kidnappers in El Salvador. Among other things.

"You have two purple hearts," Rumsfeld said. "Where'd you get those?"

"Grenada, 1983, and Mogadishu, Somalia, 1993."

"You know, I still don't understand that, how Mogadishu was considered a failure," he said. "When you consider the statistics, it appears to me that we won that battle."

"Well, that's always been an issue with me," I told the Secretary. I felt fairly certain Rumsfeld knew that the popular version of the events—both the book, *Black Hawk Down*, and the movie made from it—omitted my role as mission commander. "We killed or wounded eleven hundred, but lost eighteen and had seventy-six wounded. It's an example of how you can win a battle and lose a war because of politics."

"Yes, I agree with you," Rumsfeld said, smiling grimly. "We're dealing with some of that right now."

Exactly thirty minutes after it began, my interview was politely terminated by the Secretary. I walked out of his office and didn't hear another word about our meeting for weeks. I was excited about the reason for the timing of my promotion. The chief of staff of the Army, General Rick Shinseki, had offered me a plum assignment as deputy commander of the Training and Doctrine Command at Fort Monroe, Virginia. Not only was it an opportunity to work directly with soldiers again, it was in the Tidewater region of Virginia, where my brother and sister and their kids lived. My wife, Ashley, and I had long wanted to buy a home in Virginia, with space for nieces, nephews, and grandchildren. The TRADOC assignment seemed like the ideal twilight tour—a low-key but productive way to wind up what would by then be a thirty-five-year Army career. I immediately said yes.

Then, in late February at a military convention in Fort Lauderdale, Army vice chief of staff General Jack Keene walked up and put his hand on my shoulder. "Jerry, Secretary Rumsfeld told me he was very impressed with your interview. You did well."

I was pleased. All the pieces appeared to be falling into place: it looked as if I'd be promoted to lieutenant general, serve my final Army tour in a command that would leave an important legacy for future troops, and retire to a house in the country. Perfect.

Or so it seemed at the time.

2

A COUPLE OF WEEKS LATER, as the defense department built up for operations in Iraq, the Pentagon called. "Secretary Rumsfeld would like to see you again," his military assistant told me over the phone.

Unusual, I thought. I hadn't heard of any three-star nominee being called back for a second interview. But Rumsfeld was the boss, so I was off again to Washington.

"I want to talk more about your time at CIA," he said after we'd settled into his office in mid-March, two days after the U.S. launched operations in Iraq. I had worked for the CIA from November 1995 until June 1997, and I briefed Rumsfeld on my responsibilities there. Then he told me a story.

The rest of the federal government was rich in spy agencies—the CIA; the National Security Agency; the National Geospatial-Intelligence Agency; the State Department's Intelligence and Research; and other outfits totalling fifteen agencies in all. But the military intelligence problem became clear to Rumsfeld, he said, when he wanted to send Army Special Forces into Afghanistan to link up with the Northern Alliance to fight against the Taliban.

"My staff told me that the only way to do it was to send them in with CIA," Rumsfeld told me. "I said, 'Why do I have to put military people in harm's way under the authority of George Tenet?'" Tenet was still Director of Central Intelligence at the time.

He didn't have to, Rumsfeld's advisors said, except that he really had no choice. Military intel had never established the kind of liaison with the Northern Alliance that CIA had. And it had been doing it for years. In other words, CIA had its spooks deployed all over the globe, building relationships with key factions that might become strategically important in future conflicts. After 9/11, the Northern Alliance became strategically important, and CIA was the only game in town.

"I don't want that to happen in the future," Rumsfeld told me. "To prevent it, I'm forming a new undersecretary for intelligence and I'm nominating Steve Cambone for the position. I want you to go down and talk to him."

Rumsfeld meant right then, so I did.

Steve Cambone was one of those PhDs who is brilliant, sometimes abrasive, and usually right. Earlier in his career, he worked at Los Alamos Laboratories. But by the time I walked down the E Ring corridor to see him that day, he had been on Rumsfeld's team in one capacity or another for about seven years and was his most trusted staff officer. A visionary, Cambone was a rare breed in the defense department: a person who was able to say no to things that didn't make sense to him. He was fiercely loyal to Rumsfeld, but one of the few people who could actually influence him even when he didn't want to be influenced.

When we sat down in his office, Cambone asked me about my background, and I gave him the twenty-five-cent biographical sketch. Then, without any kind of run-up or drum roll, he said, "We're trying to put together a team here that will help this department in the area of intelligence. I'd like to know if you'd be willing to be part of that team."

The next thing I knew, Cambone offered me the position of deputy undersecretary of defense for intelligence.

Believe it or not, my heart sank. I could see the TRADOC dream tour crumbling away. It was clear Cambone and Rumsfeld had already talked about me, and I was professional enough to know that I needed to serve where I was asked to serve.

"Yes, sir," I told Cambone. "I'm willing."

It was the only right answer. Had I known that by fall my answer would lead directly to the greatest trial of my life, I might have given him a different one.

3

THE OFFICE WAS STILL GETTING ORGANIZED when I arrived in July. I was back on the E Ring, this time in an office of my own. But on a corridor housing more brass than the Queen Mary, my three stars didn't rate fancy accommodations. I had what they call a "breadbox" office. Temporary, they said, a tiny room just big enough to hold a desk, two chairs, and a bookcase. I had a nice view, though, with a window facing the Potomac.

That's where I was when my phone chirped on October 14, 2003. My secretary, Sandy, was on the line. "General, Aram Roston from NBC News is on the phone for you."

For more than three decades, I managed to keep a low media profile. Even during the *Black Hawk Down* uproar—the book, the movie, and all that—I tried hard to steer clear of reporters and writers, preferring to let the facts speak for themselves. Unfortunately, I learned that doesn't always happen. As much as anything, that got me wondering what Roston wanted.

"General Boykin, I'm Aram Roston from NBC," he said when I picked up the phone.

"Hi, Mr. Roston. What can I do for you?" I said.

"I'd like to talk to you about high-value targets."

"What do you want to talk about?"

"It's your responsibility to track these people down," he said.

CIA and NSA would be surprised to hear that, I thought.

"You're getting into a classified area here," I told him. "It's really not something I can talk about. But so that you know, chasing HVTs is not my primary task." What I didn't say was that the undersecretary for intelligence neither collected nor analyzed intelligence. We were a policy organization.

Then the conversation turned a weird corner: "You know, you're a controversial character," Roston said.

Controversial? In nearly thirty-three years, I'd hardly poked my head into public view. How controversial could I be?

"Why am I controversial?" I asked Roston.

"They've chosen you to go after these high-profile Islamic figures, and you have a track record of hating Islam," he said. "Are you suitable for this job?"

Hating Islam? What was he talking about? I had hunted down war criminals who tortured and murdered Muslims in Bosnia, and helped train Muslim Special Forces in Sudan. And hadn't I just told him I wasn't in charge of pursuing HVTs? Apparently this reporter considered himself so savvy he wasn't going to let a simple thing like honest answers throw him off track.

"I respect the right of everyone including Muslims to worship as they choose," I told Roston. "I've spent thirty-three years defending those rights."

He went on, "You've made a statement to a Somali warlord that your God was bigger than his."

He had to be talking about Osman Atto, chief financier and glorified henchman for the Somali warlord Mohamed Farrah Aidid. Atto ran the profiteering end of Aidid's theft of United Nations food shipments, brokering the sale of food taken from the mouths of starving people to make money for Aidid, who during the early 1990s brutalized and murdered the leaders of rival clans in order to consolidate his own power in the Somali capital.

As commander of Delta Force, on assignment with Task Force Ranger in the fall of 1993, I oversaw the hunt for Atto during the U.S. attempt to capture Aidid. Whenever news cameras were near, Atto mocked us.

"The Americans will never catch me," he boasted on CNN. "Allah will protect me."

So, when Allah failed to do so, and Atto was in our custody, sure—I confronted him with a message of my own. But it wasn't the one the American media reported, the one Roston was now repeating.

"I didn't say that to him," I told Roston. "I made that statement in a church."

I hadn't run an op since 1998 (as a general, you fire off more memos than bullets), but my talks before churches and civic groups were my way of helping regular citizens join in an epic battle. I urged Christians to pray not only for our troops, but for the leadership in America. I sometimes ended my talks by saying, "Fight with me!" I didn't mean through some kind of holy war. I meant spiritually, through prayer, interceding with God that He would keep our men and women safe, and help our leaders make just decisions.

At every event, people would come up after my talk and say something like, "I have a son serving in Afghanistan. I am so encouraged to know that there are Christian leaders in today's military who believe in prayer. I'll be praying for my son and praying for you, too."

But I didn't have a chance to explain all that to Roston, who then said, "You've made statements like, 'God put George Bush in the White House.'"

"Yeah, I believe that." I also believed He put Bill Clinton in the White House, Tony Blair at Number 10 Downing Street, and Pol Pot over Cambodia. I believe God is sovereign over the affairs of men. Generals from George Washington to Stonewall Jackson to Douglas MacArthur believed that, too. *When did that become controversial?* I thought.

Roston went on. "You've said that the majority of the people in America didn't vote for Bush, but God put him in there."

In my head, I'm thinking, *Come on, Roston, the entire left wing of America believes that the majority of the people didn't put George W. Bush in the White House. Bush "stole" the election, remember?*

But I said, "Yes, sir, I believe that."

Roston continued, "You've said that this is a Christian nation."

"Well, that's just a historical fact. It also happens to be an English-speaking nation. Those are just facts of our country's history."

"You're an evangelical," Roston said.

It was an accusation. His tone would have fit easily with "You're a Nazi," or "You're a Klansman."

"Yes, I'm an evangelical."

"You're a public official now. You've cast this war in religious terms. And you're the man who is being held accountable for finding these high-value targets who are Islamic leaders."

"That's just not true. You're just wrong on that."

The truth was I would've been much happier if he had been right about the HVT part. I had chased HVTs all over the world, and I was good at it. I would've enjoyed hunting bad guys a lot more than pushing paper. But there was no way I would tell him that because it had become crystal clear that Aram Roston of NBC News was going to report the story he wanted to report, no matter what I said.

I decided I'd better at least make it official.

"Tell you what you need to do," I said. "You need to call the public affairs office."

Again, he appeared not to have heard me. "I'd like to come interview you."

"You need to call public affairs, and if they clear it, I'll sit down and have a talk with you."

He would keep agreeing to talk to public affairs, but would then ask another question.

Again and again, I repeated, "Look, you need to call public affairs. You need to get them involved in this, and then I'll talk to you."

We hung up. But the next day, Cambone's military assistant walked into my office and sat down across from me. "Aram Roston called again," she said. "He still wants to come and interview you. He says the story is going to air tonight on NBC."

"Has he talked with public affairs?"

"I asked him if he had. He said no."

Of course he said no, I thought. I wondered if Roston was playing an old reporter's game: put in a couple of calls, but don't take the steps that would actually result in a real interview.

"Tell him to call public affairs and I'll be glad to talk to him," I told Cambone's assistant.

But, of course, Roston never did call public affairs. That would've ruined the story—which, I would learn by sundown, had already been written.

4

—

SINCE MOVING into the E Ring, I'd kept pretty late hours, so it wasn't unusual that I was still at the office when the *NBC Nightly News* aired. My office opened off an administrative area where the deputy undersecretaries' secretaries had their desks. They had a television bolted to the wall out there that was usually tuned to the news. At six-thirty, I stepped out of my office to see what Aram Roston had managed to cobble together. Tish Long, the civilian deputy undersecretary for policy and resources, was already standing there, looking up at the set.

In a segue from international coverage, Tom Brokaw said, "Back in this country, there's a strange new development in the war on terror involving one of the leaders of a secretive new Pentagon unit formed to coordinate intelligence on terrorists and help hunt down Osama Bin Laden, Saddam Hussein, and other high-profile targets."

Secretive new Pentagon unit? I rolled my eyes at Tish. Calling the new undersecretary job a "secretive new Pentagon unit" was like calling a new variety of apple a "mysterious new red fruit." My job wasn't a secret, I wasn't coordinating intelligence, and I wasn't leading a "unit." They didn't even get the "new" part right: the Senate confirmed Steve Cambone eight months prior, in March. Apparently, Aram Roston hadn't listened to a word I'd said.

As these thoughts flashed through my mind, Brokaw finished his segue: "NBC News has learned that a highly decorated general has a history of outspoken and divisive views on religion, Islam in particular."

NBC's Lisa Myers began her report: "He's a highly decorated officer, twice wounded in battle, a warrior's warrior. The former commander of Army Special Forces, Lieutenant General William Jerry Boykin has led or been part of almost every recent U.S. military operation from the ill-fated attempt to rescue hostages in Iran to Grenada, Panama, Colombia, and Somalia...But [his] new assignment may be complicated by controversial views General Boykin, an evangelical Christian, has expressed in dozens of speeches and prayer breakfasts around the country. In a half dozen video and audio tapes obtained by NBC News, Boykin says America's true enemy is not Osama Bin Laden...NBC News military analyst Bill Arkin, who's been investigating Boykin for the *Los Angeles Times*, says the general casts the war on terror as a religious war."

NBC then began to air audio and video clips from talks I had given at churches, interspersing them with commentary from Myers.

MYERS: "Boykin recalls a Muslim fighter in Somalia who bragged on television the Americans would never get him because his God, Allah, would protect him."

Then, audio only of me, speaking at First Baptist Church in Daytona, Florida: "Well, you know what I knew, that my God was bigger than his. I knew that my God was a real God, and his was an idol."

Inwardly, I groaned. Lifted out of context, it sounded terrible.

MYERS: "In a phone conversation, Boykin tells NBC he respects Muslims and believes the radicals who attack America are 'not true followers of Islam.'"

When did I say that?

MYERS: "Boykin also routinely tells audiences that God, not the voters, chose President Bush."

Now there's some red meat for the anti-religion Left.

Then NBC trotted out a "military analyst," Bill Arkin, the reporter who had apparently been investigating me for a month but who hadn't bothered to interview me.

ARKIN: "I think that it is not only at odds with what the president believes, but it is a dangerous, extreme, and pernicious view that really has no place."

Based on what? I thought. *Your extensive conversations with me?*

I couldn't believe what I was hearing. The report concluded. Stunned, I walked back to my office and flipped off my light. Tish walked out into the main corridor beside me. "I'm really sorry," she told me. "That's exactly one of the reasons it's hard to get good people to serve in Washington."

"Thanks, Tish," I said. I struggled to find something to add, but it seemed as if a great weight was pressing down on my soul, and I couldn't find any words. "I don't know what else to say."

That night at home, my wife, Ashley, was my comforter. She had seen the report. When I walked through the door, she hugged me. "How are you doing?"

I looked at her and shook my head. "I just can't believe it."

I skipped dinner and slumped on the couch in my living room. My mind raced. I most certainly had not been out on an anti-Islam campaign. In fact, I was on the record in print, saying the war on terror was *specifically not* a war between Christianity and Islam. I had never contradicted that, but only discussed my personal faith and tried to encourage other Christians—many of whom had sons and daughters in harm's way—with this message: they had the weapon they needed to affect the outcome of a war between good and evil—prayer. *They were not powerless.*

But now I felt completely powerless. My first instinct should have been prayer, but it wasn't. I wanted to charge in. I wanted to fight back. But I immediately realized that despite my more than two decades in special warfare, I had no idea how to fight in this situation. In my career, I had faced down warlords and drug lords, dictators and terrorists, kidnappers, guerillas, and murderers. Them, I knew how to deal with.

Osman Atto flashed into my mind. He seemed to be exhibit A in NBC's "case" against me—and yet the man was corruption in human skin. In addition to helping Mohamed Farrah Aidid starve his own people, Atto built "technicals," half-ton pickups with gun mounts in the beds Aidid and his Habr Gidr clan used to intimidate and murder members of rival clans. The warring factions often spilled each other's blood in Mogadishu's narrow, dusty streets, with Aidid's more heavily armed clan mowing down men, women, and, if they got in the way, children.

Also, Atto was a major dealer in *khat,* a narcotic weed that transformed so many otherwise strong and able Somali men into walking zombies.

A medium-sized man with eyes like onyx, Atto spoke nearly perfect

English, which made him a good PR man for Aidid when news cameras rolled through the area. Despite his dark profession, Atto, whenever possible—and especially whenever a camera was in range—invoked Allah, trying to create the impression he was a devout, practicing Muslim. In fact, Osman Atto's gods were the oldest idols of all: money and power.

In the summer of 1993, Joint Chiefs chairman General Colin Powell signed off on a plan to send an American unit, Task Force Ranger, to capture Aidid and restore peace to Mogadishu. The task force was under the command of General Bill Garrison, a cool-headed Texan who, it is rumored, has never been seen without an unlit cigar poking out of his mouth. Composed of an Army Special Operations unit, about three hundred Rangers, the task force also included 150 men from Delta Force, of which I was in command. But we'd named the entire operation Task Force Ranger to obscure that fact. In August, we set up a joint operations center (JOC) on the ragged edge of Mogadishu, and commenced operations.

As Aidid's chief of finance, Atto topped our list of high-value targets. In September, we received a snippet of intel on his location. Within thirty minutes, we launched a helo assault, dodging rocket-propelled grenade fire to land a H-6 Little Bird gunship with four black-clad Delta Force operators riding shotgun on the pods on top of one of Atto's garages.

We missed him by sixty seconds. But CNN gave Atto more time than that to crow to the world about how we would never catch him. Less than a week passed before we had an opportunity to put Atto's prophecy to the test. A CIA informant offered to lead us to Atto in exchange for a position in the new, legitimate government he hoped would be restored after Task Force Ranger booted Aidid out of Somalia. Hours later, five H-60 Black Hawks lifted skyward, their massive rotors drumming the air like thunder. Four carried the assault element—Rangers and Delta operators, including six Delta snipers. One carried a combat search-and-rescue (CSAR) package—Delta operators and Air Force PJ's, or parajumpers, medics who parachute in to tend wounded friendlies.

To that point in Mogadishu, the Rangers had been an untouchable force. With an average age of twenty-two or twenty-three years old, each had completed the Army's physically and psychologically punishing Ranger School, where they trained in air assault, close quarters combat, demolitions, and marksmanship. They were well prepared, but young and untested in the field. Still, they were ready to mix it up, kick some warlord ass. I remembered the feeling from my first Huey flights over the jungles of Vietnam.

The Delta operators weren't built quite the same way. With an average age of thirty-two, they were more circumspect. They had seen combat and knew its gritty horror. I had worked with some of them for as long as fifteen years. For them, an op wasn't a chance to test themselves in a real firefight. It was more of a craft. They were professional soldiers. Swift. Efficient. Lethal. When they rode shotgun in the Black Hawks, they surveyed the city streets as cold-eyed analysts, tabulating targets, enemy firing positions, and exfiltration routes as they went.

Back in the JOC with Garrison and our action officers, I directed the assault, watching the op unfold via a helo-mounted camera. On wall-mounted video screens, we spotted the target: Atto's two-vehicle motorcade.

I keyed my mike and gave the order: "Execute."

As all eyes in the JOC focused on the screens, a Black Hawk swooped into the picture over the top of the two vehicles. With no audio feed, its sudden appearance was silent, but I knew its beating rotors sounded like hellfire to Atto and his men. In only seconds, the big helo squared off facing the Mercedes, flared and dropped to the street, sending up thick tornadoes of dust.

The car braked to an abrupt halt and in the same instant, I knew the Delta snipers snapped off warning shots. Two more Black Hawks roared in behind the motorcade. The car's doors flew open. Two men spilled out of the Mercedes and darted for the nearest building. Another man exited the rear vehicle and sprinted toward the adjacent structure. Both were office buildings, about three stories high.

On the JOC monitors, I saw a man from the Mercedes fall in the street. A sniper's bullet had ripped into his right thigh, a potentially mortal wound. The man clutched his leg, rolling back and forth, but the camera was too far away to see his face.

I hope that's not Atto, I thought. *I want him alive.*

The other men disappeared into the buildings, one in each, just as the three Black Hawks touched down in the street, disgorging an assault force of twenty men. Black-clad Delta operators and green-clad Rangers surrounded the vehicles and poured into the buildings, now hunting just two targets.

The assault force radio crackled: "Sir, we've got somebody. We're not sure it's Atto."

The assault commander radioed back. "I'm in the other building. Take him up to the roof."

Within moments I saw two Delta operators burst onto the roof of the left-most building, holding a docile captive. Then the assault commander, a Delta officer, emerged from a stairwell door atop the other building. He jogged to the edge of the roof, and on the other roof, the young Rangers hustled their captive over to meet him.

Two seconds passed, then: "We got him," the commander radioed. "It's Atto."

A character named Osman Atto appears in the movie *Black Hawk Down*. There is a scene in which Atto, captured by Task Force Ranger, has a brief confrontation with Garrison, played by actor Sam Shepherd. That scene, with an erudite and condescending Atto puffing on a Cuban cigar while sneering at Garrison's cheaper Miami brand, is pure Hollywood fiction. When that confrontation really happened, there were three people in the room—not two, as the film depicts—and Garrison was not one of them.

Instead there was only Osman Atto, Captain Mike Steele, and me.

I did not participate in the making of the movie, but I did attend the private premiere. When I saw the way director Ridley Scott portrayed Atto, I didn't know whether to be angry or amused. The *Black Hawk Down* Atto was cool and arrogant, unfazed by the fact the most powerful Army in the world held him captive.

The real Osman Atto was terrified.

After we captured him, I wanted him to know I saw him brag to the world that the Americans would never capture him because of the great and powerful Allah. And I wanted him to know that he was not the only fighter in the conflict who claimed to serve a powerful God.

Our meeting did, as the movie shows, occur in a Conex, an empty steel shipping container converted into a small one-room shelter. Our security forces had put Atto in there because we knew we wouldn't hold him very long. We wanted to keep him safe from mortar attacks so we could gather intelligence from him before sending him off to be prosecuted for helping Aidid oppress and murder his own people.

I remember my first impression upon meeting Atto, perhaps the second most powerful man in all of Somalia who, it was rumored, had close ties to Osama Bin Ladin and other Muslim terrorists. When I walked into the Conex, intense equatorial sun poured through the wide doorway behind me, lighting the swirling dust motes that were as constant in Mogadishu as air. Atto was leaning over a small table, his hands resting on it.

The instant he saw me, fear stretched his eyes wider. He straightened and backed up against the opposite wall, feeling his way backward with his hands as though searching for a secret exit. In *Black Hawk Down*, the Garrison character and Atto have a tense little chat in which Atto seems to come off cooler than Garrison (which could be true only if Atto were Clint Eastwood). In reality, Atto said nothing.

I walked to the table opposite where he had been standing and looked him in the eye. "Are you Osman Atto?" I said.

He cringed back, as though he thought I was there to kill him. He nodded yes.

"Mr. Atto," I said, "you underestimated our God."

5

SO, YES, while serving in the United States Army, at the conclusion of an armed assault that bagged a thieving coward, I invoked the name of God. The same God whose name is mentioned twice in the Special Forces creed. The same God discussed in the Bible every U.S. commander-in-chief since General George Washington has placed his hand on at his swearing-in. The same God whom the Declaration of Independence says is the very author of the freedom I spent my life defending.

But now the media was using the faith that had been my anchor to club me over the head. Suddenly, I was being portrayed as some kind of religious fanatic perpetuating a holy war. I was under assault by an enemy in my own country, and already this enemy seemed huge, unaccountable, and immune to challenge—killing reputations instead of people.

I didn't know where the media's charge that I was heading up an anti-Islam crusade would lead. I did know that in the current political environment, civil liberties groups, Muslim groups, and others would accept the NBC News and *L.A. Times* reports at face value, with possibly devastating consequences for Muslims' perceptions of America's intent.

These were the thoughts racing through my head as I sat slumped on the couch in my living room on October 15, 2003, and they were bad enough. But I had no idea of the national firestorm that lay ahead—that pundits would concoct outright lies—such as that I had said the terror war was "a continuation of the Crusades," or that I had issued instructions on how to torture the detainees at Guantanamo Bay—and that I would face *criminal charges* based on those lies. I had no idea that within days, Muslim extremists across the globe would begin issuing death threats against me and my family, and that George W. Bush, my commander-in-chief, would stand in the White House Rose Garden and, without even an investigation, publicly disavow me.

FLAG BURNERS AND WAR HEROES

★ ★ ★

1948–1970

1

I NEVER KNEW A TIME when I didn't dream of being a soldier. The tradition of military service stretched back to my daddy's family and World War II. When I was growing up, Dad told the story of how, at age sixteen, he told his mama he had decided to drop out of high school and join the Navy so he could go fight the Nazis. His four older brothers, my uncles, were already serving in Europe.

"Ed and Mickey and Wilton and Martin are already *over* there!" he said to Lily Boykin, my grandmother, as she sat at the table in her country kitchen in Wilson, North Carolina, shucking corn into a paper sack. "I'm gonna go sign up!"

In her younger days my grandmother was reported to have been a beautiful woman. But the strong Roman nose that once gave her face the look of an aristocrat gave it a stern cast in middle age. She was as hardcore a Republican as she was a Baptist and could have run her husband's sizable tobacco operation with one eye closed while arguing a man into knots on politics and religion.

She turned to my daddy and gave him her famous hard gaze. "You are *not* gonna join the service," she said. "You're gonna stay right here and help your daddy."

"But the war's going to be *over*," he complained, the way a teenager today might whine about not getting to go see a movie. "I want you to sign for me."

"Well, I'm not gonna do it," Ma Boykin said. And that was that.

Except that Daddy walked into the local recruiter's office in downtown Wilson that very week, lied about his age, and walked out a Navy radarman. Back at home in the kitchen, he broke the news to Ma Boykin, who was washing pinto beans in the sink.

"Mama, I know you told me not to, but I went on and enlisted," he said. "I ship out next week."

23

Ma Boykin pulled her hands from the bean water, turned slowly, and eyed Daddy with that stern face. He braced himself.

"Well, I'll tell you one thing," she said. "You better not come home with no tattoos."

That's how five of the Boykin boys came to be serving in World War II at the same time. The whole time I was growing up, Ma Boykin kept a photograph of them all on the farmhouse mantel. In the old black-and-white, all five of them sat side-by-side on a bench, decked out in uniform. Three brothers—Ed, Mickey, and Martin—wore Army dress greens and rakish grins, their garrison caps pulled low over their eyes the way invincible young men wore them in those days. Dad and Wilton wore Navy crackerjacks, their Dixie cup caps tilted to the side like those of the sailors in *South Pacific*. No longer boys, but men: a tobacco farmer's sons, raised on biscuits and pole-fishing, farm chores and baseball, guided with a firm hand, but cutting up when nobody was looking. Plain country men proud to fight and die for a nation that blessed them with a plain country life.

I wanted to be just like them. I felt *an obligation* to be like them. Not in the way an obligation feels like a burden, but the way an obligation can become an honorable duty that, left undone, feels like a puzzle with the middle missing. It was the family tradition, an expectation that a Boykin man would serve his country.

2

GROWING UP, I SPENT A LOT OF TIME on Ma and Pa Boykin's tobacco farm, working in their tobacco fields. Summertime was high season and I wanted to be a part of what everyone else was doing. I pitched in as a "hander," the job reserved for the most unskilled people in the fields. Pa had a whole fleet of tobacco "trucks," which were really just little mule-drawn wagons, skinny enough to roll down between the rows in the fields. After workers stripped the leaves from the plants, they drove the wagons back to the barn.

All day long, I would pick up a handful of freshly harvested tobacco leaves and *hand* it to the elderly black women who worked as "tiers." (That's why they called us "handers.") Fresh from the field, the grass-green leaves oozed tobacco gum, a thick, fragrant liquid that dripped from the stems in great, sticky drops. The older black women danced the leaves onto four-foot-long tobacco sticks, their hands quick as fireflies: Loop, knot, done.

My favorite tier was Miss Cora. She was a round, motherly lady with a great big lap and the gentlest smile I'd ever seen. Miss Cora always took time out to chat with me, and when the sun got high during the harvest, we'd sit down together under a shade tree for a meal of saltines, sardines, and Moon Pies, all washed down with RC Cola.

When I wasn't working in the fields, I was hanging around with my best friend, Junior, whose family lived on the farm. Junior was just my size, with high cheekbones, big doe eyes, and mahogany skin. We had the run of the farm, which was a couple hundred acres. We loved to climb high in the oak trees or play hide and seek, darting in and out of the cool shade. But our most important job by far was building forts and defending them from the Indians. At least once a week, we expected a huge attack by the local Indians, and we spent a lot of time reinforcing our walls and ramparts. When foul weather kept us indoors, I was as happy as a duck in a puddle to hang around at Junior's house with his mama and daddy, Miss

Mildred and Mr. Sam. I don't know exactly how many brothers and sisters Junior had, but when we gathered around Miss Mildred's table for lunch, I was like a pinto dropped into a handful of coffee beans. I didn't think anything of it. Junior and I were tighter than bark on a tree.

The older I got, the more I found myself drawn to that old photo of Daddy and my uncles on the farmhouse mantel. My dad, Gerald Cecil Boykin, was what they used to call a "man's man"—a hunter, a fisherman, a lover of all sports. The best thing about my dad was that while I was growing up, I knew every weekend he and I were going to go do something—hunt quail, fish for bass, or go watch a baseball game. I just knew that. It's given me a heart for boys who grow up without a dad, as so many do today.

But Daddy would never talk to me about what happened to him during the war. Men in those days held things in. One measure of a man was that he had the inner strength to bear his own burdens. But the more Dad clammed up, the more I clamored for information.

To fill out the details, I began to imagine for myself a wartime backstory, in which my dad ran daring small-boat operations up the Rhine River with Glenn Ford, Henry Fonda, and John Wayne. I knew he didn't, really, but I had fun thinking about it. On Saturdays, I handed over my fifteen cents at the picture show and another quarter for a box of popcorn and a Coke. Then I'd hunker in the flickering dark watching *The Guns of Navarone* or *The Great Escape* with Daddy or my friend Bobby.

One television show, *Run Silent, Run Deep*, a show about submarines, also fired my imagination. The American Navy sank a German U-boat just about every week, and I added these scenes to my romantic ideas about war and fighting men.

So what I knew about what really happened to my dad on D-Day, how he became a Purple Heart winner and my hero, I set against the backdrop of wartime newsreels and movie scenes.

It was June 6, 1944. My dad was a radarman aboard a destroyer, and the ship had taken up its position off Omaha Beach at Normandy, France. From their inland artillery positions, the Nazis pounded the beach and surf. Dad, only eighteen years old, volunteered to drive a personnel landing craft vehicle, one of those defenseless small boats that carried heroes to death and victory. I was ten years old when Dad finally sketched the scene for me. I filled in the details, imagining he could feel the concussion of artillery blasts and hear the rattle of German guns from their beachside bunkers. I could see American soldiers streaming off other landing craft and onto the beach, some falling immediately, others charging up the sand, crouched low and firing. I knew from the movies that blood splashed the beach and bloomed in the water. And in the middle of it all, I could see my daddy, just a teenager, piloting his boat into the smoke and thunder.

When Dad told me the story of how he was wounded, all he remembered is something exploded in his face and the world went dark. The Howitzers' roar, the pounding shells, the bloody surf—all of it simply disappeared. The next time Daddy was fully aware, he was stretched out in a bed at Walter Reed Army Hospital in Washington, D.C. A thick cotton pad covered his left eye, held there by a belt of gauze circling his head. The blast at Normandy destroyed his optic nerve and for the rest of his life, he would see out of only one eye. My father did not complain and as a consequence, I did not know until I was twelve years old that he was technically half blind.

3

GROWING UP, I WAS ALWAYS THE "BIG KID." By the seventh grade, I was already six feet tall and 180 pounds. You'd think that might scare people off, but instead my size acted more like a trouble magnet. Seemed as if everybody who wanted to make a name for himself thought whipping the Big Kid was just the ticket. So I got in a lot more fights than I wanted and spent a good deal of time in the principal's office. I never got whipped, but in the fifth grade, I did get some teeth knocked out in a school bus fight.

One fight I got into had a silver lining.

In seventh grade, I played on the school basketball team with this kid named Jimmy Ferebee. I didn't know him very well. One day at practice, we collided under the basket a few too many times and our tempers began to heat up. We pushed and shoved a little, exchanged the required macho threats and insults. It came to a head in the locker room after practice.

"Hey, Boykin!" Jimmy Ferebee said. "Wanna take this outside?"

"I got no beef with you," I said, picking up my gym bag. "I'm going home."

But when I turned to walk out of the locker room, Jimmy shoved me in the back. In one motion, I whirled, dropped my bag, and grabbed him around the neck. Then we fell to the ground and began flailing away. He was tough and held his own. I got the upper hand only because I was bigger.

After a few minutes, though, I got tired of fighting. "If you've had enough, I'm going to let you up," I said.

Jimmy could've gone either way. "Okay," he said simply. I was glad since Jimmy was strong and quick, and I didn't know how much longer I could hold him down.

So I unfolded myself from the floor, picked up my bag, and walked out of the locker room. Don't ask me to explain the mysteries of male bonding, but from that moment on, Jimmy and I were inseparable. We did *everything* together including our two great passions: sports and music.

We both lettered in baseball, basketball, and football, but liked football best. I was pretty good at linebacker and loved to mow down anyone who had the bad taste to still be in possession of the ball behind the line of scrimmage. Because of my size, I also played fullback, blocking for—guess who?—Jimmy.

Jimmy was outgoing and gregarious, and the older we got, the better looking he got. (I just got taller.) Besides being the school's star running back, all the girls thought he looked like the teen heartthrob Bobby Darin, and he could sing like him, too. One day when we were sophomores, Jimmy said, "Let's get us some ukuleles and learn to play."

So we did, then we moved up to guitars. After that, Jimmy bought a banjo, and a girl named Anita Johnson joined us to form a trio. It was the era of folk music: Bob Dylan; Joan Baez; Peter, Paul, and Mary. The three of us sang "Puff the Magic Dragon" at every country fair and talent contest in a tri-county area. (I wanted to sing country music, but Jimmy and Anita hated it and wouldn't let me.) In 1965, our little group traveled all the way to New York City and sang at the World's Fair. We sang together until we graduated. Jimmy went on to a twenty-year professional music career. Anita went on to become Miss North Carolina.

By then, I'd fallen in love with Lynne Cameron, a beautiful blonde who'd transferred into our country school from New Haven, Connecticut. During my junior year, her father took over management of the Stanley Power Tools plant in New Berne. Lynne was a year behind me in school and thought I talked funny. But since she was from New Haven, everybody thought *she* talked funny. That was okay by me, because she was shy and sweet. I asked her out after the first football game of my senior year and after that, didn't date anyone else.

During my senior year, our high school integrated. But it was still the South and it was still the 1960s, and we were as steeped in racism as frogs in a swamp. There were only a few black students and only one was a boy. John was a likeable guy, and I felt for him as he struggled to fit in. At the end of the school year, one of the other seniors—a kid named Tim who, ironically, had moved to our town from up north—decided to challenge the "black kid" to a fight. Word got around quickly. By afternoon, it seemed as though everybody in the school was buzzing about it. The time was set for three-thirty in the afternoon by the gym.

The whole thing disgusted me. All day long, I pondered the situation and tried to decide what to do. I thought about the fact that the whole time I was growing up on the farm, my best friend was a black kid. I thought about Indians and forts and Miss Mildred's collard greens. And when the hour for the fight came, so had my decision.

When the last bell rang, I walked around to the side of the gym where a crowd had already gathered in a loose circle. Girls holding their school books whispered to each other. Boys crowded their way to the front for a ringside seat. The gladiators arrived almost simultaneously, working their way to the center of the crowd. John was outnumbered a hundred to one, but he had too much pride not to show.

I couldn't wait any longer. Stepping into the center of the crowd, I confronted Tim. "This isn't right," I told him. "He hasn't done anything to you."

Tim looked at me, puzzled, but said nothing. A low murmur rippled through the crowd.

"There isn't going to be a fight," I said, looking around. "So just break this up and go home."

Now Tim got angry. He twisted his face into a sneer. "What's your problem, Boykin?" he spat. "You don't want to see this nigger get his ass beat?"

I hated that word. My face flushed red. "I'll tell you what, Tim, you better start by trying to whip my ass first, because you're going to have to get by me before you get to him."

We were just about nose to nose by then, and we stared each other down. Tim was furious, but I could see the calculation in his eyes: he'd signed up to fight someone smaller than him, not someone bigger. After a long moment, he backed down.

I turned to the crowd. "Go home. No fight today."

Then, for the first time, I looked at John. "Let's go. It's over," I said. He followed me out to the parking lot and without a word, we parted ways.

I knew I was risking scorn and accusations of being a "nigger lover." But I also knew that the whole time I was growing up on the farm, Junior's parents treated me like one of their own. And besides all that, I just couldn't abide a bully.

4

AFTER GRADUATION, I went on to Virginia Tech on a football scholarship and was accepted into the Corps of Cadets, a military program that led to an army commission. My dad and uncles had laid down the pattern for Boykin family military service and I wanted to do them proud. Since the Spanish American war, Virginia Polytechnic Institute and State University has trained officers to lead the nation's forces, and I knew VT cadets had earned a truckload of decorations for valor.

Since I was playing football on scholarship, I lived in the athletic dorm instead of the upper quadrangle with the rest of the corps. During the last weeks of the summer of 1966, while the other cadets were in indoctrination classes learning how to march and salute and so forth, I sweated my butt off in two-a-days and fell into bed at night, exhausted. In fact, I don't think I even looked at the contents of my standard-issue olive-drab duffel bag until the night before the first day of classes. That was a mistake.

Late that evening, alone in my dorm room, I thought I'd better take a look at what I had. I unhooked the top of my duffle bag, upended it, and inspected the mess: a large pile of grey shirts and trousers, some wool and some cotton. A hodgepodge of brass insignia, a saucer cap, and some kind of bizarre harness used for who-knew-what. At that moment, I made two important discoveries. First, I had absolutely no clue what went with what. Second, I didn't have any shoes. Had I been attending indoc classes like the other freshman rats, I would have known I had to go buy shoes separately. But now it was too late. And I had just two choices of my own: football cleats or penny loafers.

I had seen cadets wearing black shoes, so I thought I'd try to scare some up in the athletic dorm. After a trip down the hall knocking on doors, the best I could come up with was a big old pair of work boots from a big lineman named Shorter who was taller than me and whose feet were two sizes bigger.

The next morning, damp and smelling of shower soap, I put on an ensemble that I thought looked pretty good: a pair of charcoal gray winter-wool pants and a light gray summer shirt. Shorter's size fourteen boots poked out from under my pants legs like houseboats.

I grabbed my books and clomped outside, a light feeling of anticipation percolating in my belly. It was my first day of college, yes. But I was more excited that it was the first day of my Army career. I knew my shoes weren't regulation, but I felt I'd done a pretty good job with the rest, and was proud to finally be wearing the uniform.

Walking up to the upper quad, I saw two Army captains walking toward me. These officers were sharp as bayonet points, with tightly clippered haircuts, knife-edge creases in their slacks, and spit-polished shoes. About a car length from me they stopped dead in their tracks and stared at me, astonished. I glanced down at my clothes and back at the captains. Compared to them, I looked mighty crappy.

"Mornin'!" I said, trying to blind them with cheer. "How y'all doin'?"

"Cadet!" snapped the officer on the left, who looked as if he just stepped out of a recruiting poster. He scanned me up and down as though I had just blown in from a carnival sideshow.

"What company are you in, Cadet?" the officer snapped.

"T Company—" I ventured, now dead certain I was in for some demerits or pushups five minutes into my military career.

But then the two officers just looked at each other and chuckled, shook their heads, and walked on by.

Relieved and vowing silently to at least iron my uniforms in the future, I started walking again. When I got to my first class, I sat down next to one of the cadets from the upper quadrangle and looked him over: matching summer uniform, sharp creases, and high-gloss shoes.

I sank down in my chair. *Great start, Boykin.*

5

IN THE CORPS OF CADETS, I was drawn to the instructors who came from the infantry. All of them had recently returned from Vietnam and I noticed they were the most highly decorated. Most of them were wearing Purple Hearts. As much as I could, I followed what was going on in the war. Now I was able to get firsthand information and I peppered my instructors with questions. What was it like there? What kinds of operations were they involved in? And they would tell me their stories—of patrols and ambushes, artillery strikes and firefights.

One of my instructors had been at Ia Drang Valley during the bloody battle in which 450 American soldiers faced two thousand North Vietnamese Army regulars in November 1965. The battle had tested our new air-mobility tactics—troops dropped in landing zones by helo, then supported by air, artillery, and rocket fire called in from a distance. At the end of the four-day battle, the U.S. lost 234 men to the NVA's one thousand dead. One ambush, on November 17, would stand as the deadliest in the entire war. The first major U.S. battle in Vietnam, Ia Drang is history now. But then, my instructor's memories of raging infantry clashes and hand-to-hand combat still fell into the category of current events. I hung on every word.

I noticed there was a brotherhood among the infantry men in my cadre. These were tough men who had done tough things. They had led men, seen death, and survived. They had faced down the enemy and had the scars to prove it.

In addition to my weekly helping of war stories, I studied military history and tactics, along with my general ed courses, plus classes in my major, distributive education, which emphasized work-study programs for high school kids. On Sunday mornings, I showed up at a little Baptist church. But I didn't pray outside of a crisis and I didn't read the Bible. My mother, Katie Gwendolyn Page, was a devout evangelical who raised me in church, starting with a plain little country church way off in the sticks of Wilson County, North Carolina. Before he went into civil service as an electronics technician, Daddy worked a small farm out there.

On Sundays, Mother would take me to this white wood-frame church where the main image that stuck in my mind was the preacher, who scared me to death. He was an older man who wore glasses, and the longer he preached, the louder he yelled. And the louder he yelled, the redder his face would get. I always felt as if he was yelling at me.

"Mother," I would say nearly every week, "I don't feel very good. Can I go sit out in the car?"

Every once in awhile, she'd let me. But even though I couldn't wait to get away from that lobster-faced preacher, I kind of liked Sunday school. I had fun filling in Bible scenes with lick-and-stick pictures—I especially liked that story about the big whale swallowing Jonah whole—and learned to give all the right answers about Moses, Abraham, Noah, Mary, and Joseph. I also learned that Jesus died on the cross for my sins, although I wasn't quite sure what "sins" were.

When I was young, Dad went to church with us—not out of any great conviction, but because that was just what people did. But suddenly, when I was in the sixth grade, he stopped. From then on, Dad read the paper and watched football on Sunday mornings. I kind of liked his style and wished I could do that, too. But I didn't want to disappoint my mom, and later, at college, I didn't want to have to lie to her if she asked about it. And I definitely didn't want the head football coach, Jerry Claiborne, to think I was a heathen. So I went to church.

Coach Claiborne was a Southern Baptist so conservative he'd make Ronald Reagan look like a liberal. He had played football for Bear Bryant when Bryant coached at Kentucky. Now in his forties, Coach Claiborne was a compact, powerful man with a coiled athleticism packed into his five-foot-ten frame. On the field, he was hard and tough, and demanded an extraordinary effort from every player. He did not tolerate laziness, half-heartedness, or prima donnas. To his way of thinking, athleticism was a gift from God, like the ability to paint or teach or build or manage investments, and he expected his athletes to be good stewards of their gifts.

Coach Claiborne was very open about his Christian faith. Enormous compassion and integrity tempered his toughness, and that's why we all respected him. If a player was injured, had family problems, or no place to go during a holiday, Coach would take care of it personally. When other football programs were breaking NCAA recruiting rules, Coach Claiborne didn't. He also was a man of few vices, a strict teetotaler who didn't use any type of profanity. The closest I ever heard him come to cursing was when he hollered at a player, "You're just fartin' around!"

I had another Christian coach, a faith-forward firebrand named Rock Royer. In the locker room, we used to joke that Coach Royer must be on amphetamines because the man was a nonstop blur of action and commentary. Coach Royer would wade in padless among the towering linemen, and slug it out with us on the field. And he was just as likely to tell you he loved you as to get up off your lazy ass and take one for the team.

Both coaches inspired me. As I said, during my teen years Dad stayed home. Meanwhile, the men in our home church were, well, church men. It was almost as though the fact that I met them in church, and not out in the "real world," cancelled their credibility in matters of real life. Meanwhile, my dad was a Purple Heart winner, an outdoorsman, a hardworking husband and a devoted father—not a man of faith, but unarguably a good man. Coach Claiborne and Coach Royer were the first men in my life who demonstrated to me a man could be both.

6

DURING THE FALL SEMESTER OF 1967, I married Lynne, my high school sweetheart. The following summer, our first child, April, was born. At first, Lynne and April lived with my mom and dad back in New Bern, North Carolina. But later they moved down to Blacksburg to be with me at school. April changed my life. Up until then, I had been a typical young athlete: The only reason to go to class and perform at all was to maintain my football eligibility. But after April made her debut, I got serious about school and surprised everyone by making the dean's list.

By 1970, I was a senior cadet, training every day to go to war. By then, antiwar protests had been boiling for a couple years on college campuses. I had nothing against the hippies who marched in them; I just didn't agree with their politics. And I definitely disagreed with the opinion of some that American soldiers were persecutors. My VT instructors had served in the mud and sweat of the jungle, surviving rocket fire, snipers, and the horror of seeing their buddies' heads blown off, all to keep a people free. I believed we were fighting in Vietnam not only to help those people, but also to hold back the global spread of communism. Subsequent world events, such as the utter devastation of Cambodia by the Khmer Rouge, proved that a worthy goal.

It wasn't until the early spring of 1970, just weeks before the tragic clash between Kent State students and Ohio national guardsmen, that the first big antiwar protest hit the VT campus. I had a late class that day and when I walked out of Burruss Hall onto the parade field, it was already dark. The smell of wood smoke hit me immediately. Looking across the field, I could see dozens of students clustered around a van-sized bonfire. Sparks whirled up into the night and I could hear chanting and clapping and the snap of burning wood.

I walked toward the blaze, offended that the protesters lit this fire on the very field where the cadets drilled, the field where we would graduate before going off to war. While privileged college kids chanted and sang protest songs, many of us would fight and bleed. Some of us who drilled on this very field wouldn't come home alive.

I walked faster.

From a distance, I could see that only about a hundred students seemed to be active in the protest. Several dozen others stood at the fringes, watching. As I got closer to the fire, I could feel my own temperature rising. I knew some of the students chanting slogans cared about the American war dead. I also knew many of them were ignorant of what their protests really meant, that there was no such thing as the armchair communism that suburban kids liked to think was a better way to run a country than the democratic republic that gave them the right to march against the government and not be executed for it.

Suddenly, to my left, I noticed two guys also walking toward the fire. One, wearing ragged jeans and shoulder-length curly hair, carried an American flag wadded up under his arm. Real anger bloomed inside me, as though someone ignited a gas flame inside my chest and was turning up the dial.

I closed in. "Hey! Where are you going with that flag?"

The two guys stopped and squared off on me. I remember their exact words: "This war sucks! We're gonna burn this flag!"

The flag my father lost half his sight for. The flag my uncles and eight million others had rushed to defend. The flag thousands of young men died for in Vietnam, and were dying for now, maybe at this minute.

"The hell you are," I said.

They stood their ground. The curly haired one glared at me. "Who are you to stop us?"

I didn't think I was anybody special. But I knew I wasn't going to let them do what they'd come to do.

"Well," I said very deliberately, "if you try to burn that flag, I'm going to kick both your asses. Take your choice."

They contemplated that scenario, then turned around and walked in the opposite direction, away from the fire.

Wise decision, I thought.

7

I DIDN'T GRADUATE THAT SUMMER as I expected, having failed organic chemistry. The subject made no sense to me at all, maybe because I was completely uninterested in things like carboxyls and the medicinal properties of willow bark. The F on my transcript meant I had to go back for fall semester. Still, when I finally graduated in December, I was a Corps of Cadets honor grad. I received my commission and headed for Fort Benning, Georgia, and the Infantry Officer's Basic course.

Shortly after I arrived, a no-nonsense officer with an unusual name began scheduling appointments with us, the freshest crop of second lieutenants. When I went in to see Captain Major, a Fort Benning assignments officer, my first thought was to wonder how long before his nametag would read "Major Major."

Captain Major was a crisply mannered paper pusher whose trade was matching names with jobs. We sat down across an industrial-looking desk from one another in a small, sparse office.

"Where do you want to be assigned?" Captain Major asked me without much in the way of preceding small talk.

"I want to go airborne, then Ranger training, then Vietnam," I said, not wasting any more words than he did.

Captain Major scribbled a bit in a file folder lying open on the desk between us. "Okay. I'll send you to jump school and Ranger training. Then I'll send you to Fort Hood, Texas. About four months after that, I'll send you to Vietnam."

And that was that.

With Captain Major's promise tucked under my hat, I felt my career was finally under way. I threw myself into my classes on infantry tactics, leadership, and logistics, absorbing every detail. I was up early each morning for physical training, and studied late into the evening. I really wanted to learn everything the Army had to teach.

Even though I was busy with classes, at Benning life slowed down some. Lynne and the baby were at home with my folks in New Bern. Now that I was on active duty, I didn't have to hold down an extra job. And, of course, football wasn't eating up my time anymore. For the first time since reaching adulthood, there was space in my life to reflect. That's when a vague disquiet began to stir in my heart.

At first, I couldn't pinpoint the problem. For days, between classes I laid on my bunk in the BOQ, the bachelor officers quarters, trying to figure out why I felt so anxious. Then one day, a thought crystallized in my brain: *You're not a boy anymore.*

Suddenly I realized that in some sense, I'd spent the last four and a half years in a bubble. Yes, I had spent that time as a husband and father, and was even technically in the Army. But I had also been a student and an athlete, pursuits in which the consequences of half measures or even failure, though embarrassing, didn't ripple far. Now college was over and I was in the real world: a husband and father earning a living for my family, and also stepping into another position that carried a lot of responsibility. As a new platoon leader, I would lead forty men whose lives literally depended on me.

At Fort Benning, I went to classes, went back to the BOQ, and sat on my bunk. I stared at the walls, grappling with the discontent I felt inside. I couldn't pinpoint the problem. I was married with a beautiful daughter, I had graduated the Corps of Cadets with honors, and my lifelong dream of military service was finally a reality. Still, sitting in my barracks room, I felt—empty.

Then one night, seeking some kind of answer, some kind of comfort, I got up from my bunk and rummaged in a box I'd brought from New Bern until I came up with a Bible. I sat back down and without knowing why, turned to the Gospel of John, and began reading. Twenty minutes later, a verse printed in red jumped off the page at me: "I am the light of the world," Jesus was saying to His disciples. "Whoever follows me will never walk in darkness, but will have the light of life."

Thanks to the diligence of my mother and my Sunday school teachers, I could recite the gospel verses in my sleep. But I had to admit: I'd taken all that on board as general principle—it didn't have anything to do with me personally.

Now a thought burst in my consciousness like a rocket: *That doesn't make any sense.*

Either the gospel story is personally true or it isn't. Otherwise, showing up for church on Sunday is nothing more than social fakery, and I am nothing more than a hypocrite.

Sitting on my bed with the Bible in my lap, I remembered the first time I thought Jesus might be more than just someone to learn about in church.

During Prohibition, Bill Page, my grandfather on my mother's side, was a bootlegging kingpin who made a mint running Canadian whiskey through Baltimore into Eastern North Carolina. Granddaddy Bill was a big man—huge, in fact—close to three hundred pounds. When he drove his old round-fendered Ford step-side pickup, distributing his whiskey to his sprawling network of local bootleggers, Granny Page rode shotgun. While Granddaddy chugged through North Carolina back country, Granny carved slices from a big stick of baloney and made him sandwiches as they went. The family lore is Granddaddy put gas in the car and Granny put gas in him.

During Prohibition, the Pages made so much money you'd have thought they were cranking off counterfeit cash in the storm cellar. Granny Page told me once she would stuff forty thousand dollars at a time into Mason jars and bury it in the backyard in case the revenuers raided the house. You'd think that after Prohibition, with all that money and a little age on him, Grandpa Bill might have turned philanthropist or at least retired on a nice-sized farm. Not so. Instead, he took all his money and bought a carnival, and spent the rest of his life trooping up and down the eastern seaboard with a Ferris Wheel, a sideshow, and a troop of hoochie-coochie girls.

After Grandpa Bill ran off with some carnie lady from Kentucky, Granny Page started drinking. I was four or five years old at the time, and I remember how Granny changed. She had always doted on me, telling me tall tales and slipping me treats, but after Grandpa Bill left, it was as though all the life drained from her eyes. In my little-boy logic, I thought maybe it had something to do with cigarettes. She had taken to smoking Raleighs like a coal train.

I remember one night Mother came into my bedroom and shook me softly. "Jerry, wake up. We have to go out for a little while, take a little trip."

I crawled out of my bed and could see stars through my bedroom window. It was still the middle of the night.

"Where are we going?" I asked sleepily.

"We're going to get Granny."

Mother bundled me in a blanket and guided me out to the car, where I crawled into the back, still wearing my favorite flannel PJs, the ones with the cowboys printed on them. Daddy made the short drive to Granny's place, which was the little house trailer she pulled for years while she was still in the carnival business with Grandpa. I stayed in the car while Mother and Daddy went in. I was wide awake by then. It was strange being out so late at night. I knew something must be wrong.

Then I saw Daddy and Granny come out of the trailer, and Mother behind them, shutting the door. It seemed as though my sweet grandmother couldn't walk right. She was staggering left and right and Daddy had to hold her up so she could make it to the car. *Granny must be awful sick*, I thought. I was very worried.

Daddy put Granny in the front seat. I could smell her perfume and another smell I couldn't quite make out.

Mother crawled in the back seat with me. "Granny, we're going to take you to the hospital," she said.

Granny tried to talk but it seemed she couldn't form any words. Now I was really worried. Daddy drove to the hospital. I later learned Mother and her sister, my Aunt Belle, had made many such trips before. Those trips ended, though, sometime in my fifth year, when a drastic change bloomed up in Granny like a sunrise. The sparkle returned to her eyes. Her smile came back. She was my grandmother again. I knew better than to ask about what was going on with the grownups. But Mother sat me down on the divan one day and told me something I'll never forget.

"Your grandmother has accepted Jesus," Mother said. "She'd been drinkin' a lot of liquor, but she's stopped now and has started to go to church."

I nodded. Mother seemed unusually serious.

"Jerry, I want you to remember somethin'. No matter what we've done, no matter what sins we've committed, no matter what mistakes we've made, Jesus will always forgive us," she said. "Do you understand that?"

I looked in Mother's eyes and nodded. I didn't have any idea about fancy theological words like "grace" and "regeneration." But I knew my granny had been changed from the inside out. That was the first time I saw a real person changed by faith, and I never forgot it.

Now, at Fort Benning, I thought about Granny Page's conversion. I also thought about my dad. He believed in God in a general way. If I chose a different path, did that mean my father was going to hell? I thought about Coach Claiborne and Coach Royer, their commitment, their passion, the way they inspired me and the young men around me. *My father is a great man*, I thought. *But these are great men, too.*

The next day, and for several after, I plodded joylessly through my class schedule at Benning as these thoughts worked themselves through the fabric of my mind. I couldn't stop thinking about God, about what I now suspected was the root of my anxiety: a deep spiritual anemia had somehow elbowed its way to the surface of my life. It wasn't as though *I* decided the time had come to place the evidence for and against the truth of Scripture into some kind of intellectual balance, and see which side dropped. I felt a *pressing* in my soul, a forceful insistence coming from somewhere outside myself that I deal with matters of eternity, and that I do it *now*.

I went to sleep thinking about it. I woke up thinking about it. Then one morning in late January, I knelt alone in my room, right down on the tile beside my bunk, and did business with God.

A HELLUVA RIDE

1971–1977

1

I'VE HEARD PEOPLE ASK THE QUESTION, "Why would *anyone* jump out of a perfectly good airplane?" After airborne training at Fort Benning, my question was, why would anyone not? From my first static line parachute jump, I thought it was an absolute blast, and I never changed my mind. I reveled in the adrenaline rush I got from leaping into space, and in the freedom I felt floating down through the Georgia sky. I was sorry the school only lasted three weeks. But I was also eager to move on. From there I was off to complete the next leg of Captain Major's training plan: Ranger school.

In March 1971, I reported to the Ranger Training Brigade at Fort Benning, Georgia. I breezed through some of the first tests—breaking down and loading an M-60 machine gun; setting and detonating a Claymore mine; encoding and decoding a radio message; and several tasks with M-16s, hand grenades, and the M-203 grenade launcher. These were basic infantry skills I had learned in ROTC, so they were no problem. Next came a confidence course, hand-over-hand rafter crossings over mud pits, and land navigation skills using a map and compass. I was still in great shape from playing football, so none of these things presented a real challenge.

In fact, I thought I was doing great. That is, until we left Fort Benning and moved to the Mountain Ranger Camp at Dahlonega, Georgia.

Our main focus there was learning how to conduct successful patrols under conditions meant to simulate combat. That meant little sleep, less food, and almost zero shelter. For two weeks, we lived, ate, and slept mostly in the open. It was April by then, but still bone-numbing cold in the deep North Georgia woods. Our only shelter was found in the green rubber ponchos we carried in our rucksacks. When it rained, we were wet and miserable. When it didn't rain, we were wet and miserable anyway from slogging through rivers and streams up to our hips.

Each patrol had an objective—attacking an enemy position, for example—and lasted three to six days. I had heard that the ranger instructors (RIs) would keep us on the move from 5:00 a.m. until 2:00 a.m., twenty-one hours a day. That was true, except when they marched us for twenty-four. Very quickly, I learned to snatch sleep where I could. It got to the point where if we stopped for five minutes, I could sleep for four of them.

Meanwhile, the grand total of our food intake on patrol was one C-ration a day. At some point during the day, we dropped our rucksacks in the dirt and squatted down for a deluxe meal of canned pork slices or canned beans and weenies, or my favorite, canned ham and lima beans. On our first patrol, it took maybe three days before I noticed that some guys' britches had started to sag. After five days, their faces were hollowed out from hunger and haggard from lack of sleep. If I'd had a mirror, I would've known I looked just as bad. Because of severe sleep deprivation, most of us started to hallucinate. And the thing we hallucinated about most was food. I imagined I could smell bacon frying or fudge cooking. I think I would've traded my boots for a piece of chocolate.

I guess I could blame all those things for my initial spectacular failure. We had been in Dahlonega for only a few days when the RIs tasked our patrol, about eighteen men, with assaulting an enemy base camp. I hadn't slept in two days. Blearily, I helped plan the mission, but when we finished, the plan was as clear in my head as oatmeal.

After dark, we moved out toward the objective, walking single file through an oak and cedar forest, underbrush crunching beneath our jungle boots. My back ached under a seventy-pound combat load. Ahead, I could hear frogs and crickets. Their night chatter stopped as we approached, then tuned up again as we passed, closing behind us like water. For me, the sound was hypnotic. As I plodded along near the middle of the pack in something like a trance, my mind drifted to nights spent in the North Carolina woods hunting with my dad. Some of his deer jerky sure would be good right now—

"Ranger Boykin!"

The patrol had clustered at a rally point just short of the objective for final preparation and a leader's recon, and an RI now demanded my attention. "You are now the patrol leader," he barked. "You have thirty minutes to brief your team and move out."

My head swam with panic. I scanned the surrounding tree stand and realized I had no idea where we were. I had not anticipated having to lead, and now couldn't remember a single detail of the assault plan.

"Yes, sir," I said miserably.

During the brief, I faked it as best I could, but when we moved out, I was completely inept. As we crossed potential danger areas, I was supposed to post security. I didn't. I was supposed to issue instructions to the soldier walking point. I didn't. On top of that, I was literally lost in the woods, and finally, my assistant leader had to take over the patrol. We did reach our objective, but without any help from me.

Later that night, I burrowed under my poncho as much to hide my embarrassment as for shelter. The next morning, the cadre called us over one at a time to give us our first formal grade in Ranger school.

"Ranger Boykin," said the RI who had observed my incompetence, "I have given you a failing grade for your patrol last night." He then proceeded to explain what I had done wrong, which was basically everything.

When he was finished, I slunk away, now not only ashamed, but worried about passing the school. Under an overcast sky, I trudged back to my position on the perimeter and sat on the ground near a cedar tree. Rummaging in my rucksack, I came up with a can of beans and weenies. Even as hungry as I was, the food seemed to go down my throat in large, mealy lumps that tasted like failure.

Since Infantry Officer's Basic, I had begun trying to deepen my faith. On patrol, when we rested and I could keep my eyes open, I often pulled out a little New Testament I kept in a plastic bag, and read a few verses. But now, very silently, I began to pray, asking God to help me get through the course.

Up until that point, I trusted God mainly with my spiritual well-being, the security of my eternal soul—"fire insurance," as the old joke goes. For everything else, I now realized, I had been depending on myself, on my own mental abilities, my athleticism, my determination. But when I failed that patrol, I suddenly understood I had been relying too much on myself and not enough on God. For me, that was the beginning of a life lived relying on God moment by moment.

I began Ranger school a colossal failure. I ended it as an honor graduate.

2

ON JUNE 5, 1971, Lynne and I left Fort Benning with a three-year-old, a brand-new baby, Randy, and a U-Haul trailer stuffed with everything we owned. We drove as far as Meridian, Mississippi, spent the night, then got up the next day and drove to Fort Hood, a huge post sprawling over 340 chalky square miles slap in the middle of Texas hill country. My orders there fulfilled a requirement that I have at least four months' experience in an infantry unit before shipping out for combat. But those 120 days spent leading a forty-man platoon ticked by slowly. The entire time, I felt like a racehorse at the starting gate.

Late September came, and the orders to Vietnam that Captain Major promised me had still not materialized. Nor did they arrive in October or November. Now I was really getting restless. Christmastime came and I took Lynne and the kids home to New Bern on leave. While I was home, I planned to travel up to Army Personnel in Washington, D.C., track down the infantry assignments officer, and tell him about the deal for orders I'd made with Captain Major. To my Southern way of thinking, there was nothing like a friendly personal visit to establish rapport and knock off any mud that might be slowing down the wheels of progress.

On January 3, the first business day of the new year, a Trailways bus carried me from North Carolina to the Capitol. I called ahead to tell the personnel office that I'd like to have a meeting to discuss my next assignment. When I arrived, a very nice secretary greeted me and pulled out my file.

"Okay," she said brightly. "Major Major will see you now."

I nearly fell over. Major *Major*? I couldn't believe it. My good-ol'-boy, personal visit plan suddenly went up in smoke. Stomach churning, I walked in to the major's office.

"What can I do for you, Lieutenant Boykin?" Major Major said, after I sat down across the desk from him.

I reintroduced myself. Then, treading carefully, I reminded the major that he had, almost exactly a year before, told me that I would have orders to Vietnam four months after my arrival at Fort Hood. Without saying so outright, I made it clear I thought maybe he had forgotten.

Maybe I made it too clear, because the longer I talked, the more disdain collected on Major Major's face. "Lieutenant Boykin, you serve the needs of the Army," he said, looking me straight in the eye. "Vietnam is winding down and we do not need as many lieutenants there as we did when you were in Infantry Officer's Basic. What you need to do is get yourself back to Fort Hood and enjoy your time as a platoon leader."

I wasn't ready to give up. "Is there *any* way you can find a slot for me in Vietnam?"

Major Major looked at me as though a large rock occupied the spot where my brain should've been. "No," he said with what sounded like his last grain of patience. "We don't have any requirements for platoon leaders right now." His last sentence came out as though a period followed every word.

"Well," I said, "I just want you to know that I'd really like to go before this war is over."

Now, a company commander or a division officer in the field might have appreciated my eagerness to go into combat. Major Major did not. He looked at me in the exact same way a complaint department clerk might at 4:59 on a Friday afternoon. "Well, I'll make a note here that you're a volunteer for Vietnam," he said, now clearly bored and ready to move on, "and that if *any* platoon leader spots open up, we'll send *you*."

Which was a polite way of saying, "Get out of my office."

3

I KEPT PUSHING FOR ORDERS TO THE WAR. And in the first week of February 1972, I got what I thought was the big phone call from personnel. But once again, I was disappointed: "We're giving you orders to Pusan, Korea," a personnel officer told me. "You're going to be an aide de camp."

An aide de camp! I thought. *I must have really pissed off Major Major.*

Nobody *wants* to be an aide de camp. Your first vision of it is that you're nothing more than some general's errand boy. As it turned out, I got a tremendous education, an exposure to the strategic level of Army operations I would never have gotten in a troop unit. My first boss was Brigadier General Jack McWhorter, a quartermaster officer and West Point grad from Mercedes, Texas. I worked for him only from March until June, but during that time, I was a back bencher during quite a number of high-level meetings on U.S. policy and strategy for the Korean peninsula.

Still, I did my share of grunt work. After McWhorter left, the new guy came: General Lloyd Faul of Sunset, Louisiana, a Cajun Catholic who loved cigars, had five kids and an infernal dog named Snoopy.

Faul first called me ahead of his arrival in Pusan. "Lieutenant Boykin, I wanted to let you know I'll be on the two o'clock flight into Osan with my wife, my kids, and my dog."

"Yes, sir. I'll be there," I said. "Looking forward to meeting you and your family."

"We'd like you to bring someone with you to transport the family," he said. "You transport the dog."

Now this *is some high-class work*, I thought. On the phone, I said, "No problem, sir. Glad to."

Lieutenant Choi Jung Yul worked as my Korea counterpart and an interpreter for the American generals. A college graduate, he spoke fluent English and was a very serious soldier. We spent hours discussing Korean culture and he helped me learn his language. The day General Faul flew in, Yul and I climbed into a Suburban and drove up to Osan to collect the new American boss and his entourage.

"Lieutenant Boykin, you take Snoopy to the quarantine," General Faul said after Yul and I had taken care of his luggage, his family, and his billeting.

Now you have to understand that I was used to hounds, pointers, and setters of various kinds—hunting dogs that knew how to track, retrieve, and generally do what they were told. Snoopy, by contrast, was quite possibly the dumbest animal I had ever met. Part Dalmatian, part something else, he gazed stupidly at me through the caged door of his transport kennel. Still, I wondered if I saw a devilish gleam in his eye.

All pets brought across the ocean had to be quarantined for thirty days. So all the Fauls crowded around the kennel to love on Snoopy before I took him away. That was when the general issued his warning. "Whatever you do," he said, "don't let Snoopy get away from you. If you do, you'll never catch him."

As I drove to the quarantine area, a hot June sun beat down on the Suburban's roof. I could hear the dog panting in the back. Five minutes later, I pulled up to the quarantine area, which bordered on Pusan's pristine, rolling golf course. Rather than try to muscle the whole kennel inside for check-in, I grabbed Snoopy's leash and opened the kennel door to snap the leash on his collar. That was my big mistake.

That animal shot past me like a convict in a jailbreak. He landed in the parking lot and took off at a dead gallop. General Faul's words flashed through my mind: *Don't let Snoopy get away... you'll never catch him.* That blasted dog had been lying in wait!

I cursed and sprinted after him, my two legs to his four. Maybe the mutt wasn't as stupid as he looked because he headed straight for eighteen holes of open range.

"Snoopy! Snoopy!" I hollered like an idiot, racing past generals and colonels teeing up. I could hear the dog ahead of me, yapping in celebration of his freedom. I raced across the first fairway, nearly sideswiping a woman who almost clubbed me with a seven iron midswing. Golfers laughed at me and cursed at me as my Army career flashed before my eyes. I chased that dog for seventeen holes, alternately calling his name, sucking wind, and picturing my new assignment handing out socks and jocks at the gym.

I don't know why, but at the eighteenth green, Snoopy suddenly faltered. Seizing the career saving moment, I launched off both feet in a commando dive and dragged him down like a felon. And as I carried that blasted animal back to quarantine, I held on so tight I was afraid the Fauls were going to wind up asking me why their dog had fingernail marks in him.

4

DURING MY TIME IN KOREA, I existed in a kind of cultural disconnect. By then, Vietnam war protesters stateside began lining up to scream and spit at soldiers returning from the war. Such incidents infuriated me when I saw them on Armed Forces television. By contrast, I was struck by how proudly the Koreans sent their men to the war. For most of a year, I was right in the thick of their comings and goings. Every Korean unit deployed from and returned to Pusan, a major port city. Every time a Korean unit shipped out or returned, Faul and I would head down to the bustling waterfront for the official ceremony.

Each of these events was almost like a holiday for the Koreans. The city turned out the schools and all the children would stream down to the port waving Korean flags. I remember one day in particular, going down and watching as a ship tied up and the citizens waited for disembarkation to begin. When the Koreans came off the ship, they always brought their wounded off first. Some were litter patients; others walked on their own, bandaged and limping; some were missing limbs. There was a message of honor in the fact that the wounded disembarked first: these were the real heroes. And their fellow citizens treated them that way, with this incredible combination of joy and reverence. Cheers went up when the first of the wounded appeared. A band struck up a patriotic song and the children began clapping and singing.

I stood there, my heart split by admiration and sadness as I pondered the kind of reception American soldiers were getting on our side of the Pacific. I really started to question why the Koreans were so proud of their soldiers and why some Americans had such disdain for ours. Interestingly, the Koreans I got to know in Pusan had the same questions. I had a driver named Mr. Kim who had been born in South Korea. When Kim Il-Sung, backed by the Soviet Union, took control of the north, Mr. Kim enlisted to fight and was later captured by the communists.

"During interrogations, they beat me," Mr. Kim told me one day. "In English, they called me 'son of bitch.' I did not know what they were talking about."

During a year in captivity, Mr. Kim was beaten repeatedly and starved nearly to death. After the armistice in 1953, he returned to the south in a prisoner exchange. Mr. Kim's hatred for communists was white-hot. He told me he didn't understand the American antiwar protesters. To him, it was a great honor that his countrymen now were fighting to keep the people of South Vietnam free from the same ideology that had nearly killed him.

Choi Jung Yul felt the same way. I remember one day sitting with him in a little cafeteria on the compound. I was munching on a hamburger with fries. Yul was having a hamburger with kimchi.

"You see the American war protests, Yul," I said. "How do you feel about the war?"

"I am proud to fight there," he said without hesitation. "My family saw what happened to our own country between 1950 and 1953. You know my father fought in that war. Now, when communism is threatening a country so close to us, we believe it is something that cannot be taken lightly."

If communism got a foothold in Asia beyond China and North Korea, Yul said, it could spread rapidly into the Korean peninsula.

"When we went into this war, many Americans felt the same way—that communism is not only a threat to Asia," I said, "but to the rest of the world. And that America is the only country strong enough to stand up to it."

Yul nodded solemnly. He felt the American war protesters were self-righteous dilettantes, impressed by their own bluster and completely uninformed by experience.

I told him I agreed with him completely.

5

WHEN I FINALLY MADE IT TO VIETNAM in November 1972, I considered sending Major Major a postcard. With the war winding down, General Faul and I went there to begin helping the Koreans redeploy three divisions back to their home country. To lighten the logistical load, we wanted to persuade the Koreans to turn their equipment over to the South Vietnamese. Our plan was to replace it with American equipment once they arrived back in Korea.

In some ways, my time in Vietnam was unusual. Faul and I, and our Korean counterparts linked up with some Americans, but I didn't find any who had been drafted and resented being there. I really found myself in a bubble, insulated from this other attitude about the war. For me that was providential, a blessing. During my time in-country working with the Koreans, I kept thinking, *This is the way it's supposed to be, like when my dad was in.* I was serving with people who were proud of what they were doing, who were committed, and who had the support of their people.

In Vietnam, the air itself seemed like a separate, living creature. Thick and damp, it curled around my shoulders on balmy days like a friendly cat and on scorching days like an anaconda. Always, beneath the smell of cordite and sulfur that floated on the winds of battle, the air seemed pregnant with the scent of rain. Nearly every day, I'd find myself in the belly of a UH-1 Huey, my stomach dropping away as the rotors bit into low humid skies. At first, rice paddies skated by beneath us in a pale green blur. Then the pilot would edge higher through jagged emerald gorges, hugging the terrain to make us a smaller target. Peering below, I often wished I had x-ray vision so I could see down through the jungle canopy and spot the men waiting to kill me.

Not every wartime soldier articulates it the same way, but at some point the crossover happens, the turning point between training and the real thing. There is a moment, sharp as a blade, when you realize: *this is not a drill.* There is a flesh and blood enemy out there with real bullets and bombs. He wants me dead. If he can, he will kill us all.

As a young lieutenant floating over secret-filled jungles, I had my pivotal moment and that moment produced fear. But fear was only a faint instinct compared with the adrenaline rush of the challenge. *Mano a mano.* Us against them. A macho territorial drive older than Moses. As much as anything, I yearned to be tested. I wanted to get out there and mix it up, walk through the fire, and live to tell about it.

That's why I so clearly remember the first time I thought I was going to die. It was only a week after I got to Vietnam. The Huey I was riding in that day lifted off from an airfield in Natrang, skimming across the rice paddies until the pilot snapped a steep climb to get us through a high saddle in some mountains directly ahead. I was crowded in with General Faul, four other soldiers, plus the aircrew and the door gunners. The helo cruised along at six thousand feet. Warm wind rushed through the open cargo doors, blending with the loud chop of the rotors. Out the port side of the aircraft, I could see the Huey's shadow flitting across the mountainside like a ghost.

Without warning, the helo plunged wildly. The wind now rushed suddenly upward, past the cargo door. The aircraft fell from the sky like an elevator car cut free of its cable. A single thought flashed through my brain: *we've been hit.* As we dove toward earth, my stomach hung in my throat and fear ripped at my heart like a vulture.

I have no idea what General Faul and the others did because I was completely engulfed by a white-knuckled terror. The bird felt in total freefall and I could still see the helo's shadow, now screaming down the mountainside. I said one of those emergency prayers—not devout, but desperate: *Lord, don't let us get killed!*

As we plunged through five thousand feet...four...three...two, my brain clung to scraps of hope: *Can the pilot crash-land? In a rice paddy? Better chance for rescue there than on the side of this mountain.*

It was not to be. As we broke through a thousand feet, the pilot pulled back on the stick and ended our nosedive, leveling off low enough for me to make out individual villagers in the paddies, and even the hoes and rakes they were using. Relief flooded through me as I realized the pilot had the helo under control. The villagers glanced up at us, then returned to their tilling, unafraid. The pilot now commenced a low, slow racetrack pattern orbiting the paddies. After about ten minutes, we climbed again, up and through the mountain pass, landing at a Korean fire base somewhere out in the jungle.

Legs shaking, I exited the helo with Faul and the others. The pilot got out and came around to where we all stood trying to figure out what had just happened.

"Helluva ride, wasn't it?" he said, smiling.

It turned out that we had nearly been the victims of friendly fire. The Koreans had a fire base on one side of that mountain pass, the pilot told us. They had received a call for artillery support from a unit engaged in a firefight on the other side of the pass.

"I saw artillery rounds crossing literally right in front of us," the pilot said. These were 105 rounds—two feet long and as big around as a fence post, passing just feet off the nose of the helicopter. "I had to take her down fast to get below them."

The chances of artillery rounds crossing our flight path at our exact altitude—and the pilot spotting them with his naked eye—were infinitesimal. I imagined what might've happened if he hadn't and thought maybe now would be a good time to change my trousers.

6

I HAD BEEN IN VIETNAM for only three months when Henry Kissinger finally hammered out his ceasefire. Just that quickly, my combat tour was over. Faul and I headed back to Korea. Four months later, I returned to the States and, in May 1973, reported to Fort Campbell, Kentucky, as the new executive officer of D Company, 1/506 infantry, in the 101st Airborne. The 101st had returned from Vietnam and was transitioning from its role as an airborne outfit specializing in parachute insertions, to becoming an air assault unit. I was privileged to be in on the ground floor of that historic shift, helping to develop Army air assault tactics and procedures built around helicopters like the OH-58 Kiowa Warrior and the lethal AH-1 Cobra.

Lynne and the kids joined me from New Bern. April was almost five years old by then, and our son, Randy, was nearly two. They were, of course, the cutest kids ever born. We rented a little house off-post, and it was great to have the family back together again. Randy was by now old enough that I could take him fishing, the way my father had taken me. I spent most of the time baiting his hook and chuckling as I untangled his line from the bushes. That's what my dad did with me, and when I was out on the creek with my own little boy, I felt like that was about as good as life could get.

Our time in Kentucky marked the first real opportunity we had to get involved in a local church. We joined an Assemblies of God congregation pastored by a slender, dark-skinned, and extraordinarily wise man named Bob Jones (no relation to the university). I got really involved in the church's bus ministry. On Saturdays, I would walk around the neighborhoods on post, asking parents' permission to invite their kids to Sunday school. Then on Sundays, I'd drive the church bus around and pick up the kids whose families had said yes. A lady from our congregation rode along, teaching the kids the songs they'd be singing at church. I got a kick out of driving through the streets with the joyful voices of twenty-five or thirty children spilling out of the bus windows into the Sunday morning sunshine. Of course, if an officer did that now, he'd likely be the subject of a federal probe. He might even get a call from William Arkin.

I hadn't been at the 1/506 long when I also started inviting members of my platoon to church. Some came, some didn't. But one of them, a young Spec 4 from Alabama named Stephen Collins, surprised me with a challenging question. I had invited him to church a couple of times. He said he'd come, but then never showed up. Then one Monday morning, I was sitting in my office when Steve walked in and sat down.

"Lieutenant, you don't know much about me," he began. "When I was real little, my daddy walked out on us."

Sitting across the desk from this young soldier, I flashed to my own father. I wasn't that much older than Steve. What might my life look like if my dad had been the kind who would abandon his son?

"We wound up going to live with my granddaddy," Steve went on. "So he raised me as long as I can remember, and he was a Christian. Went to church every Sunday, read his Bible. But he was a farmer, not a soldier. And I've never been able to figure out how you can be in the Army and be a Christian. Lieutenant Boykin, how can you believe it's okay to be a Christian and yet be in a job where you train to go out and kill people?"

His question took me completely by surprise, and I realized immediately that I had no good answer.

"You know, Steve, that's a good question," I said. "I've always just accepted that there's no inconsistency there. But to tell you the truth, I really haven't thought it through. Let me think about it and I'll let you know."

That Wednesday night, Lynne and I went to church. After the service, I caught Pastor Bob in his office and presented my dilemma.

"Jerry, one of the things people have to understand is that life is all about warfare," he said. "Life is a battle, a spiritual battle. And, at the root of every war, there is a spiritual battle."

He let me think about that for a second. Hitler ordered the murder of six million Jews. The communist regimes in Korea and Vietnam depended on V. I. Lenin's belief that religion is "opium for the people," "medieval mildew," "a sort of spiritual booze, in which the slaves of capital drown their human image." The very acceptance of the existence of God was a stake in the heart of communist ideology. If religion could truly liberate a man not from hardship but in the midst of it, there would be no need for socialism—or its dictators. And so "science" was Lenin's god.

Even wars without overt signs of religious strife—struggles for land, power, treasure, freedom—could be, at their core, spiritual battles. Attempts by men to serve mammon—or to fight for the right to liberty divinely imprinted on each person's heart.

Then Pastor Bob began to talk about America. "What you need to understand is that God ordained this nation to be a place where people could worship freely, and a place where other nations could look and see the foundation of that freedom is the belief that it is God who grants freedom to all men. He's called this country to be a light in a world of darkness. And He didn't create a country where believers could have freedom with the expectation that unbelievers would defend it."

That made so much sense to me. Biblical passages flashed through my mind: Joshua at Jericho, David and his armies. I could see that the concept of fighting for your country, of defending your land, was taught in Scripture, even ordered by God.

"It is not only right for Christians to defend this nation," Pastor Bob went on, "it's their responsibility. If God calls you to defend this country, He's not offering you a job, He's calling you to service."

7

AFTER FORT CAMPBELL, I served in a number of short assignments, and God blessed Lynne and I with a third child, Aaron. By 1977, I made captain and transferred to Florida Ranger Camp at Eglin AFB, where I became an RI and branch chief, overseeing various aspects of training and supervising patrols in the field. Outside my office, I had a great view: an alligator pond occupied by the camp mascot, Big John, a fifteen-foot gator. Big John brought back memories of hunting alligators with my dad. He would've loved to take on Big John, who on January 5, 1978, was sunning himself outside my office window at Eglin when my phone rang.

"Captain Boykin," said the man on the phone, "this is Lieutenant Colonel Gene Blackwell with the Army Personnel Center."

"Hey sir, how're you doing?" I was puzzled as to why he was calling me, but tried to sound casual, which I almost always did anyway because of my Carolina drawl.

"Fine, fine," Blackwell said. Then he got right to the point: "We want to ask you to volunteer for a new unit that's being formed at Fort Bragg. It's highly secret and I can't tell you much about it."

Instantly, he had my attention.

"What I can tell you," Blackwell went on, "is that when you get to Bragg, you'll undergo a thirty-day assessment and selection program and you need to be in top physical condition for it. At the end of that, if you make it, you'll be asked to volunteer for an assignment with this unit. We need to know your answer this afternoon."

That was exactly how he laid it out. Zero details. Take it or leave it. And almost before the last word was out of his mouth, I realized I was going to say yes.

A MEDAL AND A
BODY BAG

★ ★ ★

Fort Bragg
1978

1

I TOLD LIEUTENANT COLONEL Gene Blackwell I'd consider his offer and call him back. Whatever he was talking about, it was so secret he asked me to commit without even knowing what I was committing to. The mystery intrigued me. I wondered whether the Army was actually standing up some kind of new unit, or preparing for a sensitive mission. I knew that prior to the Son Tay raid, in which a small task force swooped into a North Vietnamese prison camp to free American POWs, Colonel Bull Simons had recruited and trained his men in secret. Man, I wanted to be part of something like that.

I also knew Blackwell had to be sitting up there at personnel reviewing records. I tried to imagine what spurred him to call me, among what had to be hundreds or even thousands of candidates. Maybe it was the combination of my Virginia Tech commission and Ranger experience. In any case, his words, "if you make it," lay before me like a dare.

So I did the thing I always do when confronted with a serious dilemma: I called my mother.

She picked up the phone on the first ring and I didn't waste words. "Mom, I've been asked to volunteer for something that's being formed at Bragg. I don't know anything about it. I don't know if this is where God wants me. But I want you to pray that if it is, I'll make it through this thirty-day program."

Right on the spot, we prayed together over the phone.

"Jerry?" she said after the amen, "I want you to know that I'm going to keep on praying."

"I know, Mom."

I hung up and decided to go tell Lynne, who was at home in our quarters, a block-long walk away through Florida sunshine. When I told her, she was completely supportive—even though she didn't know what she was supporting.

"Obviously this is something you've got to do," she said. I marveled at her patience with the Army's habit of turning life on its head. At the time, we really had no idea what that really meant.

For the next month, I trained hard with two Ranger NCOs who had also been invited to try out for whatever it was we were trying out for. Then on February 8, 1978, the three of us reported to Fort Bragg's Old Stockade, a nine-acre chunk of real estate isolated from the rest of the post and surrounded by a high fence of double chain-link topped with barbed wire.

The stockade once housed prisoners. But in contrast to the barbed wire and concrete, a cheery royal blue awning covered the building's entrance, and the walkway leading up to it featured the beginnings of a rose garden. I didn't know it at the time, but my future commander would one day have me on my hands and knees planting three different kinds of roses there. ("We want 'em to know we're steely-eyed killers here," he said. "But we also want 'em to know we're not barbarians.")

The NCOs and I walked between the roses, went inside, and checked in with a duty officer who sent us over to a guest house to spend the night.

"Be back at 0900 hours tomorrow morning," he said.

The next morning, we showed up way before that. I filled out some paperwork, then headed down to gear issue and drew seventy pounds' worth of equipment. Later in the day, I was assigned a bunk in one of six major cell blocks converted into spaces for housing, classrooms, briefings, weapons storage, and classified materials. Following a diagram, I wound my way through the corridors until I found the space holding my bunk. When I walked in, the first thing I saw was a burly, dark-haired man who was already setting up housekeeping.

I put out a hand and smiled. "I'm Jerry Boykin."

The man accepted my handshake. "Hi, there. I'm Pete Schoomaker."

"Where you comin' from?"

Pete told me he was from Army Personnel, an assignments officer in the armor branch. I told him I was coming from the Florida Ranger camp.

"Glad to meet you," I said. "Guess we're gonna be seein' a lot of each other."

In fact, Pete and I became best friends and would spend the better part of three decades in each other's career orbits. I liked him instantly. He was an Army brat who'd earned a football scholarship to Michigan State. But as a freshman, Pete got in trouble for some offense he would never confess. The college yanked his scholarship. Pete wound up walking on at the University of Wyoming and went on to star in the 1969 Sugar Bowl.

There was something charismatic about Pete; his warmth and humor immediately drew you in. He was a rare blend: a soldier who was serious about his craft, but who didn't take himself—or the minor trials of a given moment—too seriously.

"Well, that's about as screwed up as a football bat," Pete would say, chuckling.

I would learn later that Pete's charisma extended to leadership. Men *wanted* to follow him. But back then, we were both just a couple of young officers, excited and itching to find out what we'd gotten ourselves into.

2

THERE WERE RUMORS. The gossip was that a Special Forces officer named Colonel Charlie Beckwith, who had trained with the legendary British Special Air Service, was involved here. In Vietnam, the story went, Beckwith had been hit in the belly with a fifty-caliber round and survived. By reputation, he was a tactical genius with the personality of a porcupine. Low on patience, he pissed off almost everybody he came into contact with, but was also very often right. Pete heard Beckwith was forming some kind of elite unit. We couldn't wait to find out more.

The next morning at 0800 hours, dozens of recruits gathered in a small utilitarian conference room that had once been the stockade chapel. Pete and I sat down next to each other. I took an informal head count and tallied 118 men.

The room buzzed with anticipation.

"What *is* this?"

"Do you know anything?"

The name "Beckwith" floated around, but most guys shrugged and shook their heads at each other, mystified but hoping this was something big.

Suddenly, the door opened and a hush blanketed the room. I don't know what I had been expecting—brass and lots of ribbons, maybe—but I was completely unprepared for the man who slouched in looking as if somebody'd just poured him out of a duffel bag. A big fellow with a paunch hanging over his belt, he stood before us in civilian clothes—a green golf shirt, rumpled khaki slacks, and a big .45 caliber pistol hanging off his hip. I had just arrived from Ranger camp, where every man was spit-and-polished to within an inch of his life, so this man's appearance was a little disconcerting.

Another man, tall, thin, and also in civilian clothes, entered next and stood in the background. One thing you noticed right away was that this guy had a nose on him that rivaled Jimmy Durante's. It turned out he was a rather renowned Special Forces officer named Lewis H. "Bucky" Burruss.

"I'm Colonel Charlie Beckwith," said the man in disheveled clothes. "We're forming a new unit here along the structure of the British Special Air Service."

Pete leaned in close and whispered out of the corner of his mouth, "Is that really *Beckwith*?" He looked as skeptical as if a vagrant had just claimed to be George S. Patton.

After a stint with the British SAS, an elite and unorthodox unit specializing in counterterrorism and clandestine operations, Beckwith became familiar with the work of Sir William J. Slim, a British field marshal. Sir William's book, *Defeat into Victory*, was a military classic, and in a section called "Afterthoughts" he held forth on his opinion of Special Operations. Most SO units were wasteful, he wrote, saddled with more liabilities than advantages. But there was one kind of unit that the field marshal felt was an indispensable element of modern warfare. Soldiers in such a unit penetrated deep into enemy territory; blended in and collaborated with indigenous citizens; sabotaged enemy installations and disrupted operations; gathered intelligence; and, if necessary, assassinated enemy leaders.

Then they vanished. Like smoke.

Beckwith knew the American Army fielded no such unit. We had Special Forces, yes. But not the kind of secret and lethal organization Sir William meant—not an SAS. After his tour with the Brits, Beckwith wrote an after-action report that would, as he put it, "change the world." In it he explained the differences between the SAS's lean, mean, unorthodox— sometimes *unmilitary*—approach to Special Operations, and the Americans' more cut-and-dried, field-manual approach. Elite U.S. fighters were loyal, brave, and true, but they were *conventional*, Beckwith argued. Some in the Special Forces community agreed. Most thought he was full of bull. A few screamed in his face and ordered him out of their offices. Charlie Beckwith knew how to bring out the best in people.

Still, in 1965, he landed an assignment commanding an experimental Special Forces group in Vietnam. It was his first chance to test the SAS concept using American fighters. The Army gave Beckwith thirty men. The name of the unit was Project DELTA.

Now, in the stockade conference, the man who claimed to be Beckwith said this: "Our mission is counterterrorism. We're going to train to rescue hostages and perform other Special Forces operations."

A slight kick of adrenaline buzzed through me, tingling in my fingertips. Suddenly, I didn't care what this rumpled colonel looked like. This was what I'd been waiting for.

Beckwith then peered around the room, raking his eyes over each of us. "I'll only promise you two things," he said: "A medal and a body bag."

Pete and I exchanged a look: *I can live with that.*

3

MY FELLOW RECRUITS ranged from crackerjack to crackpot, with every shade of soldier in between. I remember one guy out of the 1st Ranger Battalion who liked to smear dog biscuits with peanut butter and eat them. Another fellow sat around sharpening his knife all the time. Thin and wiry, he had scarily blank eyes. He might've reminded me of a serial killer, except I'd read where serial killers are usually charming. Then there was the guy who ranted constantly about how ugly his wife was. Another would wake up in the middle of the night and argue with his rucksack: "Don't you *move*, you sombitch! I *see* you!"

Then there was the guy who baby-powdered a pair of pantyhose every day and wore them under his uniform. He was just trying to stay warm, but that still didn't go over very well in a camp full of testosterone-charged would-be commandos.

At first I didn't feel much like a commando, though. I had envisioned a lot of tests involving shooting, close-quarters combat, and clandestine insertions. But after a pretty demanding physical training test, we found that this top secret selection course involved...walking around in the mountains.

Just land navigation, and lots of it, using a simple map and a compass while carrying a heavy rucksack. *There has to be more to it than this*, I thought. There wasn't. But what there was, was more than enough.

The proving ground was this: the snowy mountains of North Carolina, through dense hardwood forests, over and through rivers and streams, tangled deadfalls, and steep, unforgiving slashes of untamed range. We each carried a full rucksack, load-bearing gear, and an AK-47 assault rifle. It being February, the mercury dropped into the teens. Icy winds whipped through the trees, blowing in the kind of miserable cold that makes you wish you could simply amputate your toes.

Early each morning, instructors would give us each an "RV," a rendezvous, to which we were to march as fast as we could using only our compass and a 1:50,000 scale topographic map that often depicted no more than a ridge-line, waterways, and some prominent clearings. Each man had to walk alone, find his own way. To be caught following another man was to be dropped from the course.

When a recruit reached an RV, instructors gave him another, with only one instruction: get there as fast as you can. There was a time limit to make each point, but never were we told what it was. The only way you'd know you didn't make it was that Burruss or one of his men kicked you out of the course. I prayed that wouldn't happen to me.

On the first night, our base camp was a primitive group of two-man poncho tents.

"Pair up and make camp," an instructor shouted.

Pete and I put up our ponchos together. But due to simple arithmetic, one staff sergeant, Pat Hurley, from the 2nd Ranger Battalion, was odd man out. He sort of stood around watching as the rest of us made camp. Finally, he edged up to Pete and me.

"I don't have anyone to pitch a tent with," he said.

I glanced at Pete, who went about six-three and 230 pounds to my six-one and 210. With just the two of us, it was going to be a tight squeeze. But I didn't hesitate. "Okay, pitch in here with us," I told Pat.

That night, freezing and deeply exhausted from what would turn out to be the shortest hump we'd make, the three of us unrolled our sleeping bags in a space big enough for two. Pat tossed his bag smack between Pete and me, burrowed in, and dropped off snoring with his boney butt wedged firmly into my back. I tried to inch away, but there wasn't much real estate for escape and evasion.

There's some strange folks out here, I thought. *But it's cold out there and I'm not going to make him move.* For two days, I slept like that, with Pat Hurley's tailbone drilling into my spine.

4

BECKWITH'S RECRUITS SPENT their average days alone and set loose on a task both simple and maddening. The course, in some ways, seemed an exercise in cruel futility. What possible purpose could it serve to make a man hump a heavy pack from one random spot to another with no particular destination, no known time limit, and no right method, only wrong ones?

Each march was successively longer, and we'd heard a rumor that the last one would stretch forty miles. We began to refer to it as the Long Walk. Aside from reaching a checkpoint, I rarely saw another human being. If I did, I wasn't allowed to speak to him. Using nothing but a crude map and a compass, I chose my own routes, trudging X number of miles to this hilltop or that trail junction. One of the rules was that we were not allowed to use existing trails or roads.

As I walked, I prayed. "If it's Your will that I be part of this organization, sustain me, Lord," I would say. "Give me strength. Keep my family safe and comforted." Those were my more spiritual moments. But there were times when I called down curses on Beckwith's mother. Other days, I made the RV times only because I was too stubborn to quit.

I worried about my knees. Achilles had his heel and I had my knees, both of which I'd had operated on in college. Playing football wore down the cartilage like old tire tread. Also, the medial collateral ligament in each knee had torn in half. If anything in my body was going to break down, it was my knees. After a ten-mile hike, they throbbed dully. After twenty miles, they screamed. I prayed fervently that God would shut them up.

I wasn't the only one with problems. Beckwith and Burruss designed the course to stretch every man beyond his physical limits. We bowed under the heavy weight of our rucksacks, which started off heavy and got heavier, rubbing rashy red holes in our backs. We lost men every day. Most of them just quit. A few didn't make their time between points and were dropped.

Others had to leave because of injuries. The biggest trouble was our feet. Mile after mile, the rough interior of our jump boots sanded the skin off our heels and toes. At night, we'd make elaborate preparations. Drying our feet, coating them in benzoin, plastering them with moleskin in places reddened to the danger point.

I remember this one guy, Jimmy. Both his feet looked like raw beef. Every evening, he'd limp back into camp, gritting his teeth to keep his face from showing how much it hurt. Each night, medics came in and peeled dead and dying skin off his feet in thick, nasty patches. Then they doused his feet with disinfectant and bandaged the bloody parts. The next day, Jimmy would haul on his rucksack, pick up his weapon, and limp off into the mountains again.

He didn't make it through the course. I was amazed when he came back three months later and tried again, fully aware of what he'd have to go through. That time, he passed. That's the kind of man the unit was looking for—the one who wants to be part of the team so badly he would endure whatever it took to get it done.

Every day, our numbers dwindled visibly as men fell by the wayside in twos, threes, and half dozens. Making the RV wasn't the only problem. Some days it seemed as if even the rocks and trees were in cahoots with Charlie Beckwith, conspiring to weed out the unfit. Branches thwacked me in the face. Shallow streams developed sinkholes that swallowed me up to my hips. Rocks snuck into my path to trip me and I'd tumble thirty yards down an embankment, ass over rucksack. Many days, I was black and blue, and nearly frozen by the time I dragged myself back to camp. I was surprised at how hard they pushed us and at how far we actually went.

One day during the course, I found myself on top of a mountain, hopelessly lost. I sat down, shed my ruck, and looked up toward heaven. "Lord, I don't know where I am, but You do," I prayed. "Now I ask You to guide me to where I need to go." Then I stood, put my rucksack back on, and walked off the mountaintop straight to my RV.

At night, Pete and I traded horror stories. He told me about the time he spent nearly half a day climbing over a wickedly thorny deadfall. I told him about the time I tried to jump a small creek and missed, landing knee-deep in icy water in the middle of a snowstorm. For another two hours, as

I trudged through the snow, my pants and boots literally froze to my legs and feet.

Since the instructors usually rousted us for the day's reindeer games at around 5:00 a.m., there wasn't time to do much else at night besides wolf down some dehydrated chili con carne, repack our rucksacks, drop into our racks and try to block out the guy at the other end of the tent who snored like a freight train.

By the fourth week, our selection class of 109 had shrunk to no more than twenty-five people. I'd lost fifteen pounds and had to cinch up my belt to keep my pants on. I saw my exhaustion mirrored in the gaunt, grizzled faces of others who had survived to this point. The punishing course cut down eighty-some warriors, most of them combat veterans; there seemed to be nothing reasonable left to say about why we few remained.

With so few men left, Pete and I suspected the Long Walk had to be coming soon. We were right. One morning when the instructors called reveille, the rest-meter in my brain told me we'd been shorted on our beauty sleep.

I pried my eyes open and turned to Pete. "What time is it?"

He fumbled for his watch. "Couple minutes after two."

"Well, this must be the Long Walk then."

"Yup," Pete said. "I'll see you on the other end."

After suiting up, I trudged out into the cold darkness. The pines cast long blue shadows in the snow and moonlight glinted between them. My breath made clouds in air. I wondered if I would make it.

The instructors loaded us into trucks and hauled us through the pre-dawn darkness to separate starting points. Although no man knew the time standard at the moment of his first step, each knew that to reach the final RV in time he had to keep moving and not stop to rest. Charlie Beckwith would later write about the Long Walk:

> Around the twelfth hour, if the pace was sufficient to meet the requirement, the man would be, in the medical sense of the term, almost totally exhausted. He began to look for excuses to quit, to slow down, even to hope he would injure himself. Anything to allow him to stop. It was then, after the twelfth hour, that many men quit, or rested too long, or slowed to a pace that prohibited them from meeting the time requirement.[1]

Charlie wasn't right about everything. Eight hours into the Long Walk, I hit the wall. Night had long since passed into day and I met total exhaustion. It's hard to explain the utter sucking, draining, dry reservoir feeling. It wasn't that every muscle hurt. Every fiber *burned*. I reached the point where the course crossed over from physical torture to mind game.

As I approached each RV, I'd see a Delta instructor waiting for me and think, *This has got to be it, the last RV.*

But when I reached the instructor, he'd just point at my map and say, "Your next point is—" Each time, I had to make this agonizing mental adjustment, to just switch off the part of my brain screaming at me to quit.

The instructors neither encouraged nor discouraged us. There was never a "Good job!" or "You can do it!" I later learned this was part of the test. Charlie Beckwith did not want men who needed cheerleaders. He wanted men who would succeed on courage, will, and guts, who reached "down inside themselves for that intangible trait that enabled them to carry on."

For me, after thirty miles, courage and guts were just theories—abstract concepts someone invented to explain miracles. As I stumbled through the forest, each step was a mile, each mile a marathon. I would have given anything to cave in. But instead I prayed, not so much willing myself forward as trying to tap into the strength of the Lord. I prayed Scripture, especially Isaiah 40: "He gives power to the faint, and to him who has no might he increases strength. Even youths shall faint and be weary, and young men shall fall exhausted; but they who wait for the LORD shall renew their strength; they shall mount up with wings like eagles; they shall run and not be weary; they shall walk and not faint."

My face sagged and my mouth hung open, lungs burning as I sucked in the icy air. My nose ran and my ears felt frozen hard to my head. At some point, I lapsed into a kind of trance, crunching under snow-laden pine branches, dragging boulder feet with rubber legs. I wanted to drop my weapon, drag my rucksack off my back and, like Elijah, lie down under a tree and wait to die.

Except that Elijah had finished his task and I had not. "Lord, just help me make it to the next RV," I prayed. "Let it be the last."

And suddenly, it was.

5

WITHOUT WARNING, I broke into a clearing where a huge bonfire blazed. I could see two instructors waiting there, and they turned to look at me when I emerged from the woods. For a second, I stopped walking. *Is this really the end?* I thought. I was afraid to be jubilant and far too tired anyway. But neither man came forward with another map. Instead, one of them brought me a canteen. It was as though a nightmare suddenly turned into a good dream.

"This is your last RV," said the man who gave me the water. "Get some dry clothes on. You'll be here for a while."

I trudged toward the ring of warmth surrounding the bonfire, dropped my rucksack, shucked my boots, and laid down flat on my back looking straight up at the sky. Clouds scudded overhead and I sipped at the canteen. It was the best water I'd ever drunk in my life.

My prayers at that point were simple: *Thank You, Lord. Thank You.*

There were no other recruits to commiserate with as I was the first to make the last RV. My time: eleven hours and twenty-seven minutes. Within an hour, though, other men checked in, including Pete.

When I saw him walking toward me, I sat up painfully and grinned. "Welcome to your final point," I said.

He peeled off his gear and sat down beside me. "Well, that was easy," he said, and we burst out laughing. Pete had every reason not to finish, but he did, completing the Long Walk with a stress fracture in his leg.

After it was over, I came to understand that the course was designed to test one thing and one thing only: a man's resolve. Even the British SAS didn't know why it was effective, but this method of selection had worked for twenty-five years. Charlie had to battle long and hard with Pentagon and Special Forces brass to get Delta up and running in the first place, and one skirmish involved the lengthy selection and training process. Why, the four-stars with veto power wanted to know, did top caliber

Special Ops men in peak physical condition, who could shoot the eye out of a Commie from half a mile away, need to be put through this senseless marching?

In a point paper that won the day, Charlie explained the psychology of successful counterterrorist operatives. At the 1972 Munich Olympics, Palestinian terrorists took eleven Israeli athletes hostage. A team of German sharpshooters descended on the scene, surrounded the terrorists, and took aim to get the hostages back. But when the shooting began, two of the Germans who had the terrorists in their sites failed to fire their weapons. Every hostage died.

The Germans had tested their commandos' marksmanship, agility, and tactical expertise. They had not tested their resolve. Charlie saw the opposite truth at work in Somalia and Vietnam when German and Australian counterterrorism operatives selected by similar methods, executed flawlessly. The Army can train a man to spy, shoot, blow things up, and kill with his bare hands. But it cannot instill in a man the series of two-sided personality coins that cash out as a successful operative: patience and aggression, precision and audacity, the ability to lead or fall in line. Above all, the Army cannot instill resolve beyond physical and mental limits.

So Beckwith and Burruss designed the Delta Force selection course to test each man's sheer willingness to *endure*, which is the common denominator that unites small groups of elite fighters who, *in extremis*, seem to have only each other to rely on.

In the freezing mountains of North Carolina, I learned to rely on God. When my legs felt made of pig iron, when I knew I couldn't take another step, I felt His strength. Many, many times, when I was unsure of which way to go, when the terrain blurred into sameness and my map meant nothing, I sensed Him shepherding me in a literal wilderness. When life gets tough, every man draws from a different well of strength, but I am not ashamed to say I depended on God.

6

THE NEXT DAY, instructors ferried us back to Bragg in trucks. In the mountains, they tested our wills. Now, they would render a verdict.

After what seemed a very short night of rest, an Army psychologist brought us in for a battery of tests. The day after that, he interviewed us one-on-one. Anxiety knotted my gut. Not only did I not cotton to the idea of a head doctor, I also knew this was the last hurdle, the final test before selection.

The psychologist was a strange, slightly overweight fellow who seemed totally out of place in this Special Operations environment, where nearly every man you saw was seriously fit. We met in his office, a small cinder-block room with a metal desk and a telephone.

"Sit down, Captain Boykin," he said, reaching down to lift the top file from a stack on his desk. I could see my name written on the border.

Most of the shrink's questions were open-ended, designed to test my ability to reason and think rather than to spit out "right" answers.

"Could you spend several days alone in a sniper position with a homosexual?" the doctor asked. It was his first question. In 1978, it was also a weird question, and it got my attention.

I thought about it. "If it was my mission, I could," I said. "But he'd better understand that I'm not like that."

He continued down a list of questions.

If you observed an illegal act by one of your soldiers during a mission, and knew that reporting it would compromise the mission, would you report the illegal act?

If you were given a cover story and asked to go on a mission where you would essentially live a lie, telling lies every day, would you be able to do that?

Could you, in a very calculated way, kill a person who posed no threat to you?

Tough questions. By then, I had wrestled through questions of deception and killing in times of military necessity, and how those issues sometimes seemed to clash with Christianity. I still struggled with them. But I answered each question as thoughtfully and thoroughly as I could. I knew the psych eval was the last weight in the balance, the factor that would tip the scales for me or against me at the Commander's Board, where Beckwith and his officers would make the final decisions on who was in and who was out. I wasn't sure how the shrink was rating my responses, but I spoke honestly, keeping integrity, humanity, and the military mission uppermost in my thinking.

The interview lasted two hours. "Major Burruss tells me you came in first on the forty-mile march," the psychologist finally said. "Impressive."

"Thank you, sir."

"I also understand you're a man of faith."

"Yes, sir. That's right."

"Captain Boykin, from my analysis of your test data, I believe you rely too much on your faith and not enough on yourself," he said. "I'm going to recommend against your being a part of this organization."

7

THE PSYCHOLOGIST'S ASSESSMENT hit me like a bullet. After the mental and physical torment of the selection course, I could hardly process it. But by the time he ended our meeting and I walked out of his office, I was certain his recommendation was the kiss of death. There was no way I was going to make the final cut.

That was on a Friday. The commander's board was scheduled for Monday. Miserable, I drove back down to New Bern. I talked it over with Lynne. Then Mom assured me she'd been praying for me. That Sunday morning, I went to our little church and during the service, I really began to pray.

"Lord, I don't know what Your will is, whether I'm to be part of this unit or not, but I'm relying on You to lead me," I said.

I left there that morning with peace in my heart, knowing that whatever happened would be God's will.

Back at Bragg on Monday, Beckwith held the board in the small conference room next door to the one where I'd first laid eyes on him. He and several of his men sat in chairs arranged in a semicircle, facing the front of the room and a lone chair. The hot seat. I assumed it was mine, and took it. Since the shrink both knocked the wind out of me and, I thought, punched my ticket back to Eglin, I expected to feel nervous—or worse, resigned to failure. Instead, I felt amazingly calm. In fact, I was even confident.

I looked around at the men who faced me. They all wore civilian clothes. There was Beckwith, of course, wearing his sidearm and, as always, looking like the inside of a laundry hamper. Bucky Burruss was there, as well as a combat medic named Glenn Nickle who had been part of the cadre that put us through the selection course. The unit's sergeant major, William "Country" Grimes, was also there, along with a handful of others.

There is only one word to describe their faces: hostile. Without prelude, they began to machine-gun me with questions. The instant I spit out an answer to one question, here came another one.

What are your strengths?

What are your weaknesses?

If a noncommissioned officer was the best man to lead a mission, would you be willing to work for him?

During an operation, a man under your command breaks a serious rule of engagement. Later on the same day, his bravery saves the lives of three men in your unit. When the op is over, do you discipline him?

Then Beckwith fired off a question. "What's your attitude toward blacks?"

"I serve in an army that is integrated," I said without hesitating. "I have no issues with race."

Beckwith rolled his eyes. "Come on, Boykin, you're from North Carolina. You're telling me that when you were growing up, you never called anybody a nigger?"

"That's not what I said," I answered calmly. "I said I serve in an integrated army and that I have no issues with race."

Beckwith was still snorting his disbelief when Burruss spoke up. "You know, last year the Germans assaulted an aircraft in Mogadishu to rescue some German hostages. One of the German troops went to the rear of the plane, jerked the toilet door open and found a woman, a known terrorist, wearing a Che Guevara t-shirt and holding an AK-47. What would you do if that happened to you?"

"I'd shoot her," I said.

Burruss's eyes got big. "You would shoot a *woman*?"

"You just said she was a known terrorist and she was armed. I'd shoot her."

Burruss scoffed. "I don't believe you'd do that."

Next, Country Grimes took a shot. "During a mission, you come across two little girls. They're lost and alone. Helping them might compromise your operation. What do you do?"

"Well, I'll tell you," I said. "I couldn't do those little girls any harm. I'd have to call the mission off."

"You would compromise a mission for *two little girls*?" Grimes sneered.

"Yes, sir. I would."

Nickle opened his mouth to launch the next salvo, but Beckwith held up his hand. "Okay, stop. Just hold on, everybody."

Looking me square in the eye, he said, "Captain Boykin, you're a religious man, aren't you?"

My confidence slipped a little. *Here it comes*, I thought. *The bottom line. This is where he tells me I'm too religious to serve in his unit.*

"Yes, sir, I guess I am," I said. It wasn't that I was unsure. I just didn't like the way he framed the question. Lots of people are religious, but have no faith in God.

"Is that the way you were raised?" Beckwith asked.

"Well, Colonel, I'll tell you, my mother is a saint, and yes, that's the way she raised me."

For reasons I couldn't guess, Beckwith looked perplexed. He looked down at the floor for a moment then back up at me. Then he said, almost softly, "Yeah, so was mine."

Beckwith stood. "Captain Boykin, we'd be glad to have you," he said. Then he walked over and shook my hand. Joy and relief washed over me. I rose from the hot seat and crossed the room to shake hands with the other board members.

When I got to Bucky Burruss, he gripped my hand firmly and without smiling said, "Welcome to Delta."

SURPRISE, SPEED, AND VIOLENCE OF ACTION

Delta Force
1978–1979

1

ONE-HUNDRED-EIGHTEEN MEN started the selection course. Twenty-five made it to the Long Walk. Of those who finished, nineteen made it into the unit. After the Commander's Board, I drove back to Eglin, packed up my wife and kids, and in a matter of two weeks, relocated to a rented house outside Fort Bragg and enrolled the kids in school. At the end of March I reported back to the stockade for the nineteen-week Operator Training Course (OTC). At about the same time Charlie Beckwith was giving me my shot, a fresh crop of a hundred new hopefuls was starting the Delta selection course. By the time my group started OTC, the dozen or so survivors of that second course came to join us, giving us around thirty men, enough to form a single operational counterterrorist element.

Project DELTA, the unit Charlie commanded in Vietnam, performed deep jungle insertions, recon, and "snatch" operations in which they would capture VC operatives, proving Sir William's theories about special operations accurate. Still, though the Viet Cong's methods were unconventional, even terrorist-like, Charlie's unit was fighting a uniformed, nationalist combatant in a theater of war. But events in the early 1970s turned the Pentagon's attention to a new kind of enemy: the international terrorist.

One trigger was the simmering Jewish-Islamic hatred that in 1970 erupted into battle in Jordan. Yasir Arafat's Palestinian Liberation Organization, backed by both the Soviet Union and Syria, planned to launch raids on Israel from inside the territory of Hussein ibn-Talal, king of Jordan. But the king ordered a full-scale assault on the PLO, and the Jordanian Army crushed Arafat's forces, chasing them back across the Syrian border. The battle returned control of Amman, the Jordanian capital, to King Hussein—but with an unpleasant aftereffect that haunts the West even today. Radical splinter cells formed, fueled now by both rabid anti-Semitism and embarrassment. Groups like Black September now added a new tactic for forcing their will on Israel and its allies: kidnapping and murdering civilians.

In September 1970, Black September hijacked three civilian airliners, and held three hundred passengers captive for a week. After releasing the hostages, the terrorists blew up the planes at an abandoned airfield near Amman, Jordan—then provided film footage of the event to television stations all over the world. Terror was no longer local; it was now world-wide and in living color, puffing up the importance of fledgling terrorist groups. They were well aware of the spectacular multiplier effect of images of ski-masked men holding hostages at gunpoint. The media became the terrorists' most effective weapon.

Two years after the Black September hijacking, the same group kidnapped and murdered the Israeli athletes at Munich. Over and over, global media broadcast the killings, shocking and terrifying the world.

Western European countries responded by forming elite counterterrorist units. The Germans formed *Grenzschutzgruppe 9*, GSG-9, led by Colonel Ulrich Wegener. The French formed the *Groupe d'Intervention de la Grendarmerie National* (GIGN). The Brits modified training for its already legendary SAS. But Americans had not yet been made targets. And internal debate over the separation of military and police power hampered U.S. military planners. One camp argued that hostage rescue was a police matter; others favored a military approach. While other countries trained, America talked.

Then in May 1972, the Baader-Meinhoff Gang, a German Marxist group, bombed the U.S. Army officers' club in Frankfurt and the U.S. Army, Europe, headquarters building in Heidelberg. The assaults underscored the need for an American military counterterrorist unit. Charlie Beckwith teamed with powerful Pentagon allies like Army Chief of Staff (and Rhodes scholar) Bernard Rogers and Deputy Chief of Staff for Operations General Edward "Shy" Meyer to argue for a unit modeled on the British SAS. Beckwith's quest was a ten-year slog through infighting, skepticism, power grabs, money grabs, and plain old bureaucratic foot-dragging. But in 1977, the 1st Special Forces Operational Detachment–DELTA, or Delta Force, opened for business.

Charlie's blueprint called for us to build a unit that could be deployed in response to a terrorist crisis anywhere in the world on a moment's notice. Delta would move in below the radar and work with local officials, military, and police to get the bad guys. Then, we would simply fade away, so that as far as anyone else knew the resulting counterterrorism action had been a local operation.

In some ways, this was a counterintuitive approach to military ops: no credit, no glory, no ticker-tape parades. There would be no public awards ceremonies or receptions. Our names would not appear in the newspapers. Success would be celebrated and war stories swapped only privately, among an inner circle of special ops and intel professionals already privy to information about SCI-level (Sensitive Compartmented Information) missions. In fact, the Pentagon did not even officially acknowledge our existence. After Delta began, a standard search of military personnel records for a "William G. Boykin" would reveal that no man with that name served in the United States Army.

But I did, of course, and here I was, one of thirty young hotshots reporting for training. Already, the selection course had forged a bond between us. In addition to being an assessment, it was a rite of passage. By the time we few emerged on the other end of it, most men had already fallen by the wayside. That in itself was enough to forge a strong connection. Each of us knew that the men beside us were cut from the same cloth we were.

Charlie put it this way: "If I'm going to put you in a spider-hole for a week and tell you that when a certain man walks out of a building, you're going to shoot him, I have to know that you're going to shoot him. I know this because I know that we're alike."

In nineteen weeks, Beckwith and an initial cadre of instructors would train us in marksmanship, room-clearing, close-quarters battle, hostage management, and forced entry at crisis points from hotel rooms to airliners, and much, much more. We would learn macro-functions like establishing and maintaining a command post and secure communications, to microskills like how to pick a pin tumbler padlock. We would learn how to drive anything from a Jeep to a track-vehicle to a diesel locomotive. Delta instructors would teach us how to blow stuff up and how to keep hostages safe from terrorists blowing stuff up. We would learn to live under a cover story, collect intelligence, conduct surveillance, and avoid it ourselves. We would climb and rappel, and learn to do it without making a sound. And perhaps most important of all, we would learn how best to disarm a hostile opponent—and if he resisted, how best to kill him.

Since we would be operating in small teams in faraway places with no backup, we would even go through emergency medical training to be able to save each other's lives. (Once, when we had to learn how to start IVs, I practiced on this giant ginger-haired fellow from Boston whose muscles were so big we called him Popeye. He was really mad when I collapsed his vein.)

On the first day, we all headed down to the arms room, where a sergeant issued us each an M-1911 .45 caliber pistol. Even though it was the old Army standard, that gun would stop a man cold with a single round. He also issued us each a .45cal M-3A1 "grease gun," a vintage automatic weapon that went out of production in the 1950s. Grease guns hadn't been used much since, but it turned out their low muzzle velocity and slow rate of fire made them a perfect weapon for room clearing. Their heavy slugs would slam into, but not through, a terrorist, and assaulters could squeeze off single shots without disturbing their aim.

Our marksmanship instructor was Ginger Flynn, a ruddy, carrot-topped Irishman on loan from the British SAS. Ginger loved his beer, but during his time in the States, he also developed an affection for American sour mash whiskey.

"Awright, chaps, you're not getting any prettier and I'm not getting any drunker," Ginger would say on the firing range. "Move your asses so I can get to the pub!"

We all knew how to shoot straight, but we had to learn how all over again—now using instinctive fire techniques rather than aimed fire. Here's the difference: In hunting or target shooting, you're developing a sight picture with your feet planted, one eye closed, aligning the front and rear sights on the target. Instinctive fire is more like the Old West, the quick draw you see in all the movies. In a gunfight, John Wayne never raised his Colt, developed a sight picture, then pulled the trigger. Instead, he drew his pistol, pointed, and fired.

Some Army training manuals call instinctive fire the least desirable way to kill bad guys in close-quarters combat, or CQB. That's because it is thought to be the least accurate, as the shooter does not develop a sight picture at all, but relies on muscle memory to tell him where to fire the kill shot. But in hostage rescue, the two seconds it takes to aim and fire are one more than it takes for a terrorist to kill a hostage. So for a month, we spent at least four hours a day on instinctive fire techniques. We started out with targets on stakes and hour after hour, reduced them to shreds. We learned to raise our weapons and fire in a single motion. We learned to fire, reload, and clear weapons jams on the run. Shooting at man-size silhouettes, we had to put two shots—a double-tap—in a "kill zone," the head or chest, within certain time and distance standards. I can't share what those standards were, but trust me: by the end of the month, accuracy wasn't a problem.

Ginger developed and honed our skills relentlessly and we calculated that before moving on to CQB training, we expended more ammo in thirty days than the entire 82nd Airborne used in a year.

By June, we were able to get rid of the target cloth and move into the "House of Horrors," a state-of-the-art CQB training ground. The four-room complex featured ballistic walls and portable, interchangeable target systems. One of the best things was the stop-motion projection target system. The instant you fired your weapon, the film froze on the screen so you could see exactly what you hit. Another system featured pop-up targets that allowed each operator only seconds to enter a room, identify hostile targets, and fire.

Ginger taught us to put two headshots into every terrorist—"Happiness is a headshot!" he'd say—to check to be sure they were dead, and to handcuff *everyone*, even dead guys. We practiced blowing doors and rolling flash-bang grenades, not only to gain entry but to stun the enemy, putting them on the defensive. We learned to hit terrorists with three spears that became Delta's motto: surprise, speed, and violence of action.

During the half of the day when Ginger Flynn wasn't teaching us to shoot straight, Wade Ishimoto was teaching us spy stuff, more formally known as "tradecraft." Born and raised in Hawaii, Ish was a Japanese-American who, after finishing his baccalaureate degree, enlisted in the Army and went to Vietnam. He served with the 5th Special Forces, a unit that was investigated after a double-agent mysteriously fell to his death from a helicopter. (The Defense Department suspected he was pushed.) Ish was one of those interrogated and later exonerated. In 1978, Charlie brought him into Delta to assist with intel and also convinced Pentagon brass that Ish, a detail oriented, no-nonsense man with a knack for planning, needed a commission. So Sergeant Ishimoto became Captain Ishimoto, and here he was with us.

From Ish, I learned "elicitation" and how to live under a cover story. Elicitation is the art of teasing information out of people without letting them know what you're really after. Once during training, I had to travel to the National Guard Armory in Richmond, Virginia, with an NCO and fellow operator-in-training from Indianapolis named Mark Gentry. Our mission was to learn the exact location of weapons storage on the post, and to actually be shown the weapons and granted access to the space. Our cover story was that we were working with an Army unit that was relocating from Fort Bragg to Fort Dix, New Jersey. We were coordinating en route logistics for the entire unit, our story went, and would need fuel, billeting for twenty people, and a place to store weapons overnight.

Mark and I showed up at the armory, were ushered in, and went to see the commanding major to tell him our bogus story. He was very accommodating, said he'd be happy to oblige, and showed us where he kept a whole cache of weapons, including M-16s and M-60's. I expected him to ask us for official Army orders showing this unit relocation, or at least for identification. I was astonished when he didn't ask for either.

This is a lot easier than I thought. Frighteningly easy, actually, from a national security standpoint.

"We'll be in touch," I said to the major as we headed out the door with detailed information about his armory. I was lying, of course, and he never heard from us again.

As a Christian, I thought a lot about that. From the time I was a little boy, I'd known that the Bible teaches that God hates lies. How then could I rectify the biblical mandate for honesty with making up a story to elicit information or infiltrate enemy territory? But that led to a broader question: in time of war, are we required to tell the truth to people who are trying to kill us or others?

Deception is often foundational to battle planning. On D-Day, planners deceived the Nazis. Should the Allies have announced their plan to storm the beach at Normandy?

Here's another example. During the Revolutionary War, women living at Bryan's Station, a Kentucky stockade, risked their lives in a ruse designed to ward off an Indian attack. As a diversion, the women were to pretend they didn't know the woods outside the fort were teeming with armed Indians, and stroll down to the spring carrying pails as they usually did each morning. That would distract the Indians and give the garrison inside time to post riflemen inside the walls. Terrified, but seeing no choice, the women agreed to the plan. And before they left the safety of the fort, they gathered to pray for God's protection.

The plan worked. While the women were outside the stockade, the attackers held their fire. And when the Indians finally attacked, the hidden riflemen cut down the first wave of raiders, and were able to defend the fort until reinforcements arrived.

The women of Bryan's Station not only deceived the enemy, but *prayed to God* before they did it. Was that wrong? Should they have instead cowered inside the station walls and resigned themselves to death? Were their actions un-Christian?

Those were the kinds of things I thought about as I wrestled with the deceptive aspects of clandestine work. In the end my philosophy boiled down to this: lying in the interest of defending others is different than lying for personal gain. As Winston Churchill said, "In wartime, truth is so precious that she should always be attended by a bodyguard of lies."

2

OUR TRAINING LASTED NINETEEN WEEKS. During that time, the dogfight continued between Charlie Beckwith and the Special Forces brass who opposed Delta on principle. In those days, Special Operations units fell under several tiers of command authority, including the John F. Kennedy Institute for Military Assistance, and (going north in the chain of command) the XVIII Airborne Corps, the U.S. Army Forces Command (FORSCOM), the Department of the Army, and the Joint Chiefs. But during his SAS training, Charlie had learned the killing nature of military bureaucracy.

Terrorists strike like lightning—hard, fast, and without warning. Time wasted coddling the sensitivities of turf-conscious generals with a penchant for paperwork meant hostages killed. So Charlie fought for, and won, the command-structure equivalent of a freeway bypass. Delta exited below the JFK Center and got back on at the Joint Chiefs. That made many, many people very, very angry.

As a direct result, a competitor to Delta was born: Blue Light, a 5th Special Forces unit under the command of Colonel Bob Mountel. Mountel was among those who felt Delta's mission belonged to the Special Forces community, not the Department of the Army. When he stood up Blue Light, a temporary unit meant to bridge America's counterterrorism gap until Delta got up and running, Mountel set out to make his unit Delta's permanent replacement.

While the brass fought it out, Delta continued to train, essentially cramming most of the Special Forces individual qualifications course into six weeks, which was no small task. Next, we gelled as an operations squadron under the command of Bucky Burruss and began training as a unit, practicing assault and hostage rescue, stealth troop movement, parachute operations, and VIP protection.

As needed, Charlie made contact with private industry and government officials who could help make our training realistic. In the late spring of 1978, Delta traveled to New York City and practiced taking down passenger jets at John F. Kennedy International Airport, courtesy of the airlines. (Aviation officials saw the growing rash of terrorist hijackings, and were only too happy to cooperate.) With the help of certain Washington, D.C. officials, we traveled to the Beltway and practiced assaults on the Metro. Once, Charlie even managed to have an actual passenger train brought onto Fort Bragg via the railhead located on-post.

It was an exhilarating time, as we were developing new concepts, laying the foundation for Delta's future—not only for how we were going to train and what we were going to train on, but also for the actual tactics we would use. We would plan an operation one week, and execute it the following week. Then we'd troubleshoot and document the results. But it wasn't as though Charlie and company had a ready curriculum and were putting us through it. In fact, no U.S. military playbook on counterterrorist operations existed.

It was our job to write it.

On Friday afternoons, Pete Schoomaker and I would get everybody together in a makeshift classroom. We'd take a big piece of butcher paper and sketch out a rough diagram of the next week's training operation. Then we would assign various operators to take pieces of the mission, both for planning and execution. The NCOs were very dedicated to making the training challenging and realistic. Once, we gave Sergeant First Class John Cupp the task of preparing a multi-day session on urban vehicle assault. But when he couldn't find a suitable car for us to train on, he brought his own car out to the training ground. We promptly wrecked it.

Different guys got different assignments, but if any part of the mission called for the use of explosives, we gave that job to Sergeant First Class Eddie Westfall. A Special Forces engineer, he was a big guy—really big— who never did anything at half speed. We called him "Fast Eddie."

Fast Eddie almost never stopped talking, but he was very engaging, so you didn't mind. And the only thing he loved better than talking was blowing stuff up. Throughout our ops training, Fast Eddie was always leaving the stockade and going up to, say, the shipyard or the air station at Norfolk and hauling back various objects for his breaching experiments. One time, he brought back a bus, and systematically reduced it to a useless heap of melted metal. Fast Eddie always used the principal of P—meaning "plenty." Once, the Army gave him an old building at Fort Knox to destroy. He dressed it with so much dynamite that when he pushed the button, the roof flew up, the walls fell in, and some power poles blew over, knocking out the lights on a good portion of Fort Knox.

Fast Eddie learned not to use quite so much dynamite. And like him, all of us gained skills by great leaps. I soaked it up eagerly. The most exciting thing for me was that I began to develop tremendous confidence in my teammates as I learned how talented these men really were. Don Simmons, Dave Cheney, Jack Joplin, Bob Little, and many more like them were dedicated, quiet professionals who wanted only to be on the front lines when the bullets started flying. Not only were they physically fearsome and without an ounce of quit, I was amazed by their ability to tackle new problems and develop strategies to solve them.

The British SAS helped develop our tactics. In terms of basic breaching, assault, and rescue tactics, Delta also enlisted the support of the FBI and Secret Service. Sometimes we went up to the Secret Service Academy at Beltsville, Maryland; other times their agents drove down to Bragg and worked with us on techniques. We traded time and facilities with the FBI in similar fashion, and also wove in some SWAT team tactics. But whatever hostage-rescue techniques we learned from law enforcement, we took them as a starting point then adapted them for use in a military situation.

After all, if Delta became involved in a rescue, there would be no "hostage standoff." And if hostage takers failed to surrender, we wouldn't be arresting them.

3

ABOUT SIX MONTHS into Charlie's two-year plan, Pentagon brass announced it was time for us to prove ourselves. But our training was far from complete. If we failed, the Pentagon could scrap Delta altogether, and that possibility loomed large when we found out that FORSCOM would conduct the evaluation. With Mountel and Blue Light under its umbrella, how fair would the evaluation be?

It turned out to be a hatchet job, the way Charlie saw it. I was less certain. As the evaluation unfolded on a hot, cloudless day in July, it appeared much of the time the evaluators simply didn't know what they were doing.

Delta trained in a highly unorthodox form of warfare, a violent strike hybrid of guerilla and law enforcement tactics. Though Charlie and Bucky sent FORSCOM a letter detailing Delta's training standards so they could design appropriate tests to measure us, it seemed that letter wound up at the North Pole.

For example, in the room-clearing portion of the evaluation, exercise controllers put terrorist targets behind hostage targets, so that when Delta stormed the room, they had to move around for several seconds in order to find and fire on the hostile targets. In a real-life hostage scenario, targets wouldn't stand still, but would move to engage us. The way it was set up, the hostages were dead meat before the "rescue" began.

I knew Mountel and Blue Light had been lobbying FORSCOM hard to keep their mission. Between the hostage-rescue demo and later, an equally impossible scenario designed to test our snipers, I began to wonder if the evaluators wanted us to fail.

Later in the day, after a Delta NCO sent the FORSCOM martial-arts evaluator to the hospital with a concussion, a key part came in our test: a double-hostage scenario. South American terrorists had seized both a building and an airliner. Delta assault teams were tasked to take down both—and rescue the hostages—at the same time.

As I mentioned, we'd been training on real commercial airliners, the kind actually in use in modern times. But FORSCOM was doing this evaluation on the cheap. They raided a bone yard somewhere and dragged in a Lockheed Super Constellation, a WWII vintage aircraft on which the last recorded passenger flight had occurred when Lyndon Johnson was president. On the day they gave us the scenario, they gave us the Super Constellation. I was to lead F-1, the element that would take down the aircraft. I had a great team, including Popeye; Cheney, a big-hearted bear of a man; Joplin, a Special Forces medic who earned a Silver Star during the Son Tay Raid; and Mike Kalua, a huge, delightful Samoan, who spoke rapid-fire, island-accented English and always called me "Boss."

When they gave us the Connie, we knew we'd have her only for a few hours. So we had to work fast, learning the location of all the doors, hatches, locks, and how they worked, as well as the interior layout of the aircraft and every possible rat hole that might conceal a terrorist. Ish and Delta's intel staff inundated the evaluators with questions: How much fuel is aboard? How much baggage? Who are the passengers? What does the flight crew look like? And on and on. The answers were mostly "We don't know" and "We'll get back to you." That made planning difficult, but also highlighted the nitty-gritty detail of our training. The evaluators were impressed.

While my team planned the aircraft assault, Pete and a separate element laid out a plan to take down the building.

When our planning was complete, Bucky assembled the squadron and we trucked out to Camp McCall. The evaluators had already put the hostage and terrorist actors on the Connie. From the isolation site at Bragg, a trained CIA hostage negotiator, assisted by my favorite psychologist, began fielding "demands." At dusk, I put a sniper recon team on the aircraft and Pete put one on the building. For twelve hours, my snipers kept meticulous watch on the Connie, reporting every scrap of movement, every detail.

"L-1 window open." That meant the first window on the left side of the plane.

"T-1 in the cockpit." Every terrorist had a number.

"H visible at L-1." "H" was the code for hostage.

As night fell, we split into assault elements and headed toward our separate targets. Each operator wore black coveralls, black gloves, and an assault vest full of spare ammo magazines, flex cuffs, a first-aid kit, and various signaling devices. Black balaclavas covered our heads, revealing only our eyes. Underneath the balaclavas, each of us wore a MX-360 earpiece and push-to-talk mike hooked onto our vests. All of us carried .45s and six magazines, but ten men also carried grease guns.

In addition, some operators carried specialty items. Jack carried his medical gear. Popeye carried the Chem-Lights he'd use to string a glowing walkway along which assaulters would lead the hostages from the aircraft to Jack's treatment area. Mike Kalua had a PRC-77 FM radio strapped to his back; that linked us with Beckwith and Pete.

During our study of the target, we had learned that, in addition to its main door, the Super Constellation had two emergency hatches over the wings. So we carried three ladders with us, one for each entrance, each lightly padded so that they could be laid silently against the bird in preparation for the assault.

Silence was a critical part of our training. Operators not only learned to recon, breach, climb, rappel, rig explosives, and take out sentries by approaching them from behind and snapping their necks, we learned to do it without making a sound. Absolute stealth increased the chances of success in real hostage rescue. But it was also critical during an exercise, because the way you fail an exercise is to be discovered and have the terrorist/actors start mock-murdering hostages.

Now, my team of twenty-five men crept toward the airfield under cover of darkness. The low night sounds of the Carolina woods were enough to drown any hint of our approach. Observers later said we blended into the landscape like shifting shadows, indiscernible. Moving slowly because of the ladders, we finally reached a stand of high grass near the edge of the tarmac about 150 yards off the Connie's tail. Our assault plan called for us to address the plane from the rear, where it had no windows. From our distance, we couldn't see any movement aboard, and heard only the high hum of the auxiliary power unit that pumped electricity to the aircraft. As fireflies sparked in the warm, swampy air, we hunkered down in the grass for an hour, watching.

Finally, Beckwith issued the execute code word: jasmine.

F-1 swept across the tarmac like a silent black tide. I was near the rear of the formation, just ahead of Mike and his radio. The belly of the plane stood about five feet off the ramp. Bending slightly to fit, we edged underneath, dropping lower as the tail sloped toward the concrete. Suddenly, behind me, a loud scrape echoed off the Connie's metal skin. It was the PRC-77 antenna sticking up off Mike's back. Instantly, I spun around, wrapped the big Samoan in my right arm, and took him to the ground. F-1 froze. Seconds passed as I lay nose to nose with Mike. Even though his balaclava covered all but his eyes, I could see he had *I'm sorry, Boss!* written all over his face. I felt bad for him.

We listened for the telltale pop-pop of blank rounds, the sign that hostages were dying. But there was only quiet, overlaid with the noise of the auxiliary power unit. At this distance, its steady hum had been enough to mask our error. When our snipers reported no change in activity inside the plane, the op was still a go.

Lightning-quick, an assault team of a dozen operators laid ladders below the main door and against the wings. Popeye moved to the nose of the aircraft and waited underneath. Once they were in position, I made a quick radio check with Charlie to make sure Pete's team was in position for the building assault.

Then I keyed my mike, and the order filtered into each man's ear: "Execute."

The assaulters flowed up the ladders and breached the doors.

Five seconds passed.

Above us, pistol reports rang out. Muffled voices from the plane's interior. "Remain calm! We're here to get you out! Everybody place your hands on your head."

Since the hostage takers were supposed to be Latin American, Dave Cheney repeated the last command in Spanish. *"Manos en las cabezas!"*

Ten seconds gone.

Jack sprinted away, off the Connie's port side, to set up his treatment area. Popeye moved out from under the aircraft's nose and began laying his Chem-Light path. More shots.

The snipers kept their scopes trained on the breached hatches.

"All secure," Dave reported. "Ready to evacuate."

Time elapsed: fifteen seconds.

Pete's team was just as effective. The after-action report showed that the speed and violence of their assault on the building stunned the terrorist/ actors, immobilizing them like headlight-speared rabbits on a country road.

After the exercise, we immediately trucked back to the isolation site at Bragg. Tired, dirty, and still in our assault gear, Delta gathered in the conference room. The FORSCOM evaluators were there: General Volney Warner, General Guy S. "Sandy" Meloy, a couple of colonels. The room was packed. By then, Delta's tactical teams had been twenty-four hours with no sleep and forty-eight with little. It was clear we'd executed the dual takedown scenario with stunning efficiency. But how would the evaluators balance that with our earlier performance in the individual skills tests?

General Warner was the on-scene observer with F-1. "That was the most professional cross-country movement I have ever seen," he said of our approach to the Connie. "Never heard a person say a word."

When Meloy spoke up, he was less effusive, but still gave us pretty decent marks overall.

But that wasn't the way Charlie saw it. He was still pissed off about the individual tests, and still stinging from the clear indications that no one had bothered to read his letter detailing Delta's training. Also, he was dead certain this entire early eval was a set-up, designed to dismantle Delta and clear the way for Mountel and Blue Light.

Colonel Beckwith stood and faced the generals. And when he opened his mouth, he said, "I never knew there were so [expletive] many counter-terrorism experts in the Army."

Inwardly, I rolled my eyes. *There's going to be one hell of a fight before we get out of here tonight.*

4

CHARLIE HAD HIS SAY and so did a couple of the generals. But in the end, Delta's performance on the evaluation proved that Blue Light was redundant. Mountel's rival force was disbanded.

Delta went back into training, now focused on upgrading equipment and improving strategies. Pete and I devised more complex training scenarios, and Charlie and Bucky encouraged all of us to innovate. Staff Sergeant Terry Hall improved the efficiency of the grease guns, developing a quick-operating thumb safety. Pat Hurley, the guy who slept with his boney butt in my back during the Delta selection course, invented battery-operated pop-up targets we could take to remote sites for training. Delta became the counterterrorism equivalent of a brain trust as all the guys worked on new concepts and techniques.

We also began a kind of foreign exchange program with the other elite counterterrorist units: West Germany's GSG-9, France's GIGN, and the predecessor to us all, the British SAS. Those units also sent observers when, on November 1, 1979, our final evaluation began. This was the real deal, finally, with representatives from CIA, FBI, the Secret Service, Treasury, and Justice in attendance. The State Department sent Ambassador Anthony Quainton. The three-day test was rigorous. In addition to the individual skills tests, we had to plan and perform another dual takedown scenario, this time on a building and a Boeing 727. Apparently, we were moving up in the world.

Delta wowed the evaluators in every phase. Oohs and aahs all around. We finally wrapped up at around 2 a.m. on November 4. A lot of folks piled into vehicles and drove into Hinesville to grab some Waffle House breakfast. But I hadn't slept in more than forty-eight hours. Somehow, I managed to drape my six-one frame across a little loveseat in an office somewhere and drop into the deathlike sleep of total exhaustion.

"Jerry..."

Am I dreaming?

"Jerry, wake up." Someone was shaking my shoulder, trying to rouse me out of my deep stupor.

I cracked my eyes and could see daylight.

"Hey, get your stuff packed," Bucky Burruss said. "We're going back to Bragg. The American Embassy in Tehran has just been seized."

WELCOME TO
WORLD WAR III

★ ★ ★

Iran Hostage Crisis

1979–1980

1

IN 1978 IRAN, REVOLUTION WAS IN THE AIR. For thirty years, the Americans and the Soviets had been locked in nuclear stand-off, playing out a game of trench-coat chess, each side working to block the other from gaining control of the Islamic third world and its oil resources. America allied itself with mainly Sunni Islamic powers who held to the concept of civil government—their version of separation of church and state. But beneath the surface, the anger of Shia fundamental-ists simmered, then boiled up into rage. To them, America was a greedy and power-mad infidel, not an ally but the "Great Satan" that must be driven from Islamic lands. In place of Iran's whorish foreign alliances, the Shias envisioned a glorious government under Sharia—or Koranic—law, led by fundamentalist clerics, an order author Mark Bowden would later call "totalitarianism rooted in divine revelation." In 1978, led by the Aya-tollah Ruhollah Khomeini, this Islamist revolution swept aside the gov-ernment of Mohammad Reza Pahlavi, the shah of Iran, forcing him into exile.

As it had in the U.S. for the previous ten years, the intoxicating scent of revolution seized university campuses in the Iranian capital, and many students embraced the spiritual and political fervor. With the shah gone, the dream of Islamist utopia was within reach, they felt. But in the heart of Tehran sat a cancer: the American embassy. Certain the diplomats there were actually counterrevolutionaries working to overthrow the new regime, a small inner circle of Islamist students hatched a plan. They would overrun the embassy, seize it, and occupy it for three days.

During that time they would broadcast a series of communiqués denouncing the United States. Khomeini, in a speech he gave a few days after the students discussed their plan, urged "all grade-school, university, and theological students to increase their attacks against America." The student revolutionaries rejoiced. The Ayatollah had surely heard of their plan and was with them!

It wasn't true. Khomeini knew nothing of them.

On November 4, 1979, hundreds of Iranian students, led by a small hardcore group, poured over the embassy walls, breached the buildings, and took sixty-six Americans hostage. Ordered to stand down by their diplomatic superiors, Marine Corps embassy guards never fired a shot.

Bowden's 2006 account of the embassy seizure, *Guests of the Ayatollah*, revealed that though this brief occupation was supposed to be peaceful, at least one of the students, Mohammed Hashemi, "prepared himself to die." Following Islamic instruction for *jihadi* martyrs, Hashemi performed the same ritual washing and prayers that nineteen hijackers would perform two decades later, on September 11, 2001, before murdering nearly three thousand Americans on U.S. soil. By the time Delta got news of the embassy takeover, reports had begun trickling in that the students were armed. Some hostages had been threatened at gunpoint and others severely beaten.

And so, on November 4, 1979, literally within hours of Army and intel evaluators certifying Delta ready for action, we loaded up in C-130s and flew from Georgia back to Bragg to launch our first mission.

Logan had been planning to take his squadron to Colorado for "winter warfare training" after the final eval. It was actually a ski trip to celebrate Delta's official inauguration. Bucky recalled them immediately. Most of Delta redeployed to the Farm, a secure CIA isolation site. I didn't go with them. Instead I went to Washington, D.C., joining Charlie and a Delta colonel named Chuck Whittle to meet with Pentagon brass and begin planning a rescue operation. That was how quickly it happened. Though the hostages' captivity stretched into weeks, then months, and Americans clamored for their government to storm in and get them back, the rescue planning actually began within days of the attack.

On November 8, I arrived for the first time on the Pentagon's innermost "E Ring," just past the offices of the Joint Chiefs. I was a little in awe just being there and felt a sense of history as I passed the portraits of past JCS chairmen, including General Omar Nelson Bradley, an officer who had such compassion for his men during World War II they called him "the soldiers' general." I admired that.

Normal wooden doors punctuated the walls of Corridor 8 until the end. There stood a steel door secured with a spin-dial cipher lock. I pressed a button and an Air Force sergeant opened the door then escorted me into another smaller interior hallway with a second steel door. Behind that door was Room 2C840.

I half expected to step into a sleek secret-agent kind of space. Instead, I found a tiny, cramped room with exposed pipes running along the ceiling, mismatched government-issue furniture, and filing cabinets crammed into every possible space. On the wall, a row of white clocks announced the time in strategic locations around the world. The center of the room held a warren of desks and a small conference table. A secure telephone sat in the corner. The stale cigarette smell of a thousand planning sessions hung in the air.

I had just taken a seat at the conference table when the service chiefs began streaming into the room, including Joint Chiefs chairman General David Jones and Harold Brown, the Secretary of Defense.

With everyone seated, Secretary Brown spoke first. "What do we know? What kind of intel do we have?"

The answer was, very little. But CIA was working the problem. The U.S. had three CIA agents stationed inside the American embassy in Tehran. But since all three were now hostages, very little intel was coming out of Iran. We did not know, for example, that the students who seized the embassy originally meant to stage only a three-day sit-in. Nor did we know one of the students may have been Mahmoud Ahmadinejad, who in 2005 would be elected president of Iran. But some embassy officials, offsite at the time of the takeover, spoke with embassy employees by phone before they were overrun and communications cut off. From that, we did know of the violence against the Americans.

Brown then asked who, exactly, the hostage takers were and what it was they wanted.

"Iranian students of some kind, sir," an intel officer said. "Loyal to Khomeini. Their demands are unclear at this point."

Brown scowled, unsatisfied with the vague answer.

"Has the Iranian government made any public statements?" Chairman Jones said.

"Nothing of substance," the same intel officer answered.

Then Jones asked the money question: "What do we have in terms of capabilities?"

"We've put Delta in isolation at the Farm and they're starting to do the tactical planning," a Special Ops colonel said. "We're looking at going in on Air Force helos. Spec Ops has CH-53s, so we're looking at those and Army Chinooks to see if they can play a role."

These planning considerations were aimed at two problems that, on a difficulty scale of one to ten, made this mission a fifty. First, this was not like the hostage scenarios that played out in Entebbe or Mogadishu, with not only a friendly host city, but also a handy beach perfect for a coastal insertion. Tehran was tucked away in the dry heart of Iran. A thousand miles of desert waste separated the city from the nearest coastline, which lay south. To the north was central Asia, the gateway to the Soviet Union. Afghanistan and Pakistan formed Iran's eastern border, and to the west sat Turkey and Iraq. The Soviets weren't going to help, of course, except maybe to cheer for Iran. And while America had friends in Iraq, involving other Islamic governments was, from a security standpoint, out of the question. The only regional allies willing to support us were Egypt and Oman.

This dovetailed with the second problem: Delta trained for operations in permissive environments with the support of local government, military, and police. Now, suddenly, we found our first mission was not only in a *non*-permissive environment with no support, but also the local government was going to be the enemy. Not only that, but the embassy itself was buried in a city of five million people who hated America. We would face either informants or outright armed resistance at every corner.

All those problems meant any rescue attempt would have to begin in the air from a logistically nightmarish distance. What kind of aircraft could cover the kind of distances we were talking about? Long-range transport aircraft need long, weight-stressed runways. None of those were lying around in countries that would let us use them. And even if one would, where would we land them in Iran? It was a pretty good bet the Ayatollah wasn't going to open Mehrabad International Airport for us. Meanwhile, short-range aircraft presented trouble of their own: where and how would they refuel?

Given the distances, any aircraft involved in the mission would either have to launch from friendly turf within flying range of Iran, or from aircraft carriers in the Persian Gulf. We didn't yet know how all that would come together, but those were our only options.

"We're going to have to bring State into this," Joint Chiefs vice chairman Jack Vessey said. "They'll have to coordinate the staging bases."

"All right, call State," Brown said. "Start working the staging areas and overflight approvals." Then he looked at Charlie, Chuck Whittle, and me. "You guys keep working the plan. We'll get back together tomorrow."

As the meeting broke up, Charlie began speaking in low tones about the critical lack of intel with an Army two-star I recognized as Jim Vaught, a staff officer with the Joint Chiefs. A rugged-looking combat veteran of three wars, Vaught wore a chest full of decorations. Listening in to his conversation with Charlie, I learned that Vaught had been named commander of the rescue mission.

As planning began, the knowledge that the Iranians could begin executing hostages at any moment haunted us. It meant we might have to launch any day, using an emergency mission plan slapped together with duct tape and chicken wire. Because procedure required it, we came up with a plan like that. It involved blasting our way into Mehrabad airport, blasting our way through Tehran, snatching the hostages, and blasting our way out. The chances of success were zero. Less than zero. But we were pretty sure we'd have time to come up with a better plan. Because unless the Iranians forced his hand by executing a hostage, none of us thought Jimmy Carter had the guts to order us in.

2

THE SECRET MEETINGS at the Pentagon went on. Room 2C840 became a hive of ringing telephones, clattering typewriters, and spirited debate. Somebody from on high officially dubbed the overall planning sessions "Rice Bowl." Meanwhile, Delta had to plan and train for the rescue operation itself. But because of the Kremlin's satellite surveillance on Bragg, there was no way Delta could plan and train there. After discarding several alternative sites as inadequate, we settled on the Farm. But any mass exit with a failure to return might raise suspicions that America's new door-busters were en route to Iran. So Charlie and Bucky came up with an elaborate plan by which the operators left Bragg in rented vehicles at staggered times, and over the course of two days reassembled at the Farm. To fool the Russians into believing that Delta was percolating along normally, we left a good-sized support staff behind. For the benefit of the Kremlin, they went through the motions of our daily routine.

Meanwhile, planning continued. Just getting to the embassy remained a tall order: How would we get into Iran undetected? How would we cross the vast open country into Tehran—again, undetected? How would we breach the hardened portions of the embassy? Where were the terrorists holding the hostages inside the complex? How do we neutralize resistance? How do we get back out of the embassy? Out of Tehran? Out of the country?

If each of those questions seemed difficult, the answers to them opened up huge vacuums waiting to be filled with even more answers. Take the embassy problem, for example. The complex included fourteen buildings strewn across twenty-seven heavily wooded acres, surrounded by a high wall. Getting in and out was not a problem: Delta could simply slip over the walls and Fast Eddie could blow our way out. But regarding the actual rescue op inside the compound, a storm of questions swirled: Were the Iranians holding the hostages all in one place or in separate locations?

What kind of doors were on the rooms where the hostages were held? Which way did they open? What kind of locks did they have on them? To breach the doors, would we need explosives, or would a shotgun do?

Each question was like a stack of Russian nesting dolls: one solved puzzle opened onto dozens of smaller puzzles each of which was frustrated by the lack of intelligence coming out of Tehran. But fuzzy details began to resolve themselves when we received an eight-by-twelve foot model of the embassy compound and the surrounding streets. Army engineers also constructed separate scale models of each embassy building. Inside the models, the floor plan of every story in each building was reproduced in detail. Delta memorized every one of them.

We also memorized the names, faces, and biographies of every hostage. We tacked their photos to a wall in Beech Tree, a guest house at the Farm we converted into our planning center. Every operator and action officer learned to recognize and name each hostage on sight.

My heart ached for the hostages and their families, and I prayed for them daily, especially one, a Jewish CIA man. I was really concerned that the hostage takers had figured that out from his name. How long would his status as an American protect him? If they began killing hostages, would they kill him first?

3

ON NOVEMBER 18 AND 20, we caught a break. The terrorists released thirteen hostages, and with them, a treasure of intelligence, including details on the interior layout of the embassy and valuable details about the Iranian students: what they looked like, their routines, who seemed to be in charge, who seemed weak, strong, or just going along for the ride.

At the top of our list of planning priorities: transport. Getting to Iran then getting the hostages out. For the second job, we chose the Navy RH-53 Sea Stallion, a monster helicopter that could fly a long way and carry a fair number of people. The RH-53 had foldable tail booms, which meant we could stash these helos below the deck of an aircraft carrier and steam to within a reasonable distance from the Iranian coastline without alerting hostile intelligence agencies. More importantly, the RH-53 was the only helicopter in the inventory with not only the load and range capabilities we needed, but also the ability to inflight-refuel.

So we'd picked an aircraft—great. But we still didn't have any pilots who knew how to fly the mission. Even working through the Chief of Naval Operations, Delta was able to find only one guy in the entire Navy who had both flown the RH-53 coast to coast, *and* completed aerial refueling along the way: Lieutenant Commander Jay Jacobson out of Naval Air Station Norfolk, Virginia.

But the mission planners couldn't just call him up: "Hey Jay, wanna fly a super secret mission of global importance from which you may never return?" If he said no, or even if he said yes, then made a single compromising phone call, the operation, by now dubbed Eagle Claw, could be over before it began. So we had to use different methods.

The Pentagon contacted Jacobson's squadron commander with orders for the pilot to report to a hotel in Richmond, Virginia. A man would approach Jacobson in the hotel lobby and say, "Are you here for the convention?"

Jacobson was to say, "No, I'm waiting for a buddy." Then Jacobson was to go with the man who approached him.

Now most of the Navy pilots I know won't take a leak without a flight plan. Jacobson, I was later told, grumbled and wanted to know why he had to do this. Of course, no one would tell him why. So his instructions were: "Just do what you're asked to do."

A CIA agent met Jacobson at the hotel, and they exchanged the bona fides. Jacobson got in the car and the agent drove him halfway to the Farm before pulling over to the side of the road in the middle of nowhere.

"Get out," the agent said. "Wait here until someone picks you up."

By now, Jacobson had had it with the cloak-and-dagger crap. "You've *got* to be kidding me!"

"No. I'm not kidding you," the agent said, as serious as an undertaker. "Do it. And hold this newspaper under your arm while you're doing it."

Exasperated and rolling his eyes, Jacobson got out of the car. Within fifteen minutes, another spook picked him up and drove him the rest of the way. After two more hours, the two men rolled into the Farm and pulled up to Beech Tree.

"Go sit over there on those steps," the CIA man told Jacobson.

Now the pilot was steaming. Still, he did what he was told. And when Pete and I happened to walk out on the porch at Beech Tree, there he sat, elbows on his knees, head in his hands. We didn't know he was coming.

"Who are you?" Pete said.

He looked at us, seeming confused and frustrated. "I'm Lieutenant Commander Jay Jacobson."

"What are you doing here?" I said.

Jacobson went off: "What am I doing here? I don't have a clue. I go to a hotel. Somebody picks me up. He drops me off on the side of the road. Another guy picks me up. He drives me for four hours and won't tell me a damn thing. Now I'm sitting here on these steps and some big fat guy just came and pissed over my shoulder!"

The pisser was Charlie Beckwith—just messing with Jacobson to amuse himself.

4

—

AS IT TURNED OUT, Jacobson eventually became part of the mission. We auditioned other Navy pilots, including one who quit in the middle of training (Charlie threatened to have him court-martialed). Eventually the bulk of the job fell to Marine Corps aviators who had more night-flying and tactical experience, including Major Jim Schaeffer, an experienced combat veteran who also had many hours in the RH-53, and a no-nonsense lieutenant colonel named Ed Sieffert, who would become the flight leader and pilot of the lead helo. This is how we assembled the rescue team— cobbling together expertise wherever we found it.

During the Rice Bowl planning sessions, it became very clear we had no chance of rescuing the hostages without human intelligence and advance ground preparations inside Iran. Dick Meadows, a retired Special Ops legend, volunteered for the job. Dick joined the army out of West Virginia at age sixteen, lying about how old he was so he could go fight the North Koreans. Later, in Vietnam, he did some sleuthing on the Ho Chi Minh Trail and brought back the breech of a Russian artillery piece, proving once and for all the Soviets were supplying weapons to the North Viet-namese. He was also a leader in the Son Tay raid.

Two others, DoD men with Special Forces backgrounds, also were selected. And there was a fourth man, who struck us all as one of the brav-est young patriots we'd ever met.

At the Farm, we began to realize we needed a native Iranian who knew Tehran and spoke Farsi. We weren't yet sure about the exact ways we would use such a person. But we needed hands and feet on the ground, someone who would blend in with the local population, collect intelli-gence, and probably arrange logistics. Immediately, we began canvassing all the services for anyone Iranian born. This was tricky since only a rela-tive handful of people knew what we were up to.

The Air Force got back to us with the name of a young E-4 who was stationed at Shaw AFB, South Carolina. A CIA background check showed him to be as clean as a nun. This young man showed up the next day at the Pentagon for a meeting with me and Bucky. We introduced ourselves simply as officers from Fort Bragg. Without our having said a word, I could see in his eyes that he knew what we wanted with him. The question was whether he was willing to do what needed to be done.

"Tell us about yourself," I said.

"I was born in Iran," he began. "When I was about twelve, my mother and father divorced. I came to America with my father."

He finished high school here and joined the Air Force, the young man said. Now, he was married and had two children. Bucky and I exchanged a look: *It would've been better if he had been single.*

I plunged ahead. "We are planning a rescue of the Americans being held in Tehran," I explained. "We're going to ask you to do something that's very dangerous. It's important to this nation and it's important to those Americans who are being held. We can't give you a lot of details right now and you're under no obligation to do this. The worst case scenario is, you might not come home."

The sergeant sat there for a minute, and I watched wheels turn behind his eyes. He looked over at Bucky, then back at me.

Finally, he gave us his answer. "I'll do whatever you ask of me. The only thing I ask is that if anything happens to me, you take care of my family."

"You have my word," I said. "If anything happens, we'll do that."

"Then I'm your man. Tell me what I need to do."

Up to that moment, this young man's life consisted of a safe and routine stateside Air Force assignment—going to work in the morning and home to his family at night. He could have said no, in which case we'd have kept him in isolation until the mission was over. But with little hesitation and no fanfare, this young airman agreed to lay his life on the line for his adopted country. I was astonished and impressed.

Just like that, we had our Iranian infiltrator. CIA codenamed him "Fred" and began preparing him for the impossible mission that lay ahead.

5

BEFORE GOING INTO ISOLATION, no man in Delta had been able to notify his family. From the perspective of our loved ones, we left one day for our final eval, came home for a single night, then left again for parts unknown. Because of security considerations, we weren't allowed to call home and tell them where we were. Our frequent disappearances, each as sudden as if we'd been kidnapped by aliens, would eventually stretch from November 1979 through the spring of 1980. I thought about Lynne and the kids, worried about her worrying, and prayed that God would give her the strength to manage three small children on her own.

For married guys like me, the timing of the hostage crisis explained our absence to some extent. Though I didn't talk with Lynne about the details of my job, she knew Delta's general mission. But other guys had girlfriends who had no idea what they did for a living. For some of them, relationships fell apart. Pete Schoomaker was engaged to be married, but when his fiancée, Cindy, didn't hear from him for weeks, she cancelled the wedding. When Charlie finally let him call, Pete begged her forgiveness and they were married in a small, private ceremony. Lynne and I were the only guests.

At the Farm, we had been taping the evening news broadcasts on what the networks quickly dubbed the Iran Hostage Crisis. While the initial group of hostage takers were students, the Islamic Revolutionary Guard, or *Pasdaran*, had now begun patrolling outside the embassy. By playing and replaying the news segments, we were able to learn what kinds of weapons the *Pasdaran* carried, whether they handled them professionally (they didn't), how the embassy gates were secured, and the amount of traffic and commerce still being allowed on the two main streets, Roosevelt Avenue and Takht-E-Jamshid. Months of round-the-clock planning and training finally yielded a plan that was as detailed as it was daring. It was also chock full of tripwires.

We considered several possibilities for getting the RH-53s into Iran.

The nearest land option was Turkey, but the Turks wouldn't allow us to launch from there. We considered flying the helicopters to a remote site inside Iran then using a C-141 to air-drop "blivets"—essentially giant rubber drums filled with aviation fuel—which we would then use to refuel the helos. To test the concept, Delta flew out to Yuma Proving Grounds in Arizona just before Thanksgiving. By then, the hostages had been in captivity for just over two weeks. As the American public clamored for action, we were taking it, but carefully and invisibly.

Yuma Proving Grounds was a sprawling desert wasteland, its wide circular horizon broken only by an occasional yucca plant or saguaro cactus, jutting up from the hard pack like a lonesome soldier. The night we tested the blivets, Delta broke into small groups and lined up alongside a barren drop zone. The C-141 aircrew was supposed to fly over while the loadmaster and his team shoved the blivets out the back. Each blivet was strapped to a small wooden pallet and equipped with a parachute that was supposed to open automatically—"supposed to" being the operative words.

The idea was that the blivets, each about the size of two fifty-five gallon drums, would float down under canopy and, one by one, plunk into the drop zone. Delta would then, in small groups, run to the nearest blivet, de-rig it from its pallet, and roll it across the desert floor to the helos for refueling.

Charlie, Bucky, and I stood together looking up into the sky, listening for the C-141's turbine engines. The night was cool. Untouched by city lights, the stars of the Western sky glittered like jewels. Finally, we heard the jet. As it flew overhead into the drop zone, I saw these huge dark shapes begin spilling from its tail. Against the starry sky, some canopies popped open. But some didn't. And the blivets without chutes hurtled toward us like five-hundred-pound bombs.

All of us bolted like jackrabbits, sprinting away from the drop zone, trying to outrun death. Close behind me, I heard splintering crashes as the pallets and blivets exploded against the hardpack. Glancing back, I saw aviation fuel spray skyward from the sand in great bursts that then showered down like flammable rain.

Against the odds, no one was hurt. When the sky was clear of falling fuel bombs, we trotted back to the drop zone. The oily tang of aviation fuel hung thick in the air. In groups of five or six, we put our shoulders against the few surviving blivets, and began trying to heave their rubbery bulk across the desert floor. It was so primitive, I felt as if we were in an episode of *The Flintstones*.

Bucky was heave-hoeing on my right. "We gotta talk to the riggers," he grumbled through gritted teeth. "They're gonna have to do better than that."

The riggers got the parachute trouble ironed out, and our next drop went a whole lot better. But in the end, we decided the blivets were too unwieldly and difficult to transport once on the ground. So the blivet idea was out.

Then we looked at the potential of parachuting in, but decided the risk of injury was too high. Finally we settled on a combination of helicopters and fixed-wing planes. Air Force C-141 Starlifters would transport the mission elements from a base in Wadi Kena, Egypt, to Masirah, Oman, where the entire force would transload onto C-130 Talons, a combat configuration of the durable cargo plane. The Talons would then carry Delta, some Rangers for security, along with Navy helicopter refueling teams to Dasht-e-Kavir, our initial insertion point in a wide stretch of desert waste located sixty-five miles southeast of Tehran. We code-named the insertion point Desert One.

While Delta was en route, the plan called for eight RH-53s to launch from the *Nimitz* in the Persian Gulf. Once we linked up at Desert One, Air Force crews would refuel the helos by pumping fuel out of soft "bladders" carried into Iran aboard EC-130 cargo planes. Then Delta would transload to the helos and fly in them to a hide site in the mountains near Tehran, while the Talons exfiltrated back to Masirah. The following night, from the hide site, Delta would load onto trucks driven by Iranians recruited by the CIA. Farsi-speaking U.S. soldiers would ride along in the cabs to disable and detain any checkpoint guards who made the mistake of failing to let us pass. The rest of Delta, organized into Red, White, and Blue elements, would ride in the truck beds, concealed by facades built to look like stacked cargo on its way to market.

Then the violence would begin.

Near midnight, a small team of Delta operators carrying silencer-equipped .45 caliber grease guns would kill the guards manning two permanent posts on Roosevelt Avenue. Once at the embassy, the Red and Blue elements would silently scale the wall and drop down the other side. Those teams would move across the compound, neutralizing any opposition along the way, and position themselves at the chancery and other buildings that might hold hostages. My team, the "LZ Party," would secure the soccer stadium across the street, making it ready for the 53s—everyone's ride out of there. Once the Red and Blue elements were in place, Fast Eddie would blow the embassy wall, opening the path to the stadium. The White element would set up road blocks on Takht-e-Jamshid and keep them clear with machine guns and grenade launchers.

If the Iranians were able to quickly mobilize an armored assault, Bucky and Sergeant Major Forrest Foreman would call in covering fire from two AC-130 Spectre gunships that would by then be circling overhead. Meanwhile, my job was to call in the 53s. Because it provided extra protection for the hostages and rescue force, the stadium was to serve as the helo landing zone. Delta operators—two to a hostage—would shield them from hostile fire, hustle them from the embassy across Roosevelt Avenue and aboard the helos, rotors turning. To open the way, an operator nicknamed "Boris" would lay down clearing fire with an MAG-58 machine gun. A sniper by specialty and used to single-shot precision, Boris practiced for months with his new toy and fell in love with the MAG-58's ability to wreak plain old havoc.

During all this, a Ranger unit would fly into Manzariyah, Iran, where it would take and hold an airfield. Once the helicopters arrived there with their load of rescuers and hostages, Air Force Starlifters would carry everyone—including the helo pilots, drivers, advance DoD agents, and translators—back to Masirah.

Five months of intensive scripting. Preparation down to the most minute detail. Dry run after dry run until Delta could have found its way through the embassy compound blindfolded. And still the plan bristled with contingencies. Murphy's Law lurked at every turn.

6

AROUND CHRISTMASTIME 1979, another hostage, a woman, was interviewed on television. Her innocence struck me, the unfairness of her having her life stolen from her when she had done nothing wrong. Her interview brought into focus for me the plight of all fifty-three remaining hostages. To live in fear. To wonder if you'll ever see your family again. To wonder if each morning is the last you'll ever see.

None of us in Delta believed the U.S. could successfully negotiate the release of the hostages. Backed by the Ayatollah, the Iranian students were now locked in a macho standoff with America, the big kid on the block. To blink first would've been, in the Islamic mind, unthinkable. As long as they held the global limelight, as long as they held American prestige in their hands, the student rebels would hold our citizens prisoner.

Just after the embassy takeover, President Carter declared publicly that America wouldn't do anything to endanger the lives of the hostages. What he should have said was: "We will go to any length to get our people back. All options are on the table."

At the Farm, it didn't build confidence in us that Carter was unwilling to state that publicly. Most of us saw him as a weak president before the hostage crisis. Now, all of us interpreted his public comments as revealing that he didn't have the stomach for armed conflict, even if it meant the global humiliation of the nation he meant to lead.

It wasn't just Delta who thought Carter lacked the mettle to order us in. Some intelligence agencies repeatedly told us, "You can rehearse all you want, but this thing is never going to go off."

As a result, I believe those same agencies didn't go after intelligence as hard as they might have under a different president. Their resources were already stretched keeping up with the trench-coat intrigue of the Cold War. Then, in December 1979, the Soviets invaded Afghanistan, further diluting the intelligence resources that could have been directed at Tehran.

As we continued to refine the mission plan, anticipation burned in my heart. I truly believed Delta would storm the embassy and bring home fifty-three Americans. At the same time, though, I worried about the unknown. The complexity of the problem—and thus of the plan—was unprecedented. With so many contingencies, we pegged the chance that something, and probably several things, would go wrong, at about 100 percent. Still, from end to end, the strategy we hammered out accounted for every known detail. We had practiced for six months. Pete knew every inch of the embassy corridors. Fast Eddie blew up his replica of the embassy wall so many times Charlie was tired of going out to watch him do it. And Boris fell so deeply in love with the violence of the MAG-58 I started to wonder whether any woman would ever be able to compete for his affections. The attitude of the men was, *If we're going to do this thing, let's go do it.*

At the Farm, the action officers were very concerned that Carter would draw out the embassy standoff until the Iranians executed a hostage. Then Delta would have to launch without the critical element of surprise. The Iranians would then have plenty of time to move the hostages, separate them into difficult-to-rescue groups, and harden more buildings in the embassy compound. We also worried that the hostages might attempt to escape, resulting in more American deaths.

I was disappointed in Jimmy Carter. I knew he was a man of faith, and I didn't understand his interpretation of his God-given responsibility to defend the defenseless. We believed that ultimately, it would be events—and not his own courage—that would force him to act.

We were wrong. In the end, it was just the solar system.

7

IN LATE MARCH, a small CIA aircraft piloted by a legendary one-legged pilot named Jim Ryan flew secretly into Desert One to set up a covert landing strip. On board was another Special Ops veteran, Air Force Lieutenant Colonel John Carney. Landing under cover of darkness, Carney, Ryan, and a Vietnam Special Forces NCO named Bud embedded landing lights in the desert hardpack that could be remotely activated by the Eagle Claw landing force. With just the three of them flying, without cover or backup, deep into the Iranian interior, it was an amazingly brave act that impressed even the most hardened guys in the task force.

The hostages had been seized on November 4, 1979. We went into Iran on April 24, 1980. Carter gave the order only because Charlie Beckwith told him we were running out of time. Delta needed as many hours of darkness as possible to execute the mission and, as spring ticked toward summer, the span between sundown and sunup had contracted to the margins of acceptability. The clock, literally, had run out on Jimmy Carter.

On April 21, Delta rode C-141 Starlifters into the arid wastes of Egypt and bivouacked in the ramshackle remains of an old air base built in Wadi Kena by the Russians.

We still didn't know exactly where the Iranians were holding the hostages, so we planned for the worst case scenario—that they were scattered in several locations throughout the embassy compound. Pete's Red Element would hit the highest percentage spot—the chancery—then take down other buildings until they found all the hostages.

At the eleventh hour, we got a break. The night before the op was to launch, the CIA learned that the students were holding *all* the hostages in the chancery. In a scenario straight out of Hollywood, a Pakistani cook flying out of Iran told his seatmate that he knew the hostages were all in the main building. He worked at the American embassy, he explained as his seatmate listened with the wide-eyed interest of a tourist. But since the listener was actually a CIA agent (or so the story went) he also prodded gently at the edges of the cook's story to test it for authenticity.

I was in the hangar when Charlie made the announcement: "All elements, adjust your plans and let's make the chancery our primary target. If we get there and they've been moved, we'll adjust again."

The hangar hummed with the low rumble of men's voices as the element leaders adapted to the new information. The Red and Blue assault elements would now converge on the chancery. If only part of the hostages were recovered there, the Blue element would move them to meet my element at the soccer stadium while the Red element hit other buildings.

I didn't believe the Pakistani cook story—it was just too convenient. More likely the CIA was guarding its real sources. It didn't matter, though; that we had a better fix on the hostages was the important thing. In any case, it didn't change things for my element. And as I listened to Pete and Logan detail the changes in their plans, I felt a surge of confidence: *It's coming together. We're going to get these people and bring them home.*

8

APRIL 24, THE MORNING OF THE MISSION. We all slept as late as we could, which was only until 5 a.m. Immediately, we began to ready our gear. Sitting on my cot, I double-checked my weapons to make sure the wind-driven Egyptian sands hadn't scoured them into junk. I didn't like the idea of a jam in the middle of a shootout with the *Pasdaran*.

In the run-up to the mission, we all grew beards. We dressed in Levis and jump boots, field jackets dyed black and black watch caps to match. We wore no rank or military insignia of any kind. The only exterior sign that we were Americans was a small American flag sewn on the sleeve of each of our jackets. Those would remain covered with a Velcro patch until we reached the hostages. Then each operator would tear off the patch to show the hostages that their country had finally come to take them home. To comply with the Geneva Convention, we each wore our dog tags inside our t-shirts and carried our U.S. military I.D.s.

Other than those few signs that we were on legitimate U.S. government business, we could've been a crew of especially well-conditioned longshoremen or a gang of inner-city thugs.

At about 6 a.m., I was doing final checks on my gear when Charlie walked up to me. "Jerry, I'm going to get all these men together in a few minutes and I want you to say a prayer before we launch."

I was astonished. Not since he and I talked about our mothers had Charlie expressed any interest at all in religion in general or my faith in particular. In fact, most of the time, I was pretty sure he had no confidence in me at all.

At least once during the planning of Eagle Claw, he had fired me. Of course, he had fired Bucky, too. We were overseeing air-drop operations at the Farm when Charlie got right in our faces: "You're both incompetent and unprofessional! You're fired!" He didn't just mean off the mission. He meant out of Delta. Bucky and I looked at each other: *Fired? Again?*

Charlie was always firing somebody then forgetting about it five minutes later. I was used to his bluster. But even after he put me in charge of the LZ Team when there were other, more senior officers available, I still wondered where I stood with him. Now he'd startled me with a side of himself I never dreamed existed: Charlie, who depended on Charlie and whatever parts of his vision he could instill in others, conceded that he and his men would do well this time to enlist the help of a Higher Authority.

"Okay, Colonel," I told him. "I'll be ready."

About an hour later, Charlie gathered Delta in the hangar in a loose formation and climbed up on a makeshift wooden platform. I walked up to the front and stood off to Charlie's left. Dressed like the rest of us and looking as grimly confident as I'd ever seen him, Charlie addressed the group. "We're launching this operation to bring home fifty-three Americans and I don't intend to come back until we've got every one of them." His voice echoed slightly, amplified by the high contours of the hangar. "We've done all the preparations. We're ready for this mission. I have confidence in every one of you that you'll do your job and do it well."

Then he said: "I'm going to ask Jerry to come up here and say a prayer before we launch."

Before I could begin speaking, General Vaught stepped forward. "I want to quote some Scripture," the general said. "In the book of Isaiah, the Scripture says, 'And I heard the voice of the Lord saying, "Whom shall I send, and who will go for us?" And Isaiah said, "Here am I! Send me."' Men, your country's counting on you. You've stepped forward and said, 'Here am I, send me.' God bless you."

Vaught's words from one of my favorite passages of the Bible were a special blessing to me. And for the second time in less than an hour, I was surprised to find faith at work. I knew there were other men of faith in Delta, but no one really talked about it. We didn't have an active Bible study and we didn't have a chaplain. What we had—and what Special Forces had in general—was a culture of self-reliance.

But now, faced with a mission in which obstacles and danger hovered over every phase, even the senior officers among us swept self-reliance aside and acknowledged God.

Vaught nodded at me to begin. I looked out at Pete and Bucky, Jim and Logan, Ish and Jack, all of them. By that time, they were like family to me. They were my brothers. I fervently wanted God to protect them. "You know, about three thousand years ago right in this very desert where we're standing," I began, "God led the Israelites out of bondage. They traveled across this same desert to a new freedom. And I believe God has called us to lead fifty-three Americans out of bondage and back to freedom."

Then I asked them to bow their heads and pray with me. "Almighty God, we've placed ourselves in your hands. And we ask you to lead us and guide us so that we might liberate our fellow Americans. We ask for your hand of mercy to be upon us. We ask for wisdom and strength and courage. We ask you to keep us safe, and to keep safe the people we're going after. Bring us all home to our families. And I pray this in Christ's name. Amen."

I raised my head. Then Bucky stepped up on the platform and surprised me for the third time that afternoon. "Okay, men, we're going to sing God Bless America."

And we did. With gusto. I looked out at Delta and didn't see a single man with his mouth shut. After the last notes, a loud shout went up. Each man walked back to his cot, grabbed his gear, crossed the tarmac and marched into the back of the C-141.

9

IN THE STARLIFTERS, we flew from Wadi Kena to Masirah, Oman, which we immediately renamed Misery since we spent the whole afternoon trying to hide from the scorching Arab sun. The stopover also gave us plenty of time to think.

I knew I might not make it back alive. But I was less worried about dying than, in the crush of a complex mission, being left behind in Iran. The Long Walk in the North Carolina woods was one thing, but I dang sure didn't want to have to walk to Pakistan.

I didn't expect much resistance in my part of the operation. The Revolutionary Guard might have anticipated the Americans using the soccer stadium as a staging point, but our best intel showed they might post a couple of guards there at most. If those guards surrendered under our assault, we would flex-tie them and let them watch us evacuate the hostages. If they resisted, we would kill them. I didn't have a problem with that. We hadn't gotten all dressed up for nothing.

At dusk, we transloaded our gear onto Air Force C-130 Combat Talons, barrel-chested, reliable birds that needed only a short roll to get airborne and could stop on a dime. These Talons were also equipped with the terrain following radar and special navigation gear. We needed both to fly in low over the coast, undetected by Iran's defense radar, then hug the jagged walls of the canyons the pilots planned to use as their route into the interior.

Finally, the Talons launched from Misery. Charlie, Bucky, and Logan went out on the first bird. Jim Knight, Wayne Long, and I sat near the front of the second. For four hours, we flew through the night "darkhorse"—no external lights—our faces lit only with the red lights that glowed inside the cabin. All the jump seats were removed from the aircraft to make room for Delta and our gear. But the Air Force had been kind enough to line the floor with mattresses to block out the cold and give us at least some cushion against the hard ride.

There were no pep talks or last-minute tactical reviews. The only sound I heard was the propellers' drone as we sat quietly against the bulkheads, each man tending his own inner fires.

We skimmed low across the coast of Iran then climbed through known gaps in Iranian radar to navigate the maze of desert gorges leading to Desert One. Packed in shoulder to shoulder, Jim, Wayne, and I rolled and leaned in unison as the pilot flew "nap of the earth," clinging to the dark canyon contours like a shadow. Soon I heard the engines throttle back and felt landing gear thump into place.

The Talon's wheels slammed down hard on the desert floor, bottoming out the hydraulics, and rattling my teeth. We bounced once and got briefly airborne before hitting the deck hard again. The pilot reversed thrust. We taxied to a stop and the loadmaster dropped the rear ramp.

I expected to look out and see only a wide expanse of moonlit desert. Instead, I saw that the world was on fire.

10

FROM INSIDE THE TALON, I could see a giant fireball blazing about a kilometer away. My mind flashed to the worst-case scenario: the Iranians somehow discovered the mission and had been lying in wait. I listened over the prop noise for the rattle of automatic weapons, but it didn't come. Because we rode up near the cockpit, I was among the last to deplane. Bucky and Logan were waiting for me. Logan had a bloody gash on his nose, which was already muddy with the fine dust that covered his face.

"Welcome to World War III!" Bucky said, grinning.

Behind us, the four tanker birds began landing in sequence, each one multiplying the noise and sandstorm that now swirled around us.

"What's going on!" I asked Bucky, yelling to be heard.

He grinned. "Ish and the Rangers fired up a fuel tanker!"

The rest of the story came out in bits and pieces. As the first C-130 approached Desert One, the pilots spotted a fuel tanker rolling down the dirt road that bisected the landing area. Trailing it was a small pickup. The Talon circled once, landed, dropped the ramp. Ish jumped on a Yamaha motorcycle and a Ranger named Rubio, armed with a light anti-tank weapon, jumped on behind him. They raced down the ramp, followed by a Delta/Ranger security team in a Jeep. As soon as Ish pulled within range, Rubio fired the LAW and the tanker burst like a supernova.

"They chased the other truck, but it got away!" Bucky shouted.

We agreed there wasn't much to worry about. A fuel tanker with an escort rolling through the Iranian wastes at midnight? Smugglers, probably. They wouldn't be likely to alert authorities. Even if they did, we'd be long gone before the Iranians could mobilize to investigate.

The moon glowed bright, but with the tanker shooting flames three hundred feet into the night, Desert One was lit up like a Midnight Madness sale at a used car lot. Now, as Delta operators began the heavy work of dragging a massive cargo net off the second Talon, their shadows flickered off the white desert floor. The net would be transloaded to the helos, then used to cover them at the hide site. Dust devils twisted up off the desert floor as the C-130s parked and kept their props turning. Eddies of fine sand stung my eyes and I moved away from the Talons' deafening thrum. Then, strangely, I could have sworn I heard the high faint sound of...

Women.

Crying women.

I was surprised to find out that the smugglers weren't our only visitors. Before Ish's security team could finish setting up a perimeter, a passenger bus—*a passenger bus!*—also trundled across our landing site. The security team popped off warning shots then had to fire into the engine to stop the bus. Onboard were about forty-five people, mostly women, old folks, and kids. A Delta operator now guarded them closely, but the women, naturally, were terrified, and every now and then one would cut loose in hysterical wails.

We picked Desert One for its remoteness. I mean, the place was the definition of *bleak*. Now, past 9 p.m. on what should have been an unremarkable date in April, we had encountered something in the neighborhood of *fifty people*. It didn't matter, though, because we planned for this problem. Anyone we encountered at Desert One would be hauled out on the C-130's then returned to Manzariyah the next night. People have suggested the mission planners were such buffoons that we hadn't dreamed we might encounter interlopers at the landing site. That's simply not true. We expected the unexpected, and it materialized.

I was discussing this with Bucky when Charlie walked over. "On our way in here, Vaught called about the helos. Eight off the deck, he said."

Excitement surged through me. All eight helos had launched successfully off the *Nimitz*. Most of us weren't as worried about the Iranians as we were about the helos. Vietnam proved that the rotor driven birds were notoriously cranky. For this mission we needed six working RH-53s. So far, we still had eight.

Now Charlie radioed Vaught in Wadi Kena: "What's the status on the helos?"

"Fifty minutes out and low on fuel," came the reply.

A little late, but not too bad.

Delta began to break into our element groups in preparation for onloading to the helos. Boris and Fast Eddie were with me. They sat down with the rest of the LZ element to wait for their ride to the hide site. The fire-lit sandstorm swirled around us all. Every man had extra pockets sewn into his jacket lining and we all bristled with extra clips, rope, carabiners, water, and assorted widgets. Prior to leaving Wadi Kena, I weighed every man to make sure we didn't overload the helos. Fast Eddie packed so many explosive goodies into his jacket he tipped the scales at three hundred twenty-four pounds. Now, sitting in the desert, he looked like the Michelin Man.

Soon the tankers were set, the cargo net was set, the onload groups were set, and there was nothing left to do but wait. And the helos were now officially late.

We didn't worry much at first—they'd even arrived late during rehearsals. Still, time was critical: we had to get off the deck here soon in order to reach the hide sites before sunrise. Hedging our bets, Bucky searched me out. "Jerry, if we get too far behind schedule, we're going to need a different hide site," he said. "Get the map out and start looking."

I did, poring over the pictured wasteland until I found a little niche in the side of a mountain that looked flat enough to land the helos. I wasn't comfortable with it. We had no way to recon it, the way Dick Meadows had reconned the approved hide sites. There was really no way to know whether we'd find ourselves landing on top of some kind of goat-herding village. But it was our only option.

I circled the site on the map and showed it to Bucky.

He looked at it then stared off to the south. "I wish to hell they'd get here," he said.

11

DELTA SPENT THE NEXT HALF HOUR straining to hear the faintest chop of helo blades over the collective roar of the Talons and refueling birds. Minutes ticked away, compressing the mission timeline. If we waited much longer the helos wouldn't be able to refuel and reach the hide site before first light. That increased the odds that our armada of CH-53s would be spotted from the ground and reported to Tehran. It wasn't hopeless by any means. Somebody in the Eagle Claw task force had repainted the helos in the same colors as the Iranian chopper fleet. Still, arriving under cover of darkness was the highly preferred option. Now that was going to be a squeeze play at best.

While Bucky paced, I scoured the map for a better alternate hide site. Charlie stalked off to be alone.

When the helos were forty-five minutes late, Vaught popped up on the radio. "The choppers are ten minutes out!"

Bucky's face bloomed into his familiar grin. "Boys, we're still in business!"

Five minutes later, I heard the first rotor blades beating the air to the south. Across Desert One's moon-lit surface, the men of Delta rose to their feet. The rotors' steady drumming grew louder until, one by one, the helos appeared over the horizon. We counted only six. It was enough.

I watched as Charlie jogged over to meet the first one as soon as it touched down. As each bird landed it was guided to a tanker to begin refueling. Hustling to make up for lost time, the Delta elements began muscling the cargo nets and equipment toward the helos. I was standing on the road with Bucky and Don Simmons, one of the command sergeant majors, when Charlie walked up, his eyes narrow and his jaw set.

"Well, we only have six helos here, and Ed Sieffert says one of them is down with a hydraulic problem," he said. "We're going to have to scrub the mission."

His words hit like a punch in the gut. My mind flashed to the hostages, our six months of planning and training, the grueling trip from Wadi Kena. Instantly, I knew if we didn't go forward now, we'd never go at all. There were just too many moving parts. I turned to Simmons. "Don, I think we need to try and go on with five."

Don agreed. "If we don't go now, we'll never get another chance."

Just as I turned to tell Charlie what we thought, he said to Bucky, "I've talked to Vaught. Start getting everyone loaded on the C-130s."

I knew it was a waste of time to say anything else.

Analyzing it afterward, I knew Charlie was right. The decision to abort was made during planning, as it should be, when the planners' veins were less charged with anger, bravado, or unreasoning hope. We had calculated the possibility of losing helos and agreed that fewer than six meant we had to abort. The word was written in big capital letters on the mission's contingency matrix: "Fewer than six helos—ABORT."

But at the moment Charlie made the call, I was deeply, deeply disappointed. I looked at Pete and Bucky and could see sorrow and frustration written on their faces, too. We had been close enough to grab the prize, and now, in an instant, we felt crushing defeat.

Thrumming props and rotors filled the air with noise, the fuel truck still blazed in its full glory, and underneath it all, the bus women wailed. Now that the mission was off, all the noise and light suddenly seemed like beacons for Iranian fighter planes. That was no truer than it had been five minutes before, but now, urgently, we all wanted to leave. Bucky mustered the element leaders and assigned us each an aircraft for exfiltration. Having lugged the massive cargo nets to helos, some of the men now had to lug them back, three men to a net. I saw Logan and his sergeant major, Dave Cheney, begin shepherding B Squadron into the back of one of the tankers. There was a lot less room than there should've been, because the floor was still layered with partially full fuel bladders.

Behind the C-130 I could see Jim Schaefer's helo, still refueling. When B Squadron was all aboard, the loadmaster raised the rear ramp and secured the troop doors. In a hurry-up abort status, in a propeller driven sandstorm at night, we had to be careful to take the time to account for every man. I began walking toward Logan's bird to confirm that all forty-five of his men were with him. Up ahead, I could hear Schaefer's helo turning up and through the airborne grit, dimly saw its dark form begin to shift. New dust clouds churned off the Talon's tail and I figured Schaefer had finished refueling and was moving his bird out of the C-130's way.

At that moment, I heard a noise that didn't sound right: a loud popping. Then: a great rushing *whump!* A giant fireball bloomed where Schaefer's helo had been, swallowing the tail of Logan's C-130. A wall of savage heat raced thirty yards to where I was standing and snapped at my face, pushing me back. Flames cloaked the entire rear half of the Talon, trapping Logan and his men inside with thousands of gallons of aviation fuel. I couldn't see what had happened. I didn't know then that in the darkened dust storm, vertigo caused Schaefer to fly his helicopter slightly up and over into the C-130. Now the RH-53 was embedded by its rotor blades in the Talon's upper fuselage, burning like the fuse on a bomb.

The fuel bladders would detonate any second. Instinctively, I turned to run, take cover. But after a few steps, I stopped, filled with shame. *What are you* doing? I thought. *Logan's in there!* I turned to charge in, but the violent heat forced me back. I was dimly aware of others around me, shocked, staring, straining forward, but beaten back by the ferocious blaze.

In that moment, I knew two things: That my brothers were going to die in that fire, and that the only thing I could do for them was pray. "Father, please don't let these men die!" I said. "We put ourselves in your hands and now they're all going to die unless you perform a miracle!"

The Talon's starboard troop door burst open, and I saw men begin to spill out of the inferno and hit the desert floor at a dead run. I learned later that Logan and his men had opened both the port door and the rear ramp only to find walls of flame. The starboard troop door was jammed shut and the Talon crew chief couldn't budge it. But big Dave Cheney had stepped past the crew chief and rammed the door open. Then he and Logan stood on either side of it, shouting, "Don't panic! Keep moving! Single file!"

One by one, like jumpers at a drop zone, the men of Delta had crept forward inside the aircraft. Fire licked down into the fuselage. The overhead burst into flame. The cabin temperature spiked higher and higher. With each step toward the door, each man felt certain that in the next second the plane would explode with him inside it. Staff Sergeant Chris Abel later told me, "I felt the flames coming right down the tunnel of the fuselage from the cockpit direction. AVGAS fumes filled the fuselage. I didn't know where the fire was coming from, but I knew, sitting on all that fuel, it wasn't going to be long before it would explode."

Abel said that Cheney, in his booming voice, kept yelling, "One at a time! Don't panic!"

By the light of moon and fire, I saw Logan's men running toward me, away from the flaming plane. As they approached, I could see that the heat inside the fuselage was so intense that the webbing on many of their load-bearing vests melted into their field jackets. With the other element commanders, I began directing traffic, shouting, "Go get on one of the other C-130s!"

Several gave me a look that said I was crazy: getting on another fuel laden Talon was the last thing they wanted to do. But the *very* last thing they wanted to do was to be left behind in Iran. The men of B Squadron quickly distributed themselves among the other C-130s and climbed aboard.

A couple of the Talons had already begun to taxi. I ran to the nearest bird, but as I started to climb aboard, the loadmaster blocked my way.

"We're full. We can't take anymore," he said.

A little shocked, I backed away into the sand. Quickly, I scanned Desert One's moonlit surface. I saw no one else on the ground. My heart began a steady gallop as my worse fear seemed to be coming true. I spotted another C-130 about a hundred yards away, but as I bolted toward it, the pilot began to taxi away from me. I ran faster, sending up a flare prayer: *Lord, don't let me be left behind.*

The C-130 accelerated, but the soft dust covering the desert hard pack prevented the pilot from gaining too much speed. My legs pounded the sand. My lungs threatened to burst. Suddenly, the Talon stopped and I could hear its props turning faster as it prepared for takeoff. Lunging forward, I closed the distance, threw my hands up and grabbed the open door frame. Just as I thought the pilot would begin his takeoff roll with my butt hanging out over Iran, someone grabbed my arm and pulled me into the plane.

12

INSIDE, THE TALON was packed wall to wall with black-clad men, dusty and dejected, sitting on and wedged in among partially filled fuel bladders. Logan and Ed Sieffert were already onboard. I picked my way through them to the cockpit and got the pilot's attention.

"See if you can get a fighter cap to escort us out of here," I told him.

"Roger that," he said.

I knew *Nimitz* had been standing by, ready to launch F-14 Tomcats to destroy the Ayatollah's F-4 Phantoms if they tried to mobilize during the rescue operation. Now we needed the Tomcats to cover our exfiltration on the overloaded C-130s, which would make juicy targets as we limped back to Masirah.

Turning back to face the cargo area, I started counting people. Then I gave the pilot a number and told him to relay it to the C-130 that carried Charlie and Bucky.

Logan called to me, "We need to get some fighter cover."

"It's already done," I said.

Wading back into the cabin, I wedged myself in between Delta operator Rudy Rodriguez and another man, and sat down near J.J. Byers, one of the crewmembers who had been on the burning C-130. Even in the low red light, I could see that the fire had scorched his olive-drab flight suit black. His face and hands were badly burned, the scalded skin scarlet and already erupting in blisters. He began to moan, then cry out, then scream as pain drove him toward hysteria. Delta medic Glenn Nickle and Mike Vinning, an explosives specialist with medical training, picked their way through the bladders and squeezed in beside the airman to help. Suddenly, J.J. stopped screaming and I could see him descending into shock. As Glenn and Mike administered water and painkillers, I reached over and put my hand on his boot and asked God to ease his pain and spare his life.

During the flight, the fuel bladders sloshed beneath us. I sat on the edge of one of them, across from a Farsi-speaking former Iranian general, an ex-pat who escaped Iran after the Shah went into exile. He went on the mission with us to run interference with Iranian air traffic control if they picked us up on radar. As I watched, the general began shuffling his feet, kicking at something between the bladders beneath him. In the humming dark, I peered into the crack between the bladders and saw the tip of a familiar shape.

"Stop!" I shouted and reached forward, grabbing the general's foot with my left hand. Leaning in, I slid my right hand between the fuel bladders and extracted a LAW rocket. Somehow, in the scramble to get aboard, the LAW got separated from its owner. When Rudy Rodriguez saw the rocket, his face turned completely white, and he started crossing himself.

The flight to Masirah was a dismal trip, heavy with the lead blanket of a failure that could not have been more complete. Not only had the mission not made it past Desert One, but we'd left Fred and Dick Meadows in potentially fatal circumstances in Tehran. Also, six Navy helicopters now sat on the desert floor, four of them in perfect working order. Worse, I learned later, the helos contained detailed A to Z descriptions of Operation Eagle Claw.

In the dark chill of the Talon cabin, amid the steady propeller drone, men who had not slept in more than twenty-four hours now dropped off. Those who remained awake didn't say much. As we flew through the night, I wondered how many men had died. I later found out we lost eight: Five C-130 crewmembers and three men from Schaeffer's aircrew, including one who'd been with him since Vietnam. Eight Americans who put themselves in harm's way for others. *Why, Lord?* I prayed for their families.

I also worried about the hostages: The odds were sky high that when the Iranian terrorists discovered our brazen incursion, the murders would begin.

Three hours later, we landed in Masirah, and immediately set up a small medical facility. Glenn and Mike, using just the supplies they had in their kits kept J.J. alive, staying right with him all the way back. Now we put bigger treatment teams on him and the rest of our wounded. After a short time on the ground, we transloaded to Starlifters and flew back to Wadi Kena where a fully outfitted surgical unit took over.

The landing in Egypt brought good news. The Iranians issued a statement: Even though the Americans invaded their country, they would not retaliate against the hostages. For a third time since the disaster, I had reason to say a prayer of thanks.

The hostage crisis, including our failed rescue attempt, sank Jimmy Carter's presidency. Seven months after Eagle Claw, Ronald Reagan beat Carter in the 1980 elections. And two months after that, literally minutes after Reagan was sworn into office, the Iranians unconditionally released all the hostages.

Our failure at Desert One created conflicting emotions for me. I was torn between my grief over the deaths of eight good men, disappointment that the hostages were still hostages, and my elation that God saved so many who would tell you today they thought they were going to die.

Some folks have asked me, if God is so benevolent, why didn't he save them all? I've wondered the same thing. I cannot say why those eight men died. All I can say is fifty lived.

TEA FOR
TERRORISTS

★ ★ ★

Sudan
1983

1

THE MOMENT THE 737's NOSE WHEEL rotated off the Heathrow runway, the tray table on the seat in front of me broke off and landed in my lap. Sitting next to me, Navy Commander Larry Bailey chuckled. "Looks like it's going to be a great trip."

Out the window, I could see London falling away beneath us as we headed for Khartoum, the capital of Sudan. The Sudanese had asked the American military to help it stand up a special operations/hostage rescue force. The Pentagon responded with a team of five including a two-star general, a pair of lieutenant colonels, Larry, and me. I was a major by then, but on this mission, still the junior man.

This multi-service team was a direct outgrowth of the disaster at Desert One. After the failed rescue attempt, the Pentagon appointed an investigative panel led by Admiral James L. Holloway, a former chief of naval operations. The Holloway Commission blamed much of the mission's failure on the ad hoc nature of the Eagle Claw force, patched together with people from every service, some of whom were necessary and others who just wanted a shot at glory. None trained together long term. None had confidence in the others. Within weeks of the Holloway Commission's report, DoD began forming a permanent joint special operations task force with elements from the Army, Air Force, and Navy. Delta became part of that task force.

Now, Larry and I were coming in from London to link up with other task force officers flying in from the States. Larry, a Texan who spoke perfect Spanish, was a Navy SEAL officer who had served with a Swift Boat unit in Vietnam. He later went on to command the SEAL training school in Coronado, California, and also help save the nation from a John Kerry presidency. In 2004, angry over Kerry's Vietnam-era congressional testimony that Swifties and other American soldiers had, with their superiors' full knowledge, routinely razed villages, raping, killing, and dismembering as they went, Bailey would stand up with the Swifties and call Kerry to account.

But in 1983, Kerry was still just your basic left-wing irritant, a pebble in the shoe of the Reagan administration. The Camp David Accords, during which Jimmy Carter helped Egyptian president Anwar Sadat and Israeli Prime Minister Menachem Begin hammer out an uneasy peace, were only a few years old. But now Sadat was dead, assassinated by Islamic radicals angry over his concessions to Israel. Still, U.S. relations with Egypt remained positive, and the Pentagon considered the country our key Arab ally. That made Sudan a strategic gem. Not only did the country protect Egypt's southern flank, it could possibly serve as a base of operations should U.S. military intervention be required to protect Middle Eastern oil fields.

Those were America's reasons for saying yes to Sudan's requests for military training. The Sudanese had reasons of their own. In July 1976, two years before Camp David, Sudanese President Jaafer Mohammed al-Numeiry survived a coup attempt masterminded by both his former finance minister and former prime minister, who lashed out at him from exile. Two thousand heavily armed civilians ransacked Khartoum and Omdurman, but Numeiry, a tough and wily former army colonel, squashed the rebellion. The insurrection firmed up ties between Sudan and Egypt, and the two countries signed a mutual defense pact.

The backdrop to all this was renewed tension in Sudan between the Muslim-dominated north and the heavily Christian south. Years before, Numeiry fought a civil war against the Anya-Nya rebels in the south, many of whose ancestors converted to Christianity during the reign of Justinian. Now, the country was headed toward the implementation of Sharia, or Islamic law. We suspected Numeiry was bracing for more trouble from southern rebels. But within months, we would learn that a more immediate threat loomed farther south, in Ethiopia.

Larry and I landed in Sudan midmorning and linked up with the other task force officers. Then an embassy driver whisked us through Khartoum's dusty, chaotic streets to President Numeiry's office, where we met our two main contacts in the Sudanese military, Major Abu Bakr and Colonel Hassan. Our team would work closely with the two Sudanese army officers, both of whom were Muslims.

Abu Bakr was a large, round-faced African man with close-cropped hair and a broad smile. Over the next few weeks, I would come to regard him as the perfect soldier. He was fit, committed to his country, and dedicated to his soldiers. He wanted the best for them and he wanted them to *be* the best. But Abu Bakr faced high hurdles: "It is an enormous challenge," he told me privately in his perfect English. "We are using an existing airborne unit and standard army equipment, but must learn to perform as well as our counterparts in Europe and America."

As time went on, I learned that Abu Bakr preferred to communicate one-on-one. He despised large meetings, which he considered to whirl in endless circles and accomplish little. We had that in common, as well as a love for our families. In another conversation, he told me proudly that he was married and had a young son. By then, I had showed him pictures of my wife and three children back at Fort Bragg. Abu Bakr really understood and embraced the ideas of democracy. "I hope one day, we can see these freedoms in Sudan," he said. A chain of these chats—about family, politics, and Sudanese culture—forged a friendship between us that would later stretch across the Atlantic.

2

ON OUR SECOND DAY IN SUDAN, Abu Bakr and Hassan hosted us at the airborne base in Khartoum. There, Abu Bakr's airborne unit devoted the day to demonstrating what they could already do: Static line jumps, hand-to-hand combat, marksmanship, and survival skills. The Sudanese were very serious about survival skills. As part of the demo, one man killed a rabbit, skinned it and parted it out to his fellow soldiers, who then ate it raw.

Next, a slim African with a dazzling smile brought out the biggest bullfrog I'd ever seen. It blinked against the blazing sun—until the soldier raised the frog high and brought its head down hard against the edge of the table. Then he took out a long slender knife and expertly ran it around the skin. When I was growing up, we ate frog legs all the time. My dad used to go frog-gigging in the rivers near our house. He would've been proud of this Sudanese fellow. He really knew what he was doing.

After skinning the frog, I thought the Sudanese soldier would part it out to the others as he had the rabbit. Instead, he sliced off the frog's choicest leg and handed it directly to me.

The Sudanese all smiled and looked at me expectantly. One of them made a motion to his mouth: *Eat. Eat.*

For a moment, I hesitated. Was this a rite of passage? In Special Forces we talk about building rapport. Well, here was a chance for me to build some.

Time to take one for the team, I thought.

I opened my mouth and took a big, slick bite of raw frog leg. And about the time I'd choked down the second mouthful, the Sudanese—and Larry Bailey—fell out laughing. Around the frog flesh stuck in my teeth, I laughed, too. *Okay, you got me.*

I'll tell you one thing: that was the last frog leg I ever ate.

We spent the next seventy-two hours in military tours and briefings.

Larry and I began to sketch the outlines of a training plan for Abu Bakr's new hostage rescue force, and agreed to return in January with certain equipment. The rest, the Sudanese would have to purchase through the Pentagon's foreign military sales office, we explained. Abu Bakr saw a long road ahead to get his men trained up. Still, he told me, he was encouraged.

When we returned to Khartoum the next day, Abu Bakr asked, "Would you like to see more of our culture?" The five of us immediately agreed.

At sunset, he and Hassan took us to a mosque, a kind I hadn't seen before. Instead of towers and minarets, this place was more like an open pavilion. High walls of tan stucco secluded the worship area from Khartoum's teeming streets. In the center of the open space on an ornate marble floor, large pillars of polished stone supported a tiled roof, creating a covered area that was open on all four sides. The amber sunset hung near the horizon, casting gold light over at least two hundred men kneeling on tiny *sajadas*, prayer rugs. An imam, his voice like music, sang out prayers in Arabic and the worshippers bowed forward as one, then rose again.

We stood on the periphery and watched. It never dawned on me to wonder why the Muslim officers brought us to a mosque during worship. According to Islamic doctrine, we were infidels. But never was there any sense from Abu Bakr and Hassan that they thought anything odd about inviting us there. They did not treat us like infidels, but seemed to feel they were simply sharing more with us about their way of life.

As the prayer ended, several of the worshippers moved to a corner of the pavilion and, to the rhythm of drums, began a dance that reminded me of whirling dervishes. I was fascinated.

I turned to Abu Bakr. "Thank you for bringing us here."

He smiled. "Now would you like to go to a wedding?"

As it turned out, we went to two Muslim weddings that night—even danced with the brides and, according to custom, stuck paper money to their foreheads. A couple of days later, satisfied that Abu Bakr and his new hostage rescue team were on course for success, I left with Bailey and the others, and returned to the States. None of us knew that within five months, Abu Bakr and his men would be put to their first real-world test.

3

IN JULY 1984, a band of at least twenty guerillas slipped across the Ethiopian border into Sudan, kidnapped eleven Westerners, and held them hostage at a missionary compound at the summit of the Boma Hills, near Juba. From a global perspective, the kidnapping was an obscure third-world incident, scantly reported in the Western press. The guerilla group, the Liberation Front for Southern Sudan (LFSS), quickly released six of their captives, but kept five, including a West German who ran a wildlife tracking project at the foot of the mountain. The other four were Presbyterian missionaries with African Christian Relief of Southern Sudan (ACROSS). Among the remaining hostages were mission leader John Haspels, 36, of Kansas, and missionary pilot Ron Pontier, 29, of Florida.

The LFSS, this delegation at least, was really just a ragtag batch of bullies armed with AK-47s. But Sudanese officials and their allies had no way of knowing that. The head of Sudanese national intelligence asked for American help, so I took a couple of Delta NCOs and went to Washington to link up with a foreign service officer from the State Department. Together, we boarded a C-141 for Khartoum.

Ten hours later, a Chevy van whisked us through hot narrow streets teeming with vendors and beeping taxis to the U.S. embassy in Khartoum. We arrived on the Fourth of July. In a spartan government office, we met with the American ambassador and CIA deputy station chief, the head spook already having choppered down to Juba. The deputy chief laid out the guerillas' demands, which seem quaint by today's standards: The LFSS wanted $95,000 in return for the hostages' lives. It was actually quite a bargain. But governments that negotiate with terrorists only encourage copycats. So the Sudanese decided to take them out instead.

I left one of my NCOs in the embassy to monitor radio traffic, and instructed the other, Sergeant First Class Don Feaney, to jump on the next flying object going south and join me as soon as he could. Armed with the detailed drawing of the ACROSS compound provided by a deep-cover CIA agent who had recently visited the facility, I headed for the Sudanese airbase. I hopped on a rickety November model Huey piloted by a pair of Sudanese civilians, and strapped in for the 800-mile trip down to Juba.

The pilot, a small chipper man, introduced himself with a grin. "I am Fuzzy-Wuzzy from Port Sudan!"

He looked pretty pleased about that, and I was sure "Fuzzy-Wuzzy" was supposed to mean something to me. But since I had no idea what he was talking about, I just grinned back. In an hour, we were airborne, skimming south over the straight brown ribbon of the Nile.

We hadn't flown far when, looking down, I was shocked to see a Boeing 707 parked, half-submerged, in the river.

"Air Sudan," Fuzzy-Wuzzy explained cheerfully. "The pilot line up on the Nile instead of the runway."

The crash had happened months before, but no one had thought it important to pull the airliner out of the river. My experience with Sudanese aviation did not improve. During a harrowing refueling stop at a collection of mud huts called Kosti, the copilot nearly lit a cigarette while standing next to an open barrel of aviation fuel. If Fuzzy-Wuzzy hadn't reached out and physically stopped him, it would have been the biggest July Fourth fireworks show the village of Kosti had ever seen.

We survived that, barely, but hadn't been in the air long when a cockpit alarm began a frantic buzzing. As a panel light flashed, I could hear through the headset as Fuzzy and the co-pilot argued frantically in Arabic. Fuzzy reached out and depressed the alarm light, which silenced it. But a couple of miles later, the alarm began shrieking again.

Again Fuzzy and the copilot argued in Arabic, and as Fuzzy reached for the button a second time, I could understand only one snatch of what they were saying: *"Ensh' Allah"*—"God willing."

This scene replayed itself again and again: The alarm sounded, the pilots spoke worriedly in Arabic, Fuzzy pushed the button, and the copilot said, *"Ensh' Allah."* Finally, I couldn't stand it anymore. I snatched off my headset, laid it down on the seat beside me, and sent up a flare to heaven: *Lord, let this bucket of bolts stay in the air.*

For a miraculous 650 miles, it did: I prayed to God, the copilot prayed to Allah, and Fuzzy kept pushing the button, as we buzzed south over the arrow-straight contours of the Nile. Gradually, the northern desert gave way to a flat flood plain, a vast grassy savannah stretching for hundreds of miles before wrinkling itself into more undulating terrain. As we approached Juba, just north of the Ethiopean border, I could see the Boma plateau rising to 3,300 feet. Above that, the Boma Hills reached even higher, their thick evergreen forests dusky blue in the distant haze. At the summit, I knew, five hostages waited in fear for their lives.

In 1950, on Pa Boykin's North Carolina tobacco farm with my cousins Greg and Max. That's me with the Pepsi bottle.

Believe it not, this is me at my eighth grade graduation. I was already six-foot-one.

Babe Ruth League, 1961. I'm standing next to my dad, Gerald Cecil Boykin, the coach on the left. Even when Dad didn't coach my teams, he never missed a game.

Fullback and co-captain, New Bern High School, 1966. I went on to attend Virginia Tech on a football scholarship.

Jimmy Ferebee, Anita Johnson and me, just before we took our musical act to the 1965 World's Fair in New York. Jimmy's the good-looking fellow on the left. I'm the other guy.

Loading up for infantry training at ROTC Summer Camp at Fort Indian Town Gap, Pennsylvania, in 1970. That December, I graduated from Virginia Tech and received my Army commission.

Greeting Korean dignitaries in Pusan, Korea, 1972. I served as aide de camp to Brigadier General Jack McWhorter.

With 1Lt. Choi Jung Yul, the Korean aide de camp with whom I served in Pusan. Choi Jung Yul had grown up during the Korean War, and was staunchly anti-communist. He gave me a perspective on Vietnam that was different than that being presented by the U.S. media.

Training with the 101ˢᵗ Airborne at Ft. Campbell, Kentucky in 1973.

March 1978. My Delta selection course. I'm in the back row, with no cap. Pete Schoomaker is in the back row, left. Pat Hurley is in the front row, second from the left. Pat died in a helicopter crash while SCUD-hunting during Desert Storm.

My Delta squadron in December 1981. That's me, top row, far right. On the opposite end of the row is Eldon Bargewell, who led the element that rescued American Kurt Muse from a Panamanian prison in 1989. To Bargewell's right on a row alone: Command Sgt. Major Mel Wick, who was with me in Mogadishu, 1993. Second row from top, in sunglasses: Tom Corbett, a senior NCO who was wounded inside the perimeter in Mogadishu on October 3, 1993. Second row from bottom, third from the right with silver hair: Paul Lawrence, who pulled J. J. Byers out of the burning C-130 at Desert One.

Running Delta Force parachute operations in a free-fall drop zone at Eglin AFB in January 1981. We often wore civilian clothes to reduce our profile.

In 1983, with Doug Sheldon (on my right) and Col. Hassan of the Sudanese army, dancing at a Muslim wedding in Khartoum. I don't remember who the Sudanese woman was, but she looks like she was having as good a time as we were.

In 1986, after a week of survival training in the Guatemalan jungle, Delta NCO Jack Alvarez and I encountered this young boy, whose father fished and hunted to help feed the Guatemalan army. Alvarez would later play a key role in the successful hunt for Colombian drug lord Pablo Escobar.

With Pete Schoomaker on operations in Israel, 1987. We wore Israeli army uniforms to reduce the appearance of an American military presence. The Sea of Galilee is in the background.

Outside the *Nunciatura*—or Vatican embassy—in Panama City in 1989, waiting for Gen. Manuel Noriega to surrender. Pete Schoomaker is at the far left and Gary Harrell at the far right. The man with his hand on the wall is Kelly Snapp, who later became Delta XO. Pete would go on to become Army Chief of Staff.

Receiving a ceremonial guidon from Gen. Wayne Downing (right) as I took command of Delta Force in 1992. When Gen. Downing passed away suddenly in July 2007, the nation lost a great patriot, and I lost a great friend.

Before beginning operations in Mogadishu, I spoke to Task Force Rangers, and the chaplain led a prayer. Behind me is the Conex where I spoke to Osman Atto, and where I was later hit by a mortar.

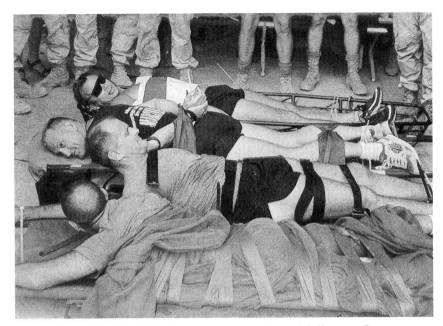

October 1, 1993 in Mogadishu: Just before the traditional Officers vs. Sergeant Majors volleyball game, the NCO's executed a takedown. Six guys grabbed each officer, flex-cuffed us, and tied us to litters. Then they brought Gen. Bill Garrison outside, pointed to us, and said, "There's your team. Let's play!" From top to bottom: Gary Harrell, me, Jim Osser (the senior Air Force officer in command of the combat controllers and parajumpers), and Danny McKnight.

In Mogadishu, briefing CENTCOM Commander, Marine Corps Gen. Joe Hoar, seated third from left.

In Mogadishu, I commanded missions from the Joint Operations Center (or JOC, pronounced "jock"). In this picture, taken prior to the Battle of the Black Sea that became known as "Black Hawk Down," we had just received new intel. I was monitoring the target area via live-video feed from helicopter-mounted cameras. In the background, the element commanders were conducting final briefings prior to launch.

In a Little Bird, turning up for my last helo flight before leaving Mogadishu. I felt I had to see the city one last time.

Tom Matthews, Bill Garrison (with cigar), and me, the day before we left Mogadishu, October 25, 1993.

November 1993, at the Oval Office with President Bill Clinton when he presented a combat award to Delta operator Brad Hallings, who lost a leg in Mogadishu. Though I was disappointed in the decisions President Clinton made after the October 3 battle, it was an honor to be there.

A farewell to George Tenet when my tour at the Central Intelligence Agency ended in June 1997. I admired and respected Tenet and was surprised when he came under fire for intelligence failures related to Iraq and WMD's. In my experience, Tenet was a serious man, conscientious about his work.

Taking command of all of Army Special Forces, April 1998. I was also a newlywed: Ashley and I had married two days earlier.

Receiving the Defense Superior Service Medal from Gen. Wesley Clark in 1998. I had worked directly for Gen. Clark while leading the hunt in the Balkans for war criminals who had systematically murdered Muslims.

My son Aaron (left) at his graduation from Army basic training. He was commissioned out of North Carolina State and served until he joined the Secret Service. My son Randy (right) served in the Army Reserves.

Target practice,
Fort Campbell, 1999.

With Command Sergeant Major Glen Nickle at Fort Carson, Colorado in 2000. Glen, a combat medic and founding member of Delta Force, helped keep J. J. Byers alive on the flight back to Wadi Kena from Desert One. Glen also took care of me in Grenada, after I was hit in the chest and shoulder with a .50 caliber anti-aircraft round.

In freefall over Yuma Proving Grounds, Arizona, in 2002.

In 2003, in Saddam Hussein's "Perfume Palace" in Iraq.

Gen. Dick Cody, at the time Vice Chief of Staff of the Army, Ashley Boykin, and Jerry during the retirement ceremony. Taken on June 8, 2007, this day marked our last day in the Army.

4

IN JUBA, THE CIA STATION CHIEF had already set up a command post in a *tugal*, a tiny adobe house with a thatched roof. A parched plains wind buffeted the little hut, spinning up clouds of dust. The head of Sudanese intel was there, along with Abu Bakr and a contingent of the men he'd put through the training plan we'd developed earlier in the year. In addition, Ron Pontier, the missionary pilot, was there, having managed to escape his LFSS captors, and fly his six-seat STOL (short take off and landing) plane off the mountain.

Via HF radio, Ron was able to talk with the remaining hostages. But with AK-47s at their heads, the hostages were limited to reinforcing the terrorists' demands. My main role was to help formulate a rescue plan and provide intelligence. In the *tugal*, I attached a crude fax machine to my satellite radio and began to receive reports that Captain Rick Zahner and his analysts transmitted from Bragg.

From the map provided by the deep-cover spook, I knew there were two airstrips, one atop Boma at the ACROSS compound and another at the base of the mountain, where the German wildlife project operated. Using satellite imagery, Bragg confirmed that and also delivered a valuable update: The terrorists, apparently amateurs, hadn't thought to block either one.

Satellite photos also showed a couple of ad hoc LFSS fighting positions that included two terrorists keeping watch from the roof of an adobe building at the missionary compound. In addition to imagery, Bragg supplied us with a detailed weather forecast. Meanwhile, Ron provided detailed information on the terrorists themselves.

"I counted at least fifteen of them, but I think there may be more," he said. "They're armed with AK-47s. They seemed high or drunk or something. I don't think they would think twice about killing any or all of the hostages."

Combined with the reports from Bragg, these details enabled the Sudanese to create an assault plan. Far from any significant body of water, Abu Bakr had only two options for insertion: overland or by air, and the land route was so risky it didn't even count. The hostage rescue team would have to climb a six-thousand-foot plateau, and it would only take one terrorist sentry to spot them and, effectively, end the mission. Abu Bakr and his officers decided they would be more likely to preserve the element of surprise if they went in fast by air.

A small band of fighters would land a Buffalo plane at the wildlife project at the base of Boma, then take and hold that facility. Simultaneously, a force of about forty fighters armed with G-3 automatic rifles would land four Puma helicopters and a Huey at the ACROSS compound and launch a direct assault on the terrorists. It was a risky plan in terms of the hostages' lives. But we calculated that the terrorists would choose to engage the assaulters and save their own skins rather than waste time shooting missionaries.

Weather was a problem. Winds atop the Boma Hills were notoriously treacherous. Using my sat radio, I contacted Bragg for another forecast and gave it to Abu Bakr. Looking it over, he chose the best weather window for the strike: twenty-four hours away, just after first light.

Delta was there strictly for support. But I wanted to go along to see how Abu Bakr's men performed, and to help if they needed it. A Sudanese general whose name I don't remember okayed it.

"You may go with us," he said. Then he delivered some of the best news I'd ever heard in my life: "But there is no room on our helicopters."

Thank God.

After my trip down the Nile, I'd seen enough of Sudanese helos. I talked to Ron Pontier and he agreed to fly a small four-seat missionary bush plane to Boma with Don Feaney and me on board.

H-Hour came and the Sudanese launched. An hour later, Ron guided our tiny plane toward the ACROSS compound. As we approached the Boma Plateau, I could see the Sudanese helicopters flying around in irregular patterns. Then I saw our runway, just a dirt strip hacked into the jungle with machetes. Swallowing hard, I cinched my seatbelt a little tighter.

After a light touchdown and bumpy rollout, Ron brought the bush plane to a quick stop. Don and I jumped out, .45s drawn, and scrambled to find the missionaries. In the search, we saw a Sudanese soldier lying dead near the airstrip. We later learned he was the first rescuer to charge into battle and was killed as soon as he jumped off the aircraft. But he was the only Sudanese casualty and LFSS resistance crumbled fast. The Sudanese cut down at least twenty terrorists and the others escaped into the evergreens.

As we moved around the missionary station, Don and I heard from below a burst of rapid fire from an assault rifle followed by a grenade explosion. A Sudanese element was still chasing the rebels down the mountain.

Abu Bakr's voice crackled over my radio. "The hostages are all alive."

But we couldn't find them. Don and I moved with caution, entering each *tugal* prepared to clear it.

Then Abu Bakr radioed us again. "The missionaries have been moved to the wildlife center airstrip. They are on their way to Juba."

Later that day, back in Juba, I finally met John Haspels, who told me he and the other missionaries had tried to escape their captors on their own. The mission, it turned out, had a little dispensary stocked with medications, including narcotics used to treat pain. In something like a scene out of a movie, Haspels made tea for the terrorists and laced it with drugs. The terrorists drank it, promptly fell asleep, and the missionaries fled into the forest. But after waking from their nap, the kidnappers hunted them down, and beat them with rawhide whips.

The day after the rescue, the U.S. embassy sent a C-12, a small turboprop, down to collect Don and me. As we arrived at the airfield, John and the other missionaries drove up in an old Land Rover. The entire group got out and walked over to us as we stood on the tarmac in front of the plane, props already turning.

"We don't know how to thank you...," John began, shouting over the prop noise. I glanced around at the group and saw tears. "We have nothing to give you in return."

"You don't have to give us anything—" I started to say, but John went on.

"The only thing we have to give you is this," and he handed me a Good News Bible. All the missionaries had signed it.

Now I had tears of my own. "I want you to know that I'm a believer, and I prayed for your rescue," I said. "Thank you."

"Thank *you*," John Haspels said. "Thank you both."

5

I STILL HAVE THAT BIBLE, and count it as a treasured possession—not only in a spiritual sense but also from a professional perspective.
The Sudan mission was Delta Force's first successful hostage rescue—and
the first that followed Charlie Beckwith's blueprint for providing low-key
assistance to other nations.

When we got back to the States, I flew up to D.C. with Digger O'Dell,
a Marine Corps major who was the joint task force J-3, or operations officer. Digger was a Vietnam veteran who'd left the service, joined the CIA,
gone back into Laos with that agency, got tired of being a spook, and
rejoined the Marines. Now, he spent nearly every weekend at an airfield
indulging his great passion: freefalling.

We were summoned to the State Department to brief the ambassador-
at-large for combating terrorism. At State, Digger and I were ushered up
to a secure conference room, where we met the ambassador, a wiry, gray-
haired little man with a sharply boned face. Next to him, at a conference
table, sat a crisply tailored National Security Council staffer whose name I
didn't catch. A CIA agent who had been with us in Juba was also present.

"Major Boykin, please show us how the Sudanese actually executed the
rescue operation," the ambassador began.

On the conference table, I laid out an aerial photo of the Boma summit
that depicted the missionary compound. I explained the Sudanese aerial
assault, the brief firefight, and the outcome. When I finished, the CIA
guy piped up. Thinking he was doing us a favor, he launched into chapter
and verse about how much assistance Delta provided the Sudanese. The
training, the planning, the intel, the weather.

Then in full praise mode, he said. "These guys' willingness to go up to
Boma was really encouraging to the Sudanese. That made them realize
how serious we were about helping them."

At that point, the ambassador's face flushed an amazing shade of scarlet, and he proceeded to screw himself into the ceiling.

"This is *totally* unacceptable!" he barked. "We were asked by the media if there was any U.S. participation, or any U.S. personnel involved in this, and we gave them an emphatic *no*. And the one thing we don't do is lie to the American public!"

Then he zeroed in on me. "Major," he said, drilling me with his eyes, "you have created a very bad situation here!"

He paused as if contemplating his next move, which I suspected involved snatching up the nearest telephone to inform the Pentagon about what this knucklehead major had done. I kept a poker face but fumed a little inside. We followed our orders and the Sudanese got every single hostage back—alive. I couldn't believe it: Delta had just completed its first successful rescue and here I sat waiting for the guillotine to fall.

I didn't know what to say, so I didn't say anything. Neither did Digger or the helpful CIA guy. In fact, for a long moment, nobody said a word.

Then, unexpectedly, the National Security Council staffer in the dapper suit spoke coolly into the tense silence.

"Well, we at the White House are very pleased with the outcome of this operation," he said. "We don't believe there is any problem with what Delta has done."

His manner was offhand and slightly superior, as if his was obviously the final word on the subject. I thought I even heard a slight edge of arrogance that said, without using the words, "I'm speaking for the President."

The effect was like ice water thrown in the diplomat's face. Instantly, the scarlet color drained away. With visible effort, he untwisted his snarl and forced himself to arrange his features in a more collegial expression. I tried not to gape.

When he was finally able to speak, he said to me, "So...will we be getting a written report on the operation?"

"Yes, sir," I said. "I'm already working on it."

The ambassador stood, indicating the meeting was over. "All right. Thank you for coming in."

As Digger and I made a rapid exit, I imagined I could feel the diplomat's eyes boring into my back. We made our way downstairs, and outside where I think I took my first full breath. As Digger and I got into the dark sedan that would take us back to the airport, I said, "By the way, who was that guy back there that just saved my butt?"

"Him? He's a Marine Corps major detailed to NSC," Digger said. "His name is Oliver North."

.50 CALIBER MIRACLE

Grenada
1983

1

AS THE UH-60 BLACK HAWK roared toward the nutmeg capital of the world, my jump boots dangled over the dark Caribbean. The steaming heat of Barbados, our departure point, gave way to a balmy warmth that poured in through the cargo door where I sat, squeezed in among other Delta operators, all of us held in by a thick canvas strap, fatigue pants flapping in the breeze. The scent of sea salt hung in the air as I watched the star-spangled horizon skimming past.

It was October 1983. President Ronald Reagan had ordered a joint-forces strike to liberate the island of Grenada from the Marxist New Jewel Movement. In 1979, while the U.S. was busy with Iran, a charismatic Marxist named Maurice Bishop had overthrown Grenada's elected leader, Sir Eric Gairy, in a mostly bloodless coup. Bishop quickly built alliances with Cuba and the Soviet Union. Soon the regime's military, Cuban-trained and Soviet-equipped, became the largest force in the region. At Delta, we received periodic reports as U.S. intelligence kept a quiet eye on these developments. When Bishop commissioned construction of a ten-thousand-foot runway—a runway of military length in a nation without an air force—Reagan began issuing public warnings.

As usual, Reagan's critics painted him paranoid. Why should we care if Nicaragua and other countries set up communist governments? And Grenada? Why should we care about a country whose only useful contribution to the world was nutmeg?

In a March 1983 speech, Reagan explained why: "Grenada, that tiny little island...is building now, or having built for it, on its soil and shores, a naval base, a superior air base, storage bases and facilities for the storage of munitions, barracks, and training grounds for the military," he said, adding wryly: "I'm sure all of that is simply to encourage the export of nutmeg."

Reagan knew a foothold in Grenada would give the Soviets two bases within striking distance of the U.S. Already communism had a death-grip on China and Eastern Europe, and was surging in Indonesia as well as Central and South America. A significant infiltration in the Caribbean could begin turning the U.S. and Western Europe into democratic islands in a global sea of totalitarianism.

When Reagan made his nutmeg speech, I was serving as operations officer for the newly created joint special operations task force. The following August, I transferred back to Delta and became Ops O there. U.S. intel continued to monitor developments in Grenada until, in October, the situation came to a head. It turned out that poor old Maurice Bishop wasn't far-left enough to suit either his old friends or his newly trained military. Backed by that military, Bishop's former deputy prime minister and friend Bernard Coard overthrew Bishop and had him, along with his top advisors, executed.

Six hundred American medical students and a few hundred American tourists were trapped on Grenada. That put Delta and the joint task force on alert. We received orders to begin planning both to rescue the medical students, and to overthrow Coard's illegitimate government.

There wasn't much time. We started planning on a Friday night and worked through the weekend, almost without sleep. Delta would work in concert with two Ranger battalions. The Rangers were to seize and hold Point Salinas airport, while Delta's target was Richmond Hill Prison, where a number of political prisoners were being held, along with several lesser targets including the radio and telephone switching stations in the Grenadian capital of St. Georges. The operation would be Delta's first major test since Eagle Claw and many of us who had been there that night felt the weight of history.

On October 24, Delta began clustering outside the Stockade, preparing to board buses for Pope AFB to catch our C-5 to Barbados. Twilight had just passed into evening. I was standing with Delta CO Sherm Williford in the bus loading area, going over some notes on the operation, when Glen Nickle walked up.

"Sir, before we launch, are we going to get everybody together and pray? You know, those prayers really worked last time and we're going to need God on this one."

Before I could answer, Sherm piped up. "Yeah, let's get em all together and do it right now."

Both Nickle's question and Sherm's response surprised me. I hadn't known our prayer at Wadi Kena had meant as much to other folks in Delta as it had to me. The command sergeant major rounded everyone up, about a hundred men, and they gathered at the foot of the stockade loading dock, their faces detailed by the building's ambient light. As I climbed up on the loading dock, an impromptu dais, guys put their hands on their buddies' shoulders and bowed their heads. Then I led the men of Delta in our second prayer for God's guidance and protection. And just as he had in Wadi Kena, Bucky stepped up and led us in singing "God Bless America."

It was the first time we had done that as a unit since our failure at Desert One. I think we all hoped this would be our chance to regain something we lost in the flames of Iran.

2

FROM POPE, we took off for Barbados on C-5s loaded with men and Black Hawks. After a miserably muggy stopover at the airfield there, I boarded one of the helos with about a dozen Delta operators. We were so crammed in that bird that hanging our feet out the door wasn't a matter of romance and daring—it was what we had to do to fit.

Sergeant Major Don Simmons, a tough and serious Special Forces veteran, sat on my right. Squeezed in on my left was Master Sergeant Dennis Wolf, a wiry, gray-haired explosives specialist. Dennis knew nothing about infantry tactics when he joined Delta, but once in the unit, he took to it like a bird to flight and became a first-rate operator. Just behind us sat Sergeant First Class Chuck Collinwood, a lionhearted man who came to Delta from the Golden Knights, the Army's elite parachuting team. Collinwood was a world freefall champion who, after he left the Army, went on to become a sniper with a big-city SWAT team, where he famously ended a hostage standoff by nailing the hostage taker with a well-placed bullet. The poor criminal never had a chance.

Dave Cheney, the big man who forced the C-130 door open at Desert One, was wedged in among others in the open door on the port side of the Black Hawk. Somewhere in between, Glenn Nickle was in there, too. We were in the flight lead, piloted by Chief Warrant Officer 3 Bill Flannery.

As the helo's massive main rotor beat the air, I caught glimpses of the five Black Hawks in trail, their position lights red against the dark.

Designed to carry more fully armed assault troops and bigger payloads than its predecessor, the Huey, the Black Hawk had been in service since 1980. We'd been training in them since just after Eagle Claw and in fact had planned a return mission to Tehran using the Black Hawk as the primary aircraft. But when the Iranians released the hostages, the mission, like so many Delta planned, became one that never happened. Grenada would be the Black Hawk's first test in actual combat. The bird's critical components and systems were either armored or redundant, built to withstand small arms and medium-caliber high-explosive projectile fire. We would now find out whether the armor worked as advertised.

The intel section briefed us to expect little resistance, so we carried pretty standard equipment: .45s, M-4 carbines, harnesses with two canteens, four ammo pouches, a strobe light, and the medical kits we always carried. My part of the mission was to set up an alternate command post, so I had a rucksack containing some smoke grenades and a PRC-66 air-to-ground radio. We didn't see a need to wear Kevlar or even helmets, which was nice since it was hot. On the other hand, the door gunner, a member of the 160th Special Operations Aviation Regiment, was zipped up tight in an OD-green flight suit and wearing a crew helmet and goggles. I felt kind of sorry for him.

We'd been en route for an hour when the sunrise began on Dave Cheney's side of the aircraft, the light quickly turning the water from grey to aquamarine as it pushed out beneath my feet. Fifteen minutes later as we approached the Grenadian coastline, the water brightened from aquamarine to turquoise to crystal shallows. Then we crossed the beach, a white ribbon there and quickly gone.

At my two o'clock, I could see the capital city of St. George's, and beyond it, three Navy ships floating on the postcard sea. Below us, island jungle formed a lush cover, broken by tiny, square farms and occasionally a village. When we did pass over open ground, I was surprised to see people looking up at us, smiling and waving. We were low enough to see their faces.

Then I saw our target: Richmond Hill Prison, a small fortress of brick and concrete set on a hill. Three minutes straight ahead.

One of the crew chiefs yelled back into the cargo bay: "Hey, Radio Free Grenada is announcing that we're coming!"

Well, that explains the friendly villagers.

It also meant there would be zero element of surprise.

As if on cue, the sky erupted with red and green tracers, arrows of light speeding up at us. For a surreal moment, my world went quiet. Suddenly, I found myself thinking in real time, but sensing in slow motion—

Looking below, I see an anti-aircraft gun emplacement, a Quad 50.

No intel on that.

I see fatigue-clad Latin men manning it, their faces turning slowly up toward mine.

Cubans.

I raise my M-4.

On the ground, a red tracer leaves the cannon's barrel.

I aim, fire, aim, fire.

The tracer is coming up straight and slow, almost lazy. I seem to see its entire path from the gun barrel to the Black Hawk.

The tracer round misses the helo, and suddenly time snaps back into place.

Now, the air crackles with gunfire. Don and Dennis are returning fire on my right and left. The door gunner is squeezing off staccato bursts, the rattle of his M-60 muted by the furious beating of the Black Hawk's rotor.

I aim and fire. I hear others firing around me. On the ground, some of the triple-A gunners fall.

Who killed them? Was it me? It is the first time I may have killed a man. I don't know how to feel.

The smell of cordite fills the air. I begin to hear popping noises and realize that each one is a .50 caliber round punching a hole in the Black Hawk. The engine roars as Bill circles the gun emplacement.

Muzzle reports from behind me, on Cheney's side. Don, Dennis and me: Fire. Fire. Fire.

The door gunner's fire slows. He's having trouble picking out targets on the ground. Another staccato burst, then his weapon jams. He struggles to clear it.

From behind him, Collinwood looms up, yelling, "*Move!*"

Collinwood yanks the gunner from his saddle, instantly clears the jam and fires. The M-60 thunders. On the ground, two men fall.

Don's magazine is out. He reloads. Dennis reloads, then me. I brace myself on my rucksack, eject a spent magazine and snap in a full one. I pick up the empty with my left hand.

I am stashing it when an invisible sledgehammer crashes into my left shoulder.

I feel a massive jolt, but there is no pain. I try to finish stashing the empty so I can reengage, but my left hand no longer works. My left arm no longer works.

It's been shot off.

My next thought: *You're not the first guy to lose an arm, now just stay alive.*

Don and Dennis are still firing. I lay down my carbine and reach over with my right hand to find the stump of my shoulder.

Can I stop the bleeding before I bleed out?

Instead of a stump, I find an upper arm.

I've still got my arm. It is more of a factual notation than a rush of relief.

I slide my right hand down to see how much of my left arm remains. It's all there, but completely numb and useless. I lift it with my right hand and flop it into my lap.

A .50 caliber round meant to bring down aircraft had blown through the Black Hawk's floor and through my rucksack, shattering the radio inside it. The round continued its upward trajectory, carrying radio shrapnel and bullet fragments up at a slight angle through my armpit into my shoulder and chest. I would later learn I was a centimeter from death: One fragment missed my brachial artery by the width of a bullet.

The drumbeat of rotors continued as Bill banked and dove, trying to pick a way to Richmond Hill through the barrage of incoming fire. I still felt nothing. From the doorway, I could see Cuban forces reloading a Quad, a different one. M-4's cracked from both cargo doors.

Suddenly the blessed numbness in my arm vanished and pain roared in, a deep, terrible searing as though somebody stuck a blowtorch under my armpit and was steadily cranking up the flame. Pulsing fire radiated into the left side of my chest, a consuming pain worse than I had ever imagined.

On my right, Don Simmons was firing. I looked at him: "Don, I'm hit."

He pulled up his M-4 and leaned over my lap, searching for the wound. Then I heard Collinwood: "Don, he's hit in the chest and shoulder. He's bleeding bad."

Collinwood stopped shooting. The roar of guns and rotors continued around us. He plunged his hand into his medical kit, snatched out a bandage, and tore it open with his teeth. Still holding the bandage in his mouth, he used both hands to rip my shirt open.

He pressed the bandage to my chest. "Hold that!" he yelled.

I reached up with my right hand to hold the bandage in place.

Collinwood grabbed the M-60 and squeezed off three more bursts. He turned back to me and adjusted the bandage, trying to stop the bleeding. He then grabbed the M-60 again and resumed firing.

In my peripheral vision, I glimpsed Don Simmons pulling a morphine syrette out of his medical kit.

"No morphine!" I yelled as he prepped it. "No morphi—"

Don jabbed the needle into my thigh. I hadn't known whether the morphine would cause me to pass out, which was why I didn't want it. But within 30 seconds, the fire in my chest and shoulder had subsided to almost nothing.

"We're going to take you to the airfield!" Simmons shouted over the battle roar.

"No!" I said. "Go around one more time and land at the target!" I thought he wanted to abort the mission because I'd been shot. I did not want to be the reason for that.

But the pilot had already decided that the triple-A fire was too heavy. "We can't land in this stuff!" Simmons yelled and at that moment Bill cranked the Black Hawk in a looping 270 degree turn and headed back over the jungle and toward the sea.

The morphine didn't knock me out, but it made me a little dopey. Leaning back a little on my ruined rucksack, I gazed out the cargo door and could see that the invasion had begun. I knew that an earlier Ranger airdrop was supposed to have already secured the airfield at Point Salinas. Now I could see the next wave of Rangers parachuting in, popping out of a C-130 in a straight line, their gray-green chutes billowing like giant man-o'-wars.

The island is ours, I thought blearily. *There's nothing they can do to stop us now.*

3

NONE OF THE ANALYSTS AT CIA OR DIA believed we would face much resistance in Grenada. Due to that critical intelligence failure, we flew into a hornet's nest. All six Black Hawks in the Delta flight were shot to pieces. Maintenance crews later counted 54 holes in the one I was riding. I wasn't the only casualty. Bill had a slight wound to his leg, and Dave Cheney was shot through the arm. A young Delta radio operator named Scott Perry was also wounded—three times with one bullet: He had been squatting on the deck near Cheney when a .50 cal round pierced the Black Hawk floor then ripped a tunnel up through his shin and calf, his thigh, and the hand he'd had resting on it.

In addition to the casualties on our bird, ten other Delta operators and eight men from Task Force 123 were wounded. One Black Hawk pilot was killed by gunfire. His copilot, also wounded, kept the bird airborne until it smashed into a ridgeline, its rotor breaking free and pinwheeling over the ridgeline and into St. George's Bay. Miraculously, no one else was killed in the crash.

Now, as our Black Hawk went feet-wet over the water, I looked out and saw the Navy ships I spotted earlier, beyond St. George's. Soon, it became clear that's where we were headed.

In my boozy haze, I thought, *Man, I hope this Army pilot knows how to land on a moving Navy ship.*

Bill guided the Black Hawk toward the nearest vessel, the USS *Moosbrugger*. The Spruance-class destroyer was poorly equipped to care for a batch of bloody Special Ops guys, but it was the closest port in a storm.

With the morphine dousing the fire in my wound, I had time to think about other things. Right next to the bullet fragments and shrapnel, deep disappointment settled into my chest. In Iran, we'd gotten as far as Desert One. Now, on our first major test since, we'd been unable to reach the target and complete our portion of the mission.

I also began to consider the ramifications of my wound. Don Simmons's face, like Collinwood's, told me it was serious. I began to pray: *Lord, spare my life. Please don't let me die without seeing my family again.* I thought about Lynne, the kids, my mom.

After that, I started to get a little angry. *Why have You allowed this?* I wanted to know. *Have You abandoned me?*

I tend to do that—question God, wonder where He is when things go bad. Then I go through a process: *Okay, this has happened for a reason. I may not know what the reason is, but I do know that I trust God.*

When Bill set the Black Hawk down on the *Moosbrugger*, Simmons and Wolf helped me out onto the helo pad and below deck. A Navy corpsman bandaged me up as best he could and told me that a Marine Corps helo would arrive shortly to take us to the USS *Guam*, a ship with a fully equipped surgical bay.

The corpsman put me on a litter and two sailors carried me back up near the helo deck to wait. Soon I could hear the distinctive twin-rotor beat of a CH-46. A few minutes later, the helo settled its strange buglike bulk onto the ship, its rotor-wash whipping the tropical air across the deck. As the sailors carried me toward the helo, I glimpsed a man hanging part way out of the cockpit, waving his arms wildly in my direction.

I couldn't believe it: The pilot was Frank Brewer, executive officer of the helo squadron, and a close friend of mine. Frank grew up thirty-five miles from me in Greenville, North Carolina, but I didn't meet him until 1982, when we sat next to each other in a seminar class at the Armed Forces Staff College. Because I was up there without my family, I spent a lot of time with Frank and his wife and daughter. Frank was a member of the Church of Christ and we saw eye to eye on a lot of spiritual issues. We became very close.

When I saw him in the cockpit of that CH-46, I felt God saying to me, *See? I haven't abandoned you.* Then Glenn Nickle suddenly appeared beside me, and before I knew it, he was with me on Frank's helo and starting an IV. I knew there was not a better combat medic in the entire Army and a warm comfort spread through me. Between Frank and Glenn, I knew God had placed me in good hands.

No more than ten minutes later, a pair of corpsmen carried me down a series of decks and ladders to the hospital bay on the USS *Guam*.

"Hey, sir, how are you feeling?" said a doctor who came to examine my wounds.

I chuckled a little. "Except for a couple of holes in me, I'm doing okay."

A corpsman added some kind of painkiller to my IV. Then the doctor lifted my arm to examine my wound. Every time he moved my arm, I could feel crunching in my shoulder. I didn't know it then, but the ragged hole in the side of my chest was about the size of a softball. The doctor and his helper asked me at least three times if I was breathing okay. I think they were amazed that my lungs still worked.

"We're going to have to take you into surgery," the doc finally said. "We really can't tell the extent of your injuries until we get in there and take a look."

"Okay," I said. "Let's do it."

After surgery, I lay in the hospital bed all night as helos ferried in more casualties. One bird brought Delta's unit physician, Ward Dean. We discussed the extent of my injuries. The triple-A round had destroyed my bicep and shredded the long bone in my arm to kindling. Two major pieces of the bone remained, splintered at the ends and separated by a wide gap where the bone had been completely destroyed. A small piece of the round had exited at the top of my shoulder. Because the projectile carried pieces of the shattered PRC radio with it, my upper chest and shoulder were riddled with embedded metal fragments. On an X-ray, my left side looked like a chocolate chip cookie—heavy on the chips.

"Hey, uh, doc," I said to Dean twice when he came to see me. "Is this something they are going to be able to repair?"

"They'll have to determine that when you get back," he said. I couldn't read his face and he wouldn't commit. That's when I knew I might be facing the end of my career.

If they board me out, what will I be able to do? I wondered, lying alone in the hospital bay. I started trying to remember people I had seen who were unable to use one of their arms. Oddly, the first guy I thought of was Senator Bob Dole, whose right arm was mangled by German machine-gun fire during World War II. Of course, Dole was in politics now. I knew for sure I didn't want to do that.

I thought about my dad, who forged a career as a civil service electronics technician, even though he was half blind. But I knew losing the use of an arm was different, limiting in a way I wasn't sure I could tolerate. I dreaded telling my mom and dad about the wound and the possibilities I faced. And as I lay there, I prayed nobody had yet told my wife.

I also began to pray about my arm, asking God to heal it and let me return to duty. I had good reasons to believe that He could. When I was a little boy, my mother was bedridden with an acute form of hepatitis. Her illness dragged on for months and was so debilitating we went to live in Richmond, Virginia, with my aunt, who was a registered nurse. It terrified me to see that on many, many days, Mom was so weak she could barely lift her head off the pillow.

After I was grown, she told me that one day, when she was at her sickest, I stood beside her bed and said, "Mama, if you die, I'm gonna kill myself."

She told me, "Jerry, I'm not going to die anytime soon."

Not long after that, another aunt came from North Carolina and drove my mother to Baltimore to see a minister who prayed for the sick. Two days later, they came back to Richmond and my mother did not have to go back to bed. The hepatitis was gone.

4

THE NEXT DAY, A TEAM OF NAVY CORPSMEN came to the hospital bay, transferred me to a litter and carried me down to the hangar deck in preparation to move me off the ship. Frank Brewer came down to see me. I got a battle update: It took the Rangers two and a half hours to complete their drop, and just as long again to take full control of the airfield. Meanwhile, part of the 1st Ranger Btn rescued 138 medical students at the True Blue medical campus. But then they learned that 224 more were holed up in a hotel near Grand Anse, a second medical campus behind enemy lines.

The next day, the Rangers rescued them in a daring helo assault, but learned in the process that *another* 202 students were on still another campus that no one in Grenada's rightful government thought important to mention to the Americans. Twelve Rangers remained behind at Grand Anse to make enough seats on the helicopters for the students. They waited until dark, captured a boat and made their escape by sea.

After Frank and I visited for a few minutes, he reached into his pocket and pulled out a small pin, the emblem of his Marine helicopter squadron. He bent and fastened it on my hospital gown.

"Frank, you don't know how much it meant to me when I saw it was you flying that helo off the *Moosbrugger*," I said.

He grinned. "You know, when we got the call I had no idea who we were going to pick up. But all the other aircrews were already flying. It was just me and the maintenance officer left. So when we got the call, I said, 'Let's do it,' and when we got there and I saw it was you, I couldn't believe my eyes."

Now it was my turn to smile. "Frank, it was the Lord's way of letting me know He was still with me."

"Brother," he said, "anything short of murder or treason, I'll do it for you."

The corpsmen loaded me onto a CH-46 and flew me back to Grenada.

Someone unloaded my litter at the Point Salinas airfield, and I lay there, flat on the tarmac in a lineup of other litters filled with other shot-up guys.

"Boykin!" I heard my name but in the bustle of activity around me, I couldn't see who was calling me.

"Hey, Boykin!"

I lifted my head as best I could, and about five feet away saw John Carney, bent over and shooting me the moon. Carney was the Air Force combat controller who'd gone into Iran ahead of us all to embed covert lighting at Desert. Now, hooting with laughter, he pulled up his pants and walked over.

I grinned at him. "John, I hate to tell you this, but you've gotten uglier since we started this operation."

We laughed and talked a bit, then Bucky Burruss came over to check on me.

Two C-141 flights later, I was back at Bragg. During the flights, I had hours to pray, to ask God to give me use of my arm again. At some point during those hours in the air, my anxiety melted away, replaced by an absolute assurance that He would. I can't explain why I felt that way. I just did.

On the ground at Bragg, a medical team whisked me off to Womack Army Medical Center, right there on post. After a round of x-rays, another team rolled me into the OR for more exploratory surgery. Back in a regular hospital room after recovery, three doctors in white coats came to explain my injuries to me. The news wasn't good.

"The bone in your upper arm is shattered, your bicep is severely damaged and you have a significant nerve injury, which is why you can't move your arm," said a lieutenant colonel, the oldest of the three. "It would not be prudent to go in and try to repair your arm now. You have so much shrapnel in you that there is an extremely high risk of infection."

I listened, nodding as he spoke.

"So what we'd like to do is, in six to eight months, go back in and use plates and screws to repair the broken bone," the doctor went on. He stopped and took a breath, then delivered the worst news of all: "Your nerve is so damaged that it is very unlikely that it will regenerate. There's a very good possibility that you'll never use your right arm again."

I took all this in, considering what to say to this group of men who I considered able medical professionals. Finally, I broke into a smile and looked at the doctor who had given me the prognosis.

"Doctor," I said, "you will never have to go back into my arm again, because God will heal my arm."

A beat passed, and it appeared to me that the three physicians were each trying to figure out the appropriate thing to say to a patient so obviously out of touch with reality.

Finally, one of them smiled indulgently. "Well, you have the right attitude, sir," he said. "We'll come back and check on you in the morning."

After the doctors delivered their news and left my room, Lynne arrived and could barely hold back tears. I told her the same thing I told the doctors. I could tell she was skeptical, but she wanted to believe it with me in spite of the medical facts. The next day, April, Randy and Aaron stormed the room with get well cards, hugs and kisses. Then Mom and Dad showed up. Mom said everyone at church in New Bern was praying for me. Being home with my family was the best medicine of all. The outpouring of affection made me so glad Scotty Morgan, the Grenada task force J-4, the logistics officer, arranged for me to come home instead of being installed in a hospital in Roosevelt Roads, Puerto Rico.

After three days, the doctors said I could go home if I promised to come back every day for a bandage check and therapy. On my first return visit, an orthopedic intern from Canada strapped me into a medieval torture device he suggested might help the bones in my arm begin to grow together again. First, he casted my arm from shoulder to wrist. Then he wrapped some kind of harness around my torso, the sole purpose of which was to support a female receptacle that would hold the end of a long stick. Next, he raised my casted arm to shoulder-level. To hold it there, he placed one end of the stick in the ribcage receptacle and the other end into another female fitting on the cast.

My shoulder burst into flame. It was the most excruciating pain I had ever felt—worse, even, than the pain that scorched me in the Black Hawk before Don doped me. I went home and spent the most miserable night I had ever spent. With my arm sticking out that way, I couldn't lie down. I tried to sleep on the couch sitting up. The misery of the Long Walk was nothing compared to this.

All through the night, I did what I tend to do in times of trouble. *Why, Lord?* I wanted to know. *Why is this happening? Why are You letting me go through this pain?*

The night passed in a blur of prayer and agony, and the next morning, I showed up at Womack at the crack of dawn and made them cut me out of the intern's awful contraption. A nurse then gave me a sedative so I could get some sleep. And when I woke up, I met the doctor who would witness my healing—whether he wanted to or not.

5

THE DOCTOR'S NAME WAS MILLER. He was a tall, wiry-haired orthopedics resident and Duke grad who had been short-suited in the bedside manners department. But he had a new plan that didn't sound like it involved medieval torture, so I was more than happy to go along.

"Here's what we're going to do," he said in his matter-of-fact New York accent. "I'm going to cast you from your wrist all the way up to your shoulder. The only thing this cast will do is provide weight and traction to try and pull the major pieces of the humerus back together."

Miller's theory was that if he could ever get the remaining halves of the shattered bone to touch each other, they would begin to knit together and heal.

"Doc, you just do the best you can," I said, smiling. "God will take care of the rest."

Miller's face, even his eyes, remained completely blank. It appeared to me he didn't know what to say and therefore didn't say anything. On the other hand, maybe he'd already heard I was a religious nut.

Miller had the Womack staff cast me up. They bent my arm across my abdomen and secured it there with a wide band. At home, I still had to sleep sitting up on the couch. I never got used to it.

The following Friday, I went back in to see the doctor. Poker-faced, he told me the bones had not moved a millimeter. But I was not at all discouraged. I knew that between the church in New Bern and my church in Fayetteville, many, many people were praying that God would heal my arm.

"Are you a man of faith, Dr. Miller?" I asked him.

"I'm Jewish," he said, and left it at that.

At the beginning of the second week I went back to work at the stockade. I mainly shuffled paper and attended meetings but from a psychological perspective, it was really important for me to feel useful and engaged. It was also early that week when my fingers began to hurt.

I was ecstatic! It was the first sensation I'd felt in my hand since being shot. By that Thursday, I was able to move three fingers on my left hand—the middle, ring, and pinky. The next day, I went to see Miller.

"Doc, you're gonna be excited," I told him. "God's healing me. Look, I can move these fingers."

I had never met a man who could keep his face so empty of expression. "That's good," Miller said. "But the bones still aren't touching."

Man, I thought, *this guy's missing his calling as a funeral director.*

I continued my Friday visits with Miller, always following the same routine: first I would stop by x-ray. Then, carrying the film with me in an oversized envelope, I would go to the examining room to meet the doc. He would pull out the x-ray, clip it to the illuminator, and then we'd have a short chat, with me on an examination table and him on a stool.

By the third week in the cast, I began moving my thumb and index finger. "Wait 'til you see this," I told Miller that Friday. I demonstrated, waggling all five of my digits. "See? I told you. God's healing my arm."

"That's good progress," he said, his face a blank tablet.

By the end of the fourth week, I was able to open and close my hand completely. On the sixth Friday, I hiked myself up on Miller's table and handed him my x-ray envelope.

"Hey, Doc, wait 'til you see these x-rays today," I said. "The bones are going to be touching. I can feel it."

At that point, he likely thought I had lost my mind, but I will never know since he said nothing. As usual, he quietly clipped the x-ray to the illuminator and looked at it.

Then he looked at me.

Then he looked at the x-ray again.

Slowly he turned back to face me. "The bones are touching," he said. "I think it's starting to heal."

"I told you! Hey, Doc, get this cast off," I joked. "I wanna go play some golf!"

"Well, uh, I'll take the cast off," he said reluctantly. "But I really wouldn't want you to play any golf."

The man never even cracked a smile.

6

—

WITH THE CAST REMOVED, my recovery accelerated. I began going to physical therapy two to three times a week. I still didn't have a left bicep, so I had to use my right arm to make my left one move. For example, I would grip a long stick with my left hand. I would then grasp the stick with my right hand and use it as a kind of handle to raise my left forearm up and down in a curl motion.

A couple of weeks passed. Then Walter Reed Army Medical Center sent a hand specialist named Dr. Chin down to give me a "nerve conduction test." In an exam room at Womack, the doctor explained that the purpose of the test was to check the functioning of my radial-ulnar nerve, the one that controls the movement of the hand and fingers.

"If the nerve is regenerating, the electrical pulses will stimulate it and your hand will involuntarily open and close," Chin said.

I lay down on a table, and Chin came to me with needles. They resembled acupuncture probes, except that each slim metal spike had a wire attached to it, through which electrical current was supposed to flow from the machine Chin brought with him from D.C. I felt slight pricking as, one by one, Chin slid the probes through my skin into my nerve. Then he stepped away from the table and positioned himself on the side of the machine, whose readout I couldn't see.

"How's that?" he said.

"How's what?" I said, looking over at him.

"Do you feel anything?"

"Nope. Not a thing."

I could see Chin manipulating something on the other side of the machine.

Ouch!

I felt something all right—an electrical shock. But not in my hand—in my neck. Then it zapped into my chest, then my torso. My legs began to heave and buck. My toes started to twitch and buzz. Chin kept cranking up the power until my whole body flopped on the table like a fish on a beach.

All the while my fingers remained perfectly still.

"Turn that thing off!" I finally shouted. "You're electrocuting me!"

Instantly, the current stopped, but all over my body, my muscles seemed to quiver and I felt slightly nauseated.

Dr. Chin walked over to the table and looked down at me. "You have no nerve conduction whatsoever in that arm," he said. "What you have is bruised nerves from the shock and the trauma of the bullet. It is worse than having a severed nerve. If it was severed, there would be a chance it could grow back or be reattached. But in your case, the nerve is too damaged. There's nothing we can do to help you."

"Well, thank you," I said, "I appreciate you looking at me."

There was no discussion of how, with no conductivity in the nerve that controlled my hand, I was able to move it on my own.

By February, my x-rays showed that the humerus had mended itself. I kept working with weights, and in March made a water jump, parachuting into a lake on Fort Bragg. And though I still had a tough road ahead, I was able to use my arm again—even doing push-ups.

Doctors at Womack now told me it appeared I would make a full recovery. They would not need to go back into my arm to put in plates and screws. Now where had I heard that before?

MERRY CHRISTMAS, NORIEGA

Panama

1989–1990

1

PETE SCHOOMAKER WAS DELTA'S C.O., and I was deputy commander by the time Manuel Noriega's goons tossed Kurt Muse into a tiny cell at *Carcel Modelo* and murdered a man in front of him. Outfitted with rape and torture rooms, the ironically named "Model Prison" was a hellhole—the Angola Prison of Panama. Starving, beaten prisoners were packed into tiny cells, dressed in rags, and sleeping on filthy pallets of thin foam. The prison was not so much a correctional institution as a retribution center for enemies of Noriega, Panama's military dictator. Noriega paid judges to convict innocent men of trumped up charges then send them to *Modelo*, where the corridors often echoed with screams. Most men who went in never came out again. Not alive, anyway.

That was clearly what Noriega had in mind for Kurt Muse. But the dictator had a little problem: Muse was an American citizen under the protection of the Panama Canal Treaty. Three weeks after the cell clanged shut behind him in the spring of 1989, Delta was tasked to rescue him.

We sent Jim Knight, a guy I had known since my first day in the Army, and a small team down to the U.S. Southern Command in the capital, Panama City. Perched high on Quarry Heights, the dominant hill in the city, SouthCom offered an eagle-eye view of *Carcel Modelo*, no more than half a mile away. Using spotting scopes and cameras, Jim and his team began filling in the intel blanks. What were the possible entry points to the prison? Where were the potential landing zones, and what were the obstacles? Were the prisoners, particularly Kurt Muse, ever brought outside? How many guards patrolled the prison? What were their patterns of movement?

In one report back to Bragg, Jim noted the presence of a small cupola with a door in it located on the prison roof. In five days of constant surveillance, not a single guard had ever gone up there.

I smiled at the news. Noriega might as well have put out a welcome mat.

As we began planning the rescue, we got to know a lot about our guy.

Kurt Frederick Muse moved to Panama at age five with his mother, Peggy, and father, Charlie, who wanted to escape the American rat race and raise their kids in a simpler way of life. Though they lived near the Panama Canal Zone, which was full of Americans who associated mainly with each other, the Muses lived on the local economy. Charlie Muse ran a successful printing business; Kurt attended Panamanian schools and grew up playing in the streets with the local children, a big blond kid in a sea of dark-eyed, brown-skinned friends.

As he grew up, Muse fell in love with the lush tropical country and considered it home. He married Annie, an American schoolteacher, and they had two kids, Kimberly and Erik. As years passed, the Muses watched as Manuel Noriega rose to power, putting more and more of Panama under his thumb. U.S. intelligence agencies also kept close tabs on Noriega's rise, and at times even enabled it. The general made nice, allowing the U.S. to set up listening posts in Panama. He funneled U.S. money to pro-American forces in El Salvador and Nicaragua. He also pretended to oppose cocaine trafficking and fed tips to the U.S. Drug Enforcement Administration and CIA, ostensibly to help the agencies in their battle against the Colombian cartels. For this he earned annual payments from then–CIA director George H.W. Bush.

The truth was, Noriega only tipped the Americans to enough trafficking to make the "War on Drugs" look like a success. Meanwhile, he became closely allied with Colombia's ruthless Medellin cartel, where a young thug named Pablo Escobar was busy moving up from car theft to murder.

By the mid-1980s, Muse and patriots across Panama had grown to hate Noriega. Along the way, somebody stuck him with a nickname, "the Pineapple," which referred to his acne-scarred face. Then a series of events began chilling American relations with Noriega. The body of Hugo Spadafora, a vocal Noriega critic, was found tortured and decapitated. A former member of Noriega's inner circle revealed that the general ordered Spadafora—and many others—murdered.

As Delta compiled background on Muse, it quickly became clear how he'd gotten his butt in a sling. He despised the Pineapple's increasingly martial rule and the way his Panamanian Defense Force (PDF) goons now lurked on every street corner, harassing peaceful citizens. Muse and a close circle of friends took to harassing the PDF in return. Using portable radios, they played tricks on the soldiers, sending them on snipe hunts, or pretending to be superior officers and chastising them on the air.

But in 1987, the radio game turned serious.

By accident, Kurt and his friends discovered a radio link to the repeater station used by *Radio Nacional* to carry Noriega's propaganda-packed public speeches live. The friends instantly realized what their discovery meant: If they could obtain a transmitter powerful enough to do the job, they could override Noriega's speeches with their own messages. They could rally the citizens of Panama to reject the dictator, band together at the next election and take back their country. That they could humiliate Noriega in the process was like a cherry on top of the whole plan, a plan they knew could mean death, or worse, for them and their families.[1]

Their first opportunity came on October 11, 1987. Noriega was scheduled to address a captive audience of thousands in a Loyalty Day speech at a baseball stadium. The speech would be broadcast live across Panama. In preparation, Kurt and his friends secretly obtained a transmitter—contraband, since only Noriega's cronies could obtain radio licenses—and recorded a special inaugural message that would launch *La Voz del la Libertad*, the Voice of Liberty. On the day of the speech, the conspirators gathered around the transmitter in the home of a friend and tuned into *Radio Nacional*, waiting for the perfect moment.[2]

They waited as one of Noriega's lapdogs introduced him. They waited while the crowd broke into wild obedient cheers. They waited as Noriega waved to the stands and basked in the applause. Then, when Noriega opened his speech, Kurt pressed the transmit button, and every Panamanian listening to *Radio Nacional* heard this:

We interrupt this broadcast to bring you a message of hope from the free and democratic people of Panama. Our date with destiny approaches. One day we will finally have an opportunity to cast our vote against the tyranny of General Noriega's dictatorship...You know the many tools that the oppressors have to keep us from the polling places. We beseech you to be brave, to persevere...Together we can bury General Noriega's dictatorship under a mountain of ballots...The end of their dictatorship is near! Together we can run them out! The free and democratic people of Panama now return this radio station to its broadcast of oppression.[3]

Kurt Muse had just signed his own death warrant.

2

OVER THE NEXT FEW MONTHS, Muse and his friends continued operating *La Voz*, infuriating the Pineapple with more messages encouraging free Panamanians to take back their country. Noriega and his PDF tore Panama apart, hunting down the source of the insurgent transmissions. Meanwhile, tensions mounted between Noriega and the United States. For years, he had been allowed to manipulate his relationship with U.S. agencies, playing DoD against State—generals against diplomats. But with increasingly corrupt elections, the Spadafora murder, and mounting visible evidence of Noriega's involvement with the Colombian cartels, the little dictator had become a violent liability.

In 1988, the U.S. indicted Noriega on federal drug trafficking charges. Also, the CIA began funneling clandestine aid to *La Voz*, providing Muse with more radio equipment as well as money to pay for leases on apartments where the only occupants were rebel transmitters. Using them, Muse's group continued to stir rebellion, hoping—along with Bush 41 and the State Department—that Panamanians would dump the Pineapple in the presidential election scheduled for May 1989.

Muse and his friends counted the days until the election. They felt *La Voz* had stirred a grassroots uprising and waited to see its effect in the voting booth. But in early April, with just a month to go, Kurt Muse arrived home in Panama on a flight from Miami—then vanished. For several days, no one knew for sure what happened to him. His friends and family were certain he'd been arrested in connection with *La Voz*. Which, in Noriega's Panama, was about the same as a death sentence. In fact, death would have been high on the list of favorable outcomes compared to what happened to most Noriega prisoners.

Because high echelons of the American government had been funding Muse's radio operation, DoD, State, and CIA immediately took an intense interest in his whereabouts. At first, Noriega's power structure said they didn't know a thing. Kurt Muse? Who's that? Never heard of him.

But the U.S. government applied a little pressure, revoking all visas for Panamanians visiting the United States. Instantly, Noriega produced Kurt in a splashy press conference in which he announced he had caught "an American spy."

3

FROM THE MOMENT WE RECEIVED THE ORDER to plan Kurt Muse's rescue, Delta didn't see taking down *Modelo* as a big deal. We really didn't. Noriega's thugs were experts at torture, but they were amateur soldiers. We felt we could strike quickly, grab the "Precious Cargo" (Muse), and be gone before the PDF could react.

But we did have two concerns. Noriega's military headquarters, the *Comandancia*, sat right next to the prison. If we inserted by helicopter, PDF soldiers walking regular guard rotation would likely send some stray rounds zinging our way. We also worried about other Americans caught outside U.S. bases. The Pineapple had been ratcheting up harassment of Americans living in the Canal Zone. When he found out we'd snatched his political prize out from under his nose, no American would be safe.

In May 1989, Noriega allowed the presidential election to go ahead, and it appeared that the popular uprising aided by *La Voz* would win the day. As the vote count proceeded, the three-candidate ticket running against Noriega's puppet candidates pulled into the lead. Immediately, Noriega tried to rig the results, but his fake tallies arrived at the election centers too late: The real results were already public and the anti-Noriega ticket won. Jubilation broke out in the streets, and the next day, the winners, including president-elect Guillermo Endara, rolled through Panama City in a motorcade. But Noriega's goon squad intercepted the winners and beat them to a pulp. Pictures of the bloodied men were broadcast all over the world, bringing Noriega's brutal rule to the world's attention.

Noriega named a longtime associate, Francisco Rodriguez, as acting president. But the U.S. declared Endara the real president. That was when Delta's mission was expanded: Now President Bush wanted U.S. Special Operations not only to snatch Muse, but also to take down Manuel Noriega's entire regime.

4

FOR MONTHS, tensions between the two countries boiled up then subsided before heating up again as America alternated between saber rattling and diplomacy. During the most volatile times, Delta would deploy to Howard AFB in Panama City, and stand by in case the mission became a go. I spent time traveling between Howard, Quarry Heights, and a couple of the American installations in the Canal Zone. I had trained with Delta in the jungles of Panama many times and knew the country well. I thought it absolutely beautiful.

The tropical air there swelters almost year round. It's just a question of whether you're going to be hot and wet from sweat, or hot and wet from rain. Still, the country's quaint, narrow streets, the hacienda-style architecture, and lush jungle captivated me. I often found myself thinking, though, what a shame it was that such a brutal man controlled it with fear and oppression. A metaphor for Noriega's regime could be seen at the *Comandancia*: Graveyards flanked the small military complex on two sides, and the headquarters stood across the street from a pathetic barrio, where entire families huddled in rude shacks built of cardboard, corrugated plastic, and hubcaps.

Because Muse had possibly broken Panamanian law (such as it was), America was in no position to demand his release. But since Annie Muse was a DoD school teacher, that made Kurt Muse a DoD dependent entitled to full legal protection under the Canal Treaty. That enabled the U.S. to strong-arm Noriega and the PDF into allowing regular visits from an American doctor and a lawyer.

Under the terms of a deal negotiated by Jimmy Carter, the U.S. was about to surrender the canal to Panamanian control. Even Noriega wasn't crazy enough to want to screw that up. So, three times a week, Marcos Ostrander, a tough Army attorney, visited Muse in *Modelo*, as did Jim Ruffer, a fighter pilot turned Air Force flight surgeon.

Officially, Ostrander and Ruffer were there to ensure that the PDF didn't abuse an American in their custody. But secretly, the two men also carried messages between Muse and his family. Even more secretly, the doctor and the lawyer gathered information for Delta. How many guards patrolled the corridor where Muse's cell was located? How are they armed? Which ones are Noriega loyalists? Could any guards be turned? We even had the doctor and the lawyer count their steps as they walked from place to place within the prison. After each meeting with Muse, analysts at Quarry Heights debriefed them, and passed us the information at Bragg. In return, we relayed them more questions to ask.

The more Delta learned about Muse, the more we liked him. The information coming back from Ostrander and Ruffer told us he was tough and resilient. We also respected the fact that he had been able to withstand some of the hell the PDF had put him through before the U.S. intervened.

Like when they murdered a man in front of Muse to try to get him to confess. Before they tossed him in prison, the PDF held Muse in a small room in another facility. When Muse refused to admit he was an American spy, three Panamanian Defense Force soldiers hustled a Colombian man into the room.

Driving him forward like a tackle dummy, all three soldiers smashed the Colombian's face into a brick wall, shattering his teeth and the bones in his face. Then one soldier grabbed the prisoner's right arm, wrenched it backward and radically upward, pinning his wrist between his shoulder blades. The prisoner howled in pain. Another soldier twisted his left arm into the same excruciatingly unnatural position. The prisoner screamed. To snap handcuffs on, the soldiers had to get the Colombian's wrists to meet between his shoulder blades, so they jerked hard on both his arms at the same time. Both his shoulders popped out of their sockets.[4]

The Colombian screamed like a dying animal.

"Have you been watching?" a PDF lieutenant told Muse. "This is your future."[5]

Then, as the Colombian begged for his life, the three soldiers beat him into the human equivalent of ground meat. Over and over, they drove their steel-toed boots into his testicles, kidneys, ribs, and gut. They stomped on his head, tearing the flesh from his face with soles of their boots. They ground their heels into his eyes. And when the room smelled of blood, and the prisoner could scream no more but only moan softly, the PDF lieutenant crushed the man's chest with a lug wrench.

He made sure Muse watched the Colombian die.

We knew what kind of hell Muse had been through and we respected him for it. After awhile, Delta pinned the big guy with an affectionate nickname: Moose.

5

BY AUTUMN 1989, Noriega had stepped up his harassment of American military personnel. By then, Special Operations engineers had constructed a three-quarter scale model of *Carcel Modelo* in Middle-of-Nowhere, Florida. Over and over, Delta's assault teams blew the cupola door, poured down the stairwell to Moose's replica third-floor cell, blasted the lock off, and spirited the Precious Cargo away in an MH-6 Little Bird, double-tapping all PDF actors who got in the way. Easy pickins.

In October, an elite Panamanian police unit staged a coup, toppling the Noriega regime. But by the end of the day, the Pineapple had grabbed the reins of power again. The days and weeks that followed brought two developments: First, *Carcel Modelo* rang with the screams of torture as Noriega sent a steady stream of "political prisoners" to their doom. Second, relations between Panama and the U.S. broke down completely as Noriega blamed America for the coup. The Pineapple made militant speeches bragging about the bloody end U.S. soldiers would come to if they took on his PDF. Then he made his boldest threat yet: Any American attempt to unseat him from power would be met with violent resistance. And the first person to die would be Kurt Muse.

To show that he meant it, Noriega ordered that a chair be placed outside the bars of Muse's cell. That chair was to be occupied at all times by a guard whose only job was to wait for the order to put a bullet in Moose.

6

BY NOVEMBER, we had deployed down to Howard several times (rehearsing the prison takedown using a DoD elementary school as a stand-in for *Modelo*), then returning to Bragg when tensions subsided. During the first week of December, we held a big exercise with the Rangers and the rest of the task force. Operation Just Cause, the removal of Manuel Noriega from power, would begin with Acid Gambit, the rescue of Kurt Muse.

After that, an entire menu of mayhem would thunder down on the Pineapple. SOUTHCOM General Max Thurman's battle plan called for 4,000 Special Ops troops—Green Berets, SEALs, Rangers, Air Force commandos, and us—to execute raids all over Panama in the early hours of the invasion.

The entire Just Cause task force consisted of 22,500 troops, plus tanks, APCs (Armored Personnel Carriers), AC-130 Spectre gunships, fighters, and six F-117A Stealth bombers. The 82nd Airborne would storm El Racener prison and rescue its sixty-four captives. The SEALS would descend on Punta Patilla Airfield and disable Noriega's private aircraft. The 7th Infantry Division was tasked with hitting targets on the Atlantic side of the canal and elements of the 5th Infantry Division were assigned missions in support of the Special Ops elements. LTG Carl Stiner from the 18th Airborne Corps would be the tactical commander of all operations.

The task force, under the command of Major General Wayne Downing, rehearsed it all, debriefing and fine-tuning along the way. Then Downing got word from the Pentagon: The situation in Panama seems stable for now. Stand down for Christmas.

Yeah. Right.

On Sunday, December 17, my home phone rang.

"Jerry, it's General Downing. Looks like we're a go," he said. "They just had an incident in Panama City. The Panamanian police killed a Marine lieutenant named Paz and have physically abused his wife. President Bush has made the decision—we're going to execute Just Cause. Start assembling as quickly as you can. We're deploying tonight."

"Yes, sir. I'm on it."

I broke the connection and dialed again, reaching the staff duty officer. "Execute the unit alert."

Pete was out of town, but I was able to reach him on the satellite phone in his car.

"Come on back as quickly as you can," I told him. "It's a go."

"I'm on my way," he said. No more details were necessary.

Within thirty minutes, I was on my way, too. That's the way it often was: The phone rang and within minutes, I had to kiss Lynne and the kids goodbye and walk out the door. Though I'd been with Delta for eleven years by then, April, Randy, and Aaron still didn't know exactly what I did for a living. They just thought their dad was in the Army and had to travel a lot. I knew my comings and goings were a strain on Lynne.

I headed for the Delta compound. By then, Delta had increased its numbers to three operational squadrons—about two hundred men—and about three hundred support personnel, including logistics, communications, and engineering. Within four hours, about half of us were strapped into a pair of C-141s and on takeoff roll out of Pope AFB. Four hours after that, we touched down at Howard AFB. And three hours after that, the hangar had been transformed from an empty shell into a fully operational base, buzzing with activity. The JOC, or joint operations center, was up and running, as were training and planning areas. In one corner, the logistic folks set up a couple hundred cots in case anybody had a moment to grab some sleep.

The aviators from the 160th set up in the hangar with us. The Rangers were going to fly in from CONUS and parachute directly into the fight on D-Day. The SEALs would operate out of Rodman Naval Base, located about a mile away on the Panama Canal. Also bivouacked in the Canal Zone's various American installations: The 5th Mechanized Division and various logistics and support groups.

The sheer mass of firepower now assembling meant one thing: The Pineapple had better get busy mixing his last margarita.

7

TO REDUCE OUR PROFILE, we kept the entire force inside the hangar. A lot of Panamanians worked on the base, and we were pretty sure some might be occasional or even regular informants for the PDF and local police. We wanted to maintain the element of surprise and felt fairly sure that our arrival hadn't seemed out of the ordinary, since we'd flown in and out so frequently during the year. To Noriega, our arrival on December 18 should've appeared to be just another batch of C-141s landing and offloading the same few hundred guys who had always simply flown back out again.

On December 19, we deployed snipers up to Quarry Heights. They dug into strategic firing positions that would enable them to pick off targets along the Little Birds' flight path to the prison. Leading the sniper element was Pat Hurley, Pete Schoomaker's and my tent mate during the Delta selection course. Throughout the day, he reported movements at *Carcel Modelo* and along the flight path.

H-Hour was set for midnight. All day long, a warm breeze carried the scent of ocean salt through the hangar, which hummed with the sound of planning meetings as the various mission commanders hunkered down with their elements. Two main factors were critical to my op, the rescue of Kurt Muse, code-named Acid Gambit: The helo assault on the prison roof, and the complete destruction of Noriega's comm center, located in the *Comandancia* next door.

In the hangar, we ran a communications rehearsal to make sure all our equipment was up and running. We ran tabletop drills of the assault on the prison. We had been rehearsing for months, but it never hurt to go over the finer points one more time. Pete and I met with leaders from the SEALs, Rangers, the 18th Airborne Corps and the 82nd Airborne division to make sure their pieces of the mission were fully coordinated. In another corner of the hangar, I met with the planners for the two Spectre gunships. Their mission was to take out the *Comandancia*.

"The key is that when we call for fire, the first round you are to fire is into the communications center in the *Comandancia*," I told the Spectre planners, pointing to a precise spot on a map of Noriega's fortress. "Here's the comm center. I want you to put a 105 round right through the roof. If you have to put a second round in there, do it. But make sure you knock it out so that Noriega can't control the PDF."

Next, I met with the crews of the MH-6s, the Little Bird guns that would lead the rooftop assault on the prison. One of the known threats was a seventeen-story building flanking the flight path. We knew the building contained apartments, many occupied by PDF soldiers and their families. We also knew from intel those soldiers were armed and, as crazy as it sounds, even had crew-served weapons, including M-60 machine guns.

The lead MH-6 pilot was Randy Jones, a cheerful, stocky guy from West Point, Mississippi, who was the undisputed Davy Crockett of Little Bird gun aviation. Randy could take out an individual man-sized target using nothing more than a grease pencil mark on his windshield as a site. The thing about Randy was that he was always, *always* smiling—and not just to cover up any sort of dark side. He was a genuinely happy man. To meet him, you never would have guessed he was also absolutely lethal.

"Whatever you do, check out that seventeen-story building," I told Randy. "If anyone's firing at us from there, take them out. Once you cross the roof, I want you to punch rockets into the *Comandancia*. Take out anything you think is a threat, particularly their armored vehicles."

Randy looked at me and grinned. "*That* I know how to do."

Day melted into night and H-Hour drew closer. By 10 p.m., Delta's operators were in full battle gear and ready to roll, and the 160th aircrews were ready to board their aircraft. Then at about 11:15 p.m., Pat Hurley checked in again from Quarry Heights.

"Looks like the PDF is setting up triple-A at the road junction outside the prison," he told a Delta communicator. "Fifty cal."

Noriega knows we're coming.

That was confirmed minutes later when Wayne Downing walked over to Pete and me. "Well, guys, looks like they know we're coming," he said. "The American media has been reporting that the 82nd Airborne launched from Bragg."

So much for the element of surprise. A free press cuts both ways. That was fine. We'd deal with it.

"Can you move the operation up?" Downing asked us.

"Yes, sir," Pete said. "We can launch at any time."

"Good. Let's see if we can go anywhere from fifteen to thirty minutes early."

8

AT 2215 HRS, all of our folks and most of the aviators gathered before a platform at the end of the hangar. Pete got up there and spoke about the mission, about the people of Panama, about liberating them from a dictator.

Then he said, "Now I'm going to ask Colonel Boykin to pray."

Pete and I never discussed that. The tradition of pre-mission prayer that Charlie began now seemed to have become a torch the Delta commanders passed along to one another. This time our group was larger, about five hundred people in all.

I climbed up on the platform. "You know, when you're going into combat, you have to depend on each other," I said. "And you also need to depend on God, not only for success but for your own protection. Let's join together and ask for God's hand to be upon us tonight."

Then I prayed for our protection and the success of the mission. Bucky had retired by then, so I dusted off my singing skills and launched the first few bars of "God Bless America." Five hundred voices lifted the lyrics to the roof of the metal hangar, and the huge space echoed like a concert hall.

Then the Delta operators, wearing jungle camouflage for this mission, and the aviators, in olive-drab green, began streaming from the hangar to the flightline. I headed out to the command-and-control bird, a Black Hawk, and took my seat at the communications console with the rest of the crew. As I settled into my seat, I silently said another prayer for the success of our mission and for the safety of the man we meant to rescue.

In addition to the command-and-control helo, the Spectres and Randy Jones's four Little Bird guns, the firepower lifting off from Howard that night included two more Black Hawks and four Little Birds carrying the prison assault element on the pods. Commanding the element was Lieutenant Colonel Eldon Bargewell, who as a staff sergeant in Vietnam was wounded four times, earning the Distinguished Service Cross for his actions during heavy combat. I was honored to serve with him. It seemed that again and again, God was answering my prayer to serve with men of valor.

Among those in Eldon's element were Major Gary Harrell, an East Tennessee native who looked like a cross between a linebacker and a professional wrestler, as thick as he was tall. But as intimidating as he looked, he was also relentlessly upbeat. Every day was a great day for Gary.

Also with Eldon were Sergeant First Class Sam Joseph, Staff Sergeant Tom Caldwell, Sergeant First Class Kelly Venden, and Sergeant First Class Jim Suderth. Intensely serious about every aspect of soldiering, Jim was also an outgoing and gregarious man who laughed a lot. Manuel Noriega didn't know it, but at the moment he issued his standing execution order for Kurt Muse, he also prompted another death order: It became Jim Suderth's job to execute the executioner.

As soon as the cupola door was blown, Jim would pin his ears back, race down the steps and get to the guard before the guard could get to Muse. As a contingency, before we blew the door, operator Pete Jacobs would rappel silently off the roof of the prison carrying a CAR-15 rifle, and hover outside one of three windows into Muse's cell. If the guard appeared in the cell doorway with his weapon raised, Jacobs would take him out like a duck in a shooting gallery.

Now, in the command-and-control bird, helos in the flight began checking in.

"OSCAR 10: Ready."

"OSCAR 20: Ready."

The Black Hawk's rotor cycled up and we surged off the deck into the warm midnight sky. One by one, the other helos followed, then gelled into formation as we headed out across the Canal.

Strapped in on my left side was Gordy Hernsberger, the air mission commander with the 160th. My comm officer, Chief Warrant Four Paul Zeisman, also sat on my left along with two other characters: a five-foot-six, two-hundred-fifty-pound fireplug named Jim Owens, the communications chief from the 160th; and Ike Eisenbarth, who was literally the largest man in the Army. Ike, my fire support officer, was the human equivalent of a redwood. Seven feet tall and two hundred eighty pounds, he had to get a waiver every year just to stay in the Army.

Gordy was in contact with all the helos, while Big Ike was on the AC 130 Gunship frequency. As the mission commander, I was in charge of the whole shooting match, so I kept the radios on the command frequency so I could talk to Pete, as well as one on the sniper channel to talk to Pat Hurley. Paul and Jim had comms with the rest of the world.

We were airborne for less than two minutes when I called Pat at Quarry Heights. "X-RAY 9, X-RAY 3. Take out the gun emplacement down there at the intersection."

Pat came back, "Roger. Executing now."

Less than thirty seconds later, the PDF soldier manning the fifty cal trigger fell dead on Fourth of July Avenue. His companions fled, then came back. Bad move: Pat's team took them out, too.

"XRAY 03, we just took out the gun and are standing by for more targets," Pat said.

"Roger. Good shootin'."

In the command-and-control bird, we crossed the canal then roared over Panama City proper at four hundred feet. I could see the high-rise apartments across from the prison. A quarter-mile out, tracers needled toward us, announcing gunfire from the roofline and in the same instant, small-arms fire pinged up from the streets. We banked right, veering out of the hail of incoming.

From my right, I saw the Little Bird guns screaming toward the high-rise, and the *Comandancia* directly behind it. They attacked in pairs, muzzles flashing red and blue, raining tracer-fire down on the PDF shooters. The helos skimmed the high-rise roof, then fired rockets into the *Comandancia* on the back side, each one exploding in a multi-colored burst with a fireball center. Each pair of helos then separated, breaking right and left, then looping back around in a butterfly pattern to join up for another attack run.

I turned to Ike, who was talking to the AC-130's: "Fire on the *Comandancia*."

He gave the order. A Specter gunship fired.

Bullseye.

The roof of the comm center vaporized and a massive explosion visibly shook the compound, sending up a volcano of debris. Now thick red tracers seared down on the *Comandancia* as both Spectres unleashed fusillades of forty millimeter grenades. Rubble erupted into the sky, followed by showers of light, like confetti sparkling white against the night.

Suddenly I remembered it was the holidays. In the Black Hawk, I smiled. *Merry Christmas, Noriega.*

9

NOW, TO THE LEFT OF NORIEGA'S burning headquarters, I watched the Little Bird troop carriers zip in low over the western wall at *Carcel Modelo*. One by one, they touched down on the roof, deposited Delta operators, and lifted off again. Silently, I prayed that Jim Suderth could kill Muse's executioner before the executioner could kill Muse.

From my Black Hawk, I saw red tracer fire strafe the prison rooftop. It was coming from the *Comandancia* and I would later learn that an even heavier barrage came in from the prison kitchen located diagonally across the prison yard from Muse's cell. Pete Jacobs had already driven a spike into *Modelo's* roof, spidered down in front of Muse's cell, and was hanging there as bullets chipped the concrete wall around him. Eldon Bargewell and the assault element returned fire from the roof.

The PDF's assault was brave but suicidal. Eldon called in support from the Little Bird guns. A pair of MH-6s broke away from the high-rise and roared down on the prison kitchen, muzzles flaring as their mini-guns shredded the kitchen wall and collapsed its roof. Aftermath pictures would show several hundred narrowly grouped holes in the wall from the ground to the roof. Not even Gumby could have escaped alive.

Now from the Black Hawk, I watched as the Spectres and Little Bird guns made run after run on the *Comandancia*, systematically blasting it to rubble. Below us, civilian vehicles careened through the streets trying to escape the firestorm. A group of wood-frame buildings along Fourth of July Avenue caught fire, and flames licked up into the night.

Six minutes after Delta touched down atop *Carcel Modelo*, Eldon Bargewell called me on the radio. "We have the Precious Cargo."

They have Muse! I was absolutely elated. Still, we weren't home yet: We had Moose, but we still had to get him out alive.

I keyed my mike. "Roger that."

Then, I keyed up the Little Bird troop carriers and gave the order to extract.

Moments later, a transmission from a Little Bird gun: "This is OSCAR 20. I've lost my wingman."

"Roger two zero," I said. "Where did he go down?"

"I don't know. We made a run on the *Comandancia*, punched off some rockets, and came off-target. When we passed the apartment buildings, I went left and he went right. Haven't seen him since. I think he might have gone down in the *Comandancia*."

Gordy started trying to raise the lost Little Bird on the radio. I turned to Big Ike. "We've got a Little Bird down. Call the ACs. Tell them to fly over the *Comandancia* and see if they can spot a Little Bird."

Instantly, Ike relayed: "Check fire! Check fire on the *Comandancia* and survey the area. See if there's a Little Bird down there."

As Ike transmitted, I saw the Little Bird troop carriers touch down on the roof and begin the *Modelo* extraction. Moments later they buzzed off again with Noriega's prize hostage safely aboard.

The Spectre reported in, and Ike turned to me, "The ACs can't find anything in the *Comandancia*. Can we continue firing?"

"Yes, engage targets."

Ike to the Spectres: "That's affirmative. Continue firing."

Where had the Little Bird gone?

I knew the 5th Mech was standing by at Quarry Heights with M-113 APCs, ready to get into the fight. Our liaison there was a major whose real, honest-to-goodness name was Howard Humble.

I called him on the FM: "ECHO17, we've got a gun down. Get down by the *Comandancia*, and see if you can find a Little Bird in the streets."

"Roger," Humble said. "We're moving."

Humble and the 5th Mech rolled off the large mountain overlooking Panama City en route to the *Comandancia*. As they passed Hurley's sniper position, I learned later, they noticed a dead PDF soldier on the side of the road. Hurley and his band of merry men had caught him trying to sneak up Quarry Heights and, with a single shot, had ruined his day.

10

AT LEAST TEN MINUTES had passed since the Little Bird gun went down. Also, I hadn't heard from Eldon. I was about to radio him for an update on the Precious Cargo when Howard Humble came alive in my ear: "I've found the Little Bird and the Precious Cargo is okay."

"What?" I didn't think I'd heard him right. "Say again?"

"I've found the Little Bird and the Precious Cargo is okay," Howard repeated.

"What are you talking about? The bird we're looking for is a gun. It was a gun that crashed, not the Precious Cargo bird."

Howard's next transmission knocked me for a loop. "Well, the Precious Cargo bird crashed, too. We're policing them all up right now and are headed for Howard Air Force Base."

I had no idea that Muse's bird had been shot down. While I was looking for the Little Bird gun, Gordy was talking to the troop carriers. Both of us missed the call from Chief Warrant Three Mike Dietrich, the pilot of Muse's aircraft, when he reported he was down. Then, when another MH-6 began transmitting that he saw a Little Bird go down, Gordy and I both thought he was referring to the Little Bird gun. That's what they mean by "fog of war."

I called Howard Humble. "Get Muse back to Howard. We'll stay airborne until you confirm you're there."

"Roger that," Humble said. "We're crossing Bridge of the Americas now."

As we orbited Panama City in the command-and-control bird, watching the *Comandancia* burn, I suppressed my excitement. If we could successfully return Muse to base, and ultimately to his family, it would be Delta's first successful rescue of an American hostage. In the ten years since Delta had gone operational, we had planned many, many missions: To rescue American hostages in Beirut. To infiltrate Laos to search for American MIAs. In 1985, to rescue the hostages on TWA 847. All those operations had been called off for one reason or another (all of which could be classified under the heading, "White House Unwilling to Risk It").

The rescue of Kurt Muse had been our first direct test. Like any war, it got messy. But our tactics worked. And we hadn't gone in and snatched back a diplomat or an intel agent or the child of a dignitary. In the scheme of world politics, Kurt Muse wasn't anybody special. But we still rescued him, and for one reason only: He was an American. If only for that, everything I'd been through up until then had been worth it.

11

TWENTY MINUTES LATER, Howard Humble called me to say they were rolling through the gates.

"Roger that," I said, then turned to the Black Hawk pilot. "Take us home."

Once on the ground at Howard, I found Eldon and Gary. We gathered in the hangar for what we call the "hot-wash," the immediate after-action brief. The first thing I learned was that Suderth and his team encountered only three PDF inside *Modelo*. The first surrendered and they let him live. The other two didn't and Suderth killed them.

Then the assaulters blew the door on Moose's cell, slapped a Kevlar vest on the man, and hustled him up to the prison roof where they met a barrage of PDF fire. Bullets bit away at the concrete and pinged into the Little Birds, piercing their skin. The Precious Cargo team climbed aboard a helo and the bird took off. But just as Dietrich, the pilot, cleared the roofline, the helo plunged wildly toward the prison yard.

Engine malfunction. Catastrophic.

Just before impact, Dietrich was able to get enough lift to clear the prison wall by inches. First he set the wounded bird down in the street about a block from the inferno that had been the *Comandancia*. Then he tried to take off again, but couldn't gain altitude and was forced to steer the helo through the street just a foot or two off the deck.

Overhead, the Little Bird guns blasted away at PDF positions, trying to keep the fire away from the Precious Cargo bird. From inside the helo, Suderth, Tom Caldwell, Sam Joseph, and the rest of the team also engaged. Dietrich maneuvered to the end of the *Comandancia* block and pivoted in the air. With his damaged engine, he needed a long, running start to get some altitude. He commenced his takeoff run and bullets clanged off the Little Bird as PDF soldiers emptied their magazines in a last bid to prevent Muse's escape.

Dietrich gained speed, then lift. Ten feet, twenty feet in the air. Suderth told me that's when he thought they were going to make it.

Then a Delta operator took a PDF bullet square in the chest. The round pierced his Kevlar and he fell out of the helo, twenty feet into the street below.

Moments later, a round slammed into the back of Jim's knee. Then gunfire shattered the cowling over his head and the Little Bird fell out of the sky. The helo bounced once in the street, ejecting several men, including Suderth, who was secured to the helo by a tether. When the helo came down again, it landed on his left foot, crushing it, and trapping him in the open street.

Gunfire raged around him, but the Little Birds kept PDF troops away. Inside the helo, Kurt Muse was okay. Tom Caldwell was with him, and Muse asked Tom for a gun: "I was in the Army! I know how to shoot!"

Skeptical, but knowing they were down in enemy territory, Tom gave Muse a .45. Muse and Caldwell climbed out of the twisted Little Bird and—*bam!*—Tom's head lurched sideways. He dropped like a flour sack, taking Muse with him. Lying beside Caldwell in the roaring street, Muse could see blood trickling down the operator's face, inches away, and thought he was dead, hit by a sniper. Muse braced himself for more incoming.

Suddenly, Caldwell's eyes snapped open, and he saw Muse, already mourning him.

"Moose! You okay?" Tom said.

Muse was shocked. "What happened to you! I thought you were dead!"

"Rotor blade hit me in the head."

Little Bird guns roared overhead, but PDF bullets still zinged through the streets. They needed cover. But when Caldwell stood to walk, he couldn't make his feet work. Muse, a big man, slung Tom's arm over his shoulder and the two linked up with the pilot and the other operators, who had already established a defensive position, on a sidewalk with a brick wall behind them and some parallel-parked cars in front. They had found the operator who was shot in the chest, and carried him with them. He was alive, but barely hanging on. Minutes later, Suderth came limping in. He had managed to free his mangled foot from under a thousand pounds of helicopter, but his toes were ruined.

Overhead, the Spectres continued to pulverize the *Comandancia*. While the Little Bird guns held off the PDF, an operator used an infrared strobe to signal their position. Almost immediately, a Black Hawk flew overhead, rocking back and forth to acknowledge their position. And a few minutes after that, Howard Humble and his APCs rolled up to the rescue.

During the hot-wash, I also learned that the Little Bird gun *had* crashed in the *Comandancia*—crash-landed, actually. Shot down by PDF fire, the MH-6 slammed down in the compound grounds, skidded across the pavement, crashed *through* a wall, and into a building. Inside, the fire from their burning helo raged. Outside, the Spectres were chewing the *Comandancia* into dust. Finally, the Little Bird pilots had to make a choice.

"We decided we could either stay inside and burn up, or go outside and take our chances," one pilot said at the hot-wash.

They chose the latter. The pilots bolted outside and rushed toward the *Comandancia* wall. Tangled barbed wire ran along the top of it; a street lay on the other side. If they made it out of the compound, it would still be a long trek through enemy territory to find safety. But both men were armed with .45s, and they had them ready.

One pilot took off his Kevlar vest and flung it upward, where it landed like a drape over the barbed wire.

Behind them, they heard footsteps and a voice: "*¡No disparen! Me rindo! No disparen! Me rindo!*"

Don't shoot! I surrender!

The pilots whirled to see a PDF soldier running toward them. They raised their weapons to shoot him, but then held their fire.

The soldier had his hands up.

He was surrendering. To Americans. Who were trapped *inside* Noriega's headquarters and trying to escape.

"*Me rindo,*" the soldier said. "*¡Llévame contigo!*"

I surrender. Take me with you.

The pilots looked at each other, surprised, then at the PDF soldier. "Okay," they said.

The two American pilots and their brand new POW then hoisted themselves over the *Comandancia* wall and jumped into the street. And just at that moment, one of the 5th Mech APC's rolled up and scooped them aboard.

12

AFTER THE HOT-WASH, I went to meet the Precious Cargo. I found Kurt Muse sitting on a bloody Kevlar vest inside an empty tent, one of several, including a hospital tent, set up near the hangar. He had on khaki pants and a golf shirt, both of which told the story of the battle he'd just been through. I also noticed he was much thinner than he appeared in his photographs. Panamanian prison will do that to a guy.

He started to rise. "No, no, don't get up," I said. "You've had a rough night."

"It's been an amazing night," he said, then put out his hand. "Kurt Muse."

"Jerry Boykin," I said, smiling as we shook. "I wanted to be the first to say welcome back to freedom."

"Thank you, sir," Muse said.

"Is there anything else I can do for you right now?"

Muse didn't miss a beat. "Yes, sir, I'd like to meet my rescuers."

"I'm afraid I can't let you do that," I said. "Security issues."

Muse looked worried. "They were hurt. Badly. Some of them…"

I reassured him. "Doctor says they're all going to make it. Nothing life-threatening."

That wasn't entirely true, but again, the operators' condition presented a security issue.

Muse looked at me for a long moment. "I just wanted to thank them for saving my life."

"I'll pass that along," I said. "It will mean a lot to them."

When Muse spoke next, his voice was flushed with passion. "Words could never be enough, sir."

We shook hands again, and I left him, crossing over to the hospital tent to pass along what he'd said. Inside the tent, four of my guys were stretched out on gurneys. I could see Tom Caldwell's head injury, where the rotor blade whacked him. Jim Suderth gave me a smile, even though we both knew by then that he was going to lose the toes on his left foot. The operator shot in the chest lay there, his heavy bandages already tinged with blood. He was conscious, but a little bleary from pain meds. An operator with a bullet wound in his leg sat upright drinking water and wincing from the pain.

As I made my way among them, I told them how proud I was of what they'd done. And every man I talked to said the same thing: "Hey, how's Moose?"

After about the third one asked me that, I realized that it was just as important for them to see the man they'd risked their lives to rescue—to see him safe and free, mission accomplished—as it was for Muse to see them, here, alive, and out of the line of fire.

"Would you all like me to bring him in here?" I asked the room.

The tent echoed with one big "Yes!"

Walking out, I saw Muse standing not far away. "Moose! Come with me. I've got something I think you'll like."

I showed him into the hospital tent and when he saw his rescuers lying there, he turned and shot me a look of surprise.

I grinned. "Turns out they wanted to see you, too."

I walked him over to the first gurney and introduced him to the sergeant who had been shot in the chest. Muse reached down and took the sergeant's hand in both of his big mitts. "There's no way I can ever thank you for giving me my life back." His voice was thick with emotion.

Around him, the other operators smiled. One by one, he circled the room, stopping and thanking each man personally, always taking one of their hands in both of his. Again and again, his message was the same: his gratitude was beyond anything he could put into words.

"You being here like this says it all," Suderth told him. "Now go and have a good life."

As I watched, Muse stepped back and looked at them all, lying there, wounded for him. I could see that he was about to break down. But he collected himself enough to force out one last message. "I love you guys. I'll never forget you."

And he hasn't. Every year, on December 20, the anniversary of his 1989 rescue, my telephone rings. When I pick up the phone, Kurt Frederick Muse says, "Hey, Jerry, I just want to thank you again for saving my life."

Then we chat awhile, but not for too long because Kurt has a bunch of other phone calls to make.

13

WITH MUSE SAFE, the remaining missions in Operation Just Cause were a go. The force arrayed against Manuel Noriega swept across Panama, seizing his every strategic and tactical asset. Delta alone launched forty-two raids over the next seventy-two hours, turning inside out every known or suspected safe house where Noriega could hide. The hangar at Howard AFB buzzed like the floor of the New York Stock Exchange, with tips and intel on Noriega's location pouring into the comm center in a constant stream. The instant we received any scrap of reliable information, Pete and I scrambled the element leaders. Clustering around our display of maps and reconnaissance photos, we lightning-planned an assault, hustled out to the flight-line, and launched. Thirty minutes from tip to takeoff.

Across the city, black-hooded Delta elements struck without warning, kicking down safe-house doors, pouring in through windows, and forcing Noriega's cronies to the floor at gunpoint: *"¡En el piso! En el piso!"*

Prisoners were flex-cuffed and questioned. Those with intel value were arrested; those with none were released. Often, one raid led to another as captives suddenly became helpful: *"¡El General no está aquí! Esta en la casa de la otra mujer!"* (The General's not here! He's at his mistress's house!)

Coordinating these operations from a Black Hawk, I could see Panama City and the surrounding countryside bristling with military activity as U.S. forces swept away Noriega's defenses. As Operation Just Cause unfolded, the 82nd Airborne, the 75th Ranger Regiment, Army Special Forces, and other Joint Task Force sea, air, and land units seized Torrijos-Tocumen Airport and military airfield, as well as the Pacora River Bridge, the national television station, and a major PDF base near the village of Rio Hato. SEALs and their Special Boat assets destroyed PDF patrol boats, and seized Noriega's yachts and beach house.

Delta pressed forward, taking down Noriega friendly townhomes, village huts, and even his mountain retreat. In many hideouts, operators confiscated money, passports, weapons, maps, and intel. But the most interesting find occurred at Altos del Golfo, one of Noriega's Panama City homes.

I was circling overhead in the Black Hawk when Lieutenant Colonel John Noe's squadron reported they had uncovered stacks of hardcore pornography, $8 million in American cash, and two religious altars, one at each end of the house. One was a Christian altar. The other was an altar to Satan, decorated with jars containing human internal organs.

I knew from intelligence reports that Noriega met regularly with a spiritualist and dabbled in some form of dark religion. I'd even heard he wore red underwear because the spiritualist told him it would protect him from his enemies. Now it looked like he was playing both spiritual ends against the middle.

While none of our forty-two raids bagged the Pineapple, the speed and frequency of our door-busting drove the dictator like a hunted animal. By the fourth day after the American invasion, Noriega had no place left to hide. He also knew none of the foreign embassies located in the capital would side with him against the Panamanian people and grant him asylum. Ironically, as a last resort, he threw himself on the mercy of the church.

14

ON CHRISTMAS EVE 1989, we got intel that Noriega was headed to the *nunciatura*, or Vatican embassy, to seek asylum. Again, we scrambled the helos, six Black Hawks, plus the command-and-control bird, this time hunting the blue all-terrain vehicle we'd heard was Noriega's ride.

While we were airborne, Pete called me from the JOC. "Noriega's already in the *nunciatura*. See if you can land there. I'm sending John Noe's squadron there now by vehicle. Get the place secured, and give me a report as soon as you can."

"Roger that. We're on it."

Our helos were already in the immediate area of the *nunciatura*, a large white stucco building, two stories with a red tile roof. Cars and pedestrians scattered as we landed two birds on Avenida Balboa, the main street in front of the *nunciatura*, sending up tornadoes of dust and litter. A dozen Delta operators armed with .45s and M-4 carbines poured into the street and surrounded the *nunciatura*.

Facing north and surrounded by a high stone wall, the Vatican embassy occupied its own small block. I jumped down into the street and walked quickly up to the wrought iron gate. To my right, across a side street from the *nunciatura*, sat a large apartment building with an attached parking garage. To my left, lay the Pacific Ocean, the beach and wide mud flats separated from the embassy by a narrow street that dead-ended in front of a Holiday Inn.

In the time it took to observe this, a nun appeared on the other side of the wrought iron.

"*Quiero hablar a nuncio papal,*" I said.

I wanted to speak to the *papal nuncio*, the priest supervising the diplomatic mission.

She nodded, then turned and disappeared into the building. A couple of minutes passed before a priest appeared. He was not the *papal nuncio*.

"*Habla Ingles?*" I said.

"Yes." He smiled. Friendly enough, but all business.

"We are looking for Manuel Noriega. Is he inside?"

"Yes, señor, he has taken asylum here in the *nunciatura.*"

"Father, Manuel Noriega is wanted by the United States government and the people of Panama. We'd like for you to turn him over to us."

"I will have to speak to the *papal nuncio.*"

"That's fine. We're going to keep you surrounded here until we get Noriega."

Smiling officially, the priest excused himself and went back inside.

While we waited for the *papal nuncio*, Monsignor Jose Sebastian Laboa, to make an appearance, more firepower rolled up. John Noe and his squadron had borrowed M-113s and a pair of two-and-a-half-ton trucks from the 5th Mech. I deployed the APCs around the *nunciatura*, their .50 cal guns aimed outward to guard against a rescue attempt by Noriega loyalists. Then I called the 82nd Airborne at Fort Clayton and asked for some engineers to come out and erect a barrier of concertina wire around the embassy. Within the hour, that was done.

During my initial meeting at the gates of the *nunciatura*, I noticed a rather large group of people observing our activities from the end of the street. I looked up at the Holiday Inn, and saw that the third-floor balcony was packed with reporters. Nearly every one of them had these long boom mikes pointed directly at us, trying to listen in on my discussion with the priest. They were less than a hundred yards away, and I thought they probably stood a pretty good chance of picking up our conversations.

I knew we had a loudspeaker team from the 5th Psychological Operations Group at Fort Bragg. I sent someone to find them. In only a few minutes, two young soldiers approached me.

"Hey, can you guys point your speakers up to those boom mikes and block their reception with some kind of broadcast?" I asked.

"Sure," one young soldier said. "What do you want us to play?"

"I don't care what you play, just as long as those mikes can't pick us up."

Ten minutes later, being twenty-year-olds, the psy-ops guys started playing loud rock music. *Really* loud.

Be careful what you ask for, I thought.

Not long after I noticed the reporters, I posted Delta snipers around the *nunciatura:* one team down by the water, another in the parking garage, and another on the sixth floor of the apartment building adjacent to the *nunciatura.*

An hour passed and I spoke again with the priest, who told me the Pineapple was resting. He had no other news.

Later that night as I patrolled the perimeter with Eldon, festive lights and decorations reminded me that it was Christmas Eve. Panamanians came out of their homes to greet us.

"Thank you so much for giving us our country back," people said to us in English. They asked us earnestly to come in, eat Christmas dinner with them, or at least use their telephones to call our families. That was against policy, of course, and we couldn't accept their generosity. But it was a wonderful Christmas present to know that the Panamanians were behind us.

15

ON THE SECOND DAY, Monsignor Laboa came out of the embassy, crossing the avenue to the Catholic School where we had set up our command center. By then, a fairly large group of officers had gathered there, including Wayne Downing and U.S. Army South Commander General Mark Cisneros.

A small, older gentleman with white hair and spectacles, Laboa wore black trousers and a black shirt with a clerical collar. With regard to Noriega, he said, his hands were tied: "I am obligated to discuss this situation with the Vatican. I'm not in a position to make a decision on my own."

That sent us into a holding pattern, with the Pineapple holed up in the wire-wrapped, sniper-scoped *nunciatura* and several hundred American soldiers waiting for him outside. Several times a day, one of us would cross the street to chat with either the priest or the *papal nuncio*. They shared very little information, and showed no signs of wanting to give Noriega up.

In taking the dictator in, Laboa was upholding the Vatican tradition of offering sanctuary to anyone fleeing persecution. I wasn't sure how Noriega, Panama's chief persecutor, fit that definition. It wasn't until later I learned Laboa was all the while gently pressuring Noriega to surrender. No country would give him refuge, the priest told the dictator. The Americans had him surrounded. A peaceful, formal surrender would be the most dignified option.

Also, I learned Laboa did not mean for the Pineapple to get too comfortable: The *nuncio* housed Noriega in a room barely larger than a closet, decorated only with a crucifix. The dictator's amenities included a television that didn't work, a window that didn't open, and zero air-conditioning. Apparently, he didn't have access to a washer and dryer, either: Every now and then, one of the snipers would report that they could see a pair of red briefs hanging outside on a clothes line.

One night, I was sitting around at the school with Major Darrell Poor, a task force doctor, shooting the breeze. "You know what, Doc?" I said. "There's only one thing I want out of this whole operation."

"What's that?"

"Noriega's red drawers."

Poor burst out laughing.

16

THE PSY-OPS GUYS kept the rock music blasting day and night, keeping their speakers pointed directly at the Holiday Inn and, gradually, stirring up a political firestorm. Newscasters all over the world reported that we were trying to mess with Noriega's mind, reduce him to a mass of quivering jelly with an overdose of Guns N' Roses. On about day three of the operation, a directive sped down all the way from the Bush White House: turn the music off.

I'm not sure whether the constant noise bothered Noriega, but I'm pretty sure it was driving the *papal nuncio* crazy.

We did shut the music off, but substituted instead Spanish language news reports that carried the accurate story that Noriega's troops had stopped fighting after he abandoned them. In fact, PDF soldiers began presenting themselves at Howard AFB daily to surrender. The loudspeaker newscasts also told Noriega that American officials were moving to freeze funds he had deposited in overseas accounts.

We wanted the Pineapple to realize that his situation was hopeless. Though Laboa was trying to talk Noriega into giving up, the Vatican continued to shield him, justifying its actions by arguing that the dictator was a political refugee. On December 26, Secretary of State James Baker sent a letter to the Vatican saying Noriega was not fleeing persecution, but prosecution. He was a common criminal, wanted by the U.S. for drug trafficking. Baker later assured the Vatican that if Noriega gave himself up, we wouldn't shoot him—just arrest him.

The waiting game continued. Then on January 3, fifteen thousand Panamanians rallied on Avenida Balboa. Crowding around the *nunciatura* just outside the concertina barrier, thousands waved white handkerchiefs and chanted anti-Noriega slogans like "Kill the Hitler!" Some people skewered pineapples with long sticks and they pumped them up and down in the air, sneering, "Pineapple face! Pineapple face!"

To keep the situation under control, we posted soldiers between the crowd and the wire barrier. We didn't want the crowd to storm the *nunciatura* and attempt to capture Noriega.

That evening, after the crowd dispersed, I was sitting at the school with Wayne Downing when I saw Monsignor Laboa walking across the street. When he reached us, he drew himself up very formally and said, "Noriega has decided to surrender."

Elation surged through me. We had won. A complete victory.

"He wants to be able to surrender in uniform and only to a general officer," Laboa said.

Clearly, Noriega was trying to set himself up as a prisoner of war who would be afforded Geneva Conventions rights. In that way, he hoped to keep himself out of the U.S. courts. I knew it wouldn't work.

"That's acceptable," Downing said. "What time does he want to surrender?"

"At about 8 p.m."

"That will be fine."

Immediately, we began preparations. I posted guards at the gates of the *nunciatura*, and put out the order that there were to be no photographs. I walked a couple of Delta guys through the procedure, showing them the path along which they were to escort Noriega from the *nunciatura* gate across Avenida Balboa, and out to a school soccer field, which would be a helicopter landing zone. The school had an awning that ran from the entrance out to the sidewalk. I rustled up an American flag and hung it from the awning poles nearest the street. When Noriega walked out of the *nunciatura*, I wanted him to see it.

All right, I admit it—I was twisting the knife.

At 8:50 p.m., I saw Laboa and Noriega emerge from the front door of the *nunciatura*. Wearing his tan general's uniform with his four stars, Noriega came alone through the gate. Four Delta Operators wearing camouflage stepped up, one man in front of Noriega, one behind, and one on each side. As our men escorted him across the dark avenue, Noriega tried to hold his head high, but he stumbled twice.

The surrender was simple, yet formal.

General Cisneros had every reason to hate Noriega. Prior to Just Cause, the dictator ordered his thugs to threaten and harass the Army general and his family for months. Still, Cisneros accepted the surrender without any extra dialogue.

Noriega: *"Yo soy el General Noriega. Me rindo a las fuerza de los Estados Unidos."* I am General Noriega and I am surrendering to U.S. forces.

Cisneros: *"Su rendición es aceptada."* Your surrender is accepted.

The Delta team then escorted Noriega to the soccer field where a Black Hawk waited, rotors already turning. The helo whisked him away to Howard AFB, where a C-130 was waiting to fly him to America, and his date with the U.S. justice system.

Ten days later, I was back in my office at Bragg when Darrell Poor walked in.

"Hey, Jerry, I've got something for you," he said.

"Oh yeah? What you got?"

"Remember what you said you wanted out of the operation down in Panama?"

I shook my head, a slow smile spreading across my face. "You didn't."

"I did." Darrell grinned, and held up a plastic bag with a pair of red briefs inside. "I got them when we strip searched Noriega at Howard. I had you in mind."

Beginning in 1992, Manuel Noriega commenced a fifteen-year stint in a Miami federal prison. At the time of this writing, he is fighting extradition to France.

His underwear are still sitting in a display case at Fort Bragg.

DRUG LORDS AND FALSE PROPHETS

Colombia and Waco

1992–1993

1
—

THE BLOODSTAINS ON THE FLOOR convinced me: The world would be better off without Pablo Escobar.

In July 1992, I toured *La Catedral* prison, where Escobar, head of the Medellin cocaine cartel, had been "incarcerated" until his "escape" that same month. *La Catedral* wasn't really a prison. Escobar actually had the place custom built, and in a deal with the Colombian government to avoid extradition to the United States, agreed to confine himself there. In return, he promised to stop murdering the police and government officials who were trying to rein in his cartel's multibillion-dollar cocaine business.

It was, almost literally, a deal with the devil. Not only did Escobar come and go from his lavishly appointed prison/resort largely as he pleased, but he also continued to rule his worldwide drug empire, estimated at its height to haul in $30 billion a year. He threw festive holiday parties, with food cooked to order by his personal chef. He hosted lavish orgies, providing young teenage girls for his friends' pleasure.

Also, he kept on murdering.

The blood I saw splashed and dried on the floor at *La Catedral* may very well have belonged to Fernando Galeano and Gerardo Moncada, the heads of two families who had been trusted inside players in the cartel. The two men had been put in charge of a large share of Escobar's empire after his "incarceration." Each family paid Escobar $200,000 a month for the privilege and still grew fabulously wealthy. But with his movements somewhat limited and monitored by the government, Escobar grew suspicious even of his closest lieutenants. Paranoid at their accumulation of wealth, he invited Galeano and Moncada to *La Catedral*, and had them killed.[1] Then he had their brothers tracked down and killed. Escobar the business executive, tying up loose ends.

The blood spatter at *La Catedral* represented only drops in a river that stretched back nearly two decades. It was through murder that Escobar, a street hoodlum and car thief growing up in Bogota's Antioquia region, entered the cocaine trade in the first place. In 1975, he purchased fourteen kilos of cocaine from Fabio Restrepo, a well-known Medellin drug dealer. Then, apparently seeing a business opportunity, Escobar reportedly murdered Restrepo and commandeered his men. Charged with murder, Escobar was unable to bribe the judge. But he did succeed in having his two arresting officers whacked. The case was dropped and—bingo—Escobar's philosophy was born: *Plata o plomo*—silver or lead. Accept a bribe and step aside, or face assassination.[2]

Escobar's ruthlessness and the seemingly bottomless U.S. demand for cocaine in the disco era combined to catapult him and his early partners into control of 80 percent of the world's cocaine trade. Escobar built a fabulous ranch, *Hacienda Napoles*, featuring a private airport, helipads, and six different swimming pools. He bought the best of everything, including the best judges, police officials, and Colombian lawmakers. If they didn't play, he had them killed.

In 1989, Escobar targeted Cesar Gaviria, a young presidential candidate who was running for the post only because the former candidate, Luis Galan, had been assassinated. (His fatal error: running for office on promises of breaking the cartels.) After Galan's death, the Colombian government cracked down on the Medellin cartel, touching off an urban war. The cartel set off a long series of pipe bombs in very public places—at the entrances to offices, banks, and shopping centers, terrorizing citizens to ratchet up pressure on the government to cease its pursuit of the cartel. Between March and August, at least fifteen officials were murdered, including another presidential candidate, Jose Antequera, in addition to a lawyer, a newspaper editor, a chief magistrate, a judge's father, and the governor of Antioquia.

Bogota was a war zone. By August, more than four thousand Colombian judges had gone on strike, in fear for their lives. Escobar issued "communiques" in which he styled himself part of a humble citizen resistance whose rights had been violated by an oppressive police state, and whose families were the targets of "arbitrary raids." He asked for "peace."

Then he kept on killing.

When Cesar Gaviria took up Luis Galan's cause, Escobar decided to kill him, too. This is how ruthless Escobar was: When he learned that

Gaviria was ticketed on an Avianca Airlines flight, Escobar recruited one of his trusted *sicarios*, or assassins, a man named Carlos Alzate. This time Alzate thought he was assigned to a less lethal job—carrying a suitcase equipped with a recording device aboard the flight to record the conversation of the passenger sitting next to him. But he was wrong. When the poor stooge flipped the recorder's switch, he detonated five kilos of dynamite, blowing himself and one hundred nine other people out of the sky. All this to assassinate one man, Gaviria, who as it turned out, was not aboard, precisely because he knew the cartel meant to kill him.[3]

That was Pablo Escobar: willing to murder more than a hundred innocents, including his own man, to crush one enemy.

2

PART OF OUR JOB AT DELTA was keeping tabs on the world's bad guys, and we had been watching Escobar for years. We downloaded daily intel briefs from a dozen different agencies, concentrating on groups and individuals known to be involved in terrorism, hostage taking, and the proliferation of WMDs. Though Escobar wasn't mentioned every day, he frequently had a starring role. He wasn't a terrorist in the political sense, one who terrorized in the pursuit of some religious or political belief. Escobar had simpler tastes: Money and power. And he elevated narco-terrorism to a craft.

By the time I visited *La Catedral* in the summer of 1992, Escobar had either personally executed or ordered the deaths of more than a thousand people. The CIA and U.S. Drug Enforcement Administration had labored against the cocaine trafficking for years, and the U.S. ambassador to Colombia, Morris D. Busby, had been pushing the government to take specific action against Escobar. But in Colombia, corruption choked reform like a fast-moving cancer and those not already in Escobar's pocket were at each other's throats.

Meanwhile, Escobar's farcical imprisonment at *La Catedral* had become an embarrassment to Cesar Gaviria, who was elected president in spite of Escobar's effort to kill him. From his mountain "retreat," the drug lord still managed the shipment of millions of pounds of cocaine into the U.S. every month. By 1992, Gaviria had had enough. He ordered the Colombian army to go to *La Catedral*, take Escobar into custody, and move him to a real prison. But the soldiers, many on the take and the rest terrified of Escobar's certain retaliation, let the drug lord escape.

Gaviria was livid. While Escobar was ensconced in *La Catedral*, the country enjoyed relative peace. Now its legislature was set to rewrite the constitution, and Colombia was a nation on the verge of historic change. Desperate, Gaviria sought out Busby.

The Colombian president knew we had captured Manuel Noriega and imprisoned him for drug trafficking. He also knew that in the United States Escobar was under indictment as Noriega had been. But the Colombian constitution forbade the use of foreign troops on its soil. Still, wasn't there some way America could help?

3

UNLIKE MANY AMERICAN DIPLOMATS, Morris Busby understood the yin and yang of diplomacy and military force. I had worked with him in years past when I was operations officer in the Special Ops task force and he served as ambassador-at-large for combating terrorism. He was an experienced statesman with the warm personal style of a West Virginian, but also with the aggressive edge of a former naval officer. Complex and engaging, he loved country-boy things like bluegrass music, but you might also walk in at any moment and find him listening to Chopin.

While many diplomats considered the employment of military force the sign of absolute diplomatic failure, Busby recognized that sometimes, especially when working on behalf of an ally, it was simply another tool in the toolbox—even if it was a hammer. In this case, the hammer he selected was Delta.

During the two previous years, I attended the Army War College and served as operations officer for General William F. Garrison, the steel-jawed Texan who would turn out to be so crucial during the Somalia operation. Garrison had taken charge of the Joint Task Force, and in the early summer of 1992, I took over command of Delta Force, relieving Pete Schoomaker who headed to Texas to become assistant commander of 1st Cavalry Division at Fort Hood.

Pablo Escobar became my first major target. In July 1992, Bill Garrison called me at my office. "Have you seen the intel reports on Escobar's escape from prison?"

I said I had.

"Ambassador Busby has gotten approval for Delta to help the Colombians hunt him down," Garrison said.

Interesting, I thought. I knew that Wayne Downing had talked around a similar operation in 1989, but the idea was shot down. Now, though, Busby's request had survived the scrutiny of Joint Chiefs Chairman Colin

Powell, Secretary of Defense Dick Cheney, and President George H.W. Bush—and had come back approved. Manuel Noriega, the last drug pushing despot who thought his *cajones* were bigger than Bush's, was sitting in a federal penitentiary in Florida.

Maybe Escobar will be next.

Garrison went on, and I pictured him on the other end of the line, tall and lanky, his cigar clenched in his teeth and bobbing up and down as he spoke. Garrison never lit his stogies, and I couldn't remember ever having seen him without one.

"I want you to go down there. Select a few folks to take with you," he said. "Keep it small. I'll let you know as soon as we have the execute order."

Garrison was a special ops veteran who had worked on Phoenix, a Vietnam program that retaliated against Viet Cong who killed village leaders when they did not support communism. Under Phoenix, Viet Cong who could not be induced to surrender were assassinated. Garrison was tough. Nothing ruffled him—ever.

Between Busby and Garrison, I thought, *Pablo Escobar has met his match.*

The first man I selected for the mission was Lieutenant Colonel Gary Harrell, the big guy from East Tennessee who served in Eldon Bargewell's prison assault element in Panama. Gary selected the rest of the team, choosing from the Delta squadron that happened to be stateside on a training rotation. Sergeant First Class Joe Vega, the Julio Iglesias of Delta Force, was among his first picks. A buff, good-looking Latino who spoke fluent Spanish, Vega was a skilled operator who charmed everyone he came in contact with. The Colombians would prove no exception.

Gary also tapped Sergeant First Class Tony Mafnas, a Saipan-born operator and lethal martial artist who stood only five-four and was one of the toughest men I've ever met. While prepping for a particularly dangerous mission I can't mention here, Mafnas attended SERE (Survival Evasion Resistance and Escape) training at Fort Bragg. I had the opportunity to observe him during the interrogation phase, which is pretty brutal. The SERE instructors know they're training high-risk personnel, so they slap you around, slam you against walls, grab you by the hair and hold your head under water, that kind of thing. As three interrogators took turns battering Mafnas, I watched through a two-way mirror. After awhile, Mafnas broke down and started crying.

The interrogators eased up and, one by one, filed out. Moments later, the SERE psychologist went in to talk to Mafnas, who sat in a chair, head in his hands, shoulders heaving.

The shrink leaned down and touched Mafnas's shoulder. "Tony? How are you doing?"

Mafnas shot the shrink a quick sideways glance and his eyes were dry. "Go back to your office, doctor," he said quietly. "I've got them right where I want them."

Gary also chose for the mission Sergeant Major Jack Alvarez, another native linguist, and a veteran operator with whom Gary and I had both served for years. Known for his speed and agility, Alvarez was a former track star who had been a member of the winning team in European Counterterrorism Olympics. The man was just deadly.

I looked forward to the mission. First, I thought it was a prime opportunity to rid the world of a gory and unrestrained killer who got so rich that in 1989 *Forbes* magazine listed him as the seventh wealthiest man in the world. I hoped we would capture Escobar quickly, but I knew the best scenario for everyone was to simply kill him. If we captured the drug lord and he was imprisoned, he would simply launch another war—a bombing and assassination campaign in which hundreds more would die. Meanwhile, the Colombian justice was so corrupt it was unlikely Escobar would even be convicted (should any judge live long enough to actually do that). If he served any time at all, innocent Colombians would continue dying until the government was forced to cut a deal.

By then I had come to believe that some men in the world were simply evil. They could not be bargained with. They could not be rehabilitated. As mass murderers who killed repeatedly without regard for human systems of justice, it was possible they could not even be defeated. I came to believe such men just needed killing.

Pablo Escobar was one of those men.

4

IN LATE JULY, I flew down to Bogota with Gary and the rest of the element, eight of us in all. We deplaned at El Dorado Airport into the almost liquid warmth of a humid evening, all wearing civilian clothes. A group of officials whisked us to the embassy, a gray four-story structure hunkered in downtown Bogota like a fortress.

Gary and I were to meet with Busby in the "vault," a room normally located on an embassy's top floor, fortified by a soundproof, bulletproof Lexan bubble. No bullets in, no secrets out. When we arrived, DEA agent Joe Toft and CIA station chief Bill Wagner were already there. Busby, a tall, smooth gentleman, made the introductions. As we all took seats, he and I caught up on old times. How were things at Delta, he wanted to know. I asked him about the counterterrorism fight at State. Then we got down to business.

Busby laid out the complexities surrounding Escobar, much as an analyst would: A brief history on how Escobar came to be at *La Catedral*. His history of violent and indiscriminate retaliation against officials who tried to rein in the cartel. And the intricate web of corruption permeating every level of Colombian government. He ended on a hopeful note: The sea change in Colombian politics and society possible under Cesar Gaviria's presidency.

"Gaviria, unlike his predecessor, is truly committed to shutting down the drug trade in Colombia," Busby said. "The credibility of his administration is at stake. It's critical that you find Escobar. Do you have any limitations on what you can do?"

"General Joulwan wants to make sure this is a Colombian operation," I said, referring to the new SouthCom commander. We had stopped in Panama on the way down and met with George Joulwan, a man with a reputation as an effective leader who used a lot of football metaphors because he thought of himself as a coach. During our meeting, Joulwan told me Delta's role was to support the Colombian police and military with training and intelligence, along with some weapons and equipment.

He was crystal clear that the Colombians were to be on the front lines. Delta was to be invisible—a ghost.

Now, in the vault, Busby said he agreed with Joulwan: the Colombians had to be the public face of the hunt for Escobar. "But you guys are going to have to get up to Medellin and work with them, train them," he said.

I told them we were prepared to do that, and to offer logistical and intel support. "We have pretty good SIGINT," I said, meaning signals intelligence collected via electronic surveillance, communications intercepts, and telemetry. "What we'll need is any kind of human intel we can get from DEA and CIA. Any reports they can provide would be very helpful."

Busby glanced at Bill Wagner, the CIA station chief. "We'll provide all we have, plus they can work in our space here," Bill said. Busby seemed pleased.

We turned to the DEA agent, Joe Toft. Long and lean with a tanned leathery face, Toft was a veteran frontline agent, accustomed to the bloodbath that was the South American drug war. And yet, with all he'd seen, he considered Escobar the most notorious and lethal cocaine trafficker who had ever lived. Toft, I would learn, saw the drug lord's "escape" not as a problem, but as an opportunity to finally hunt him down. Still, I was unsure how the DEA viewed Delta's involvement.

"Yeah, we've got some sources," he said. "We can get you some information."

Toft was hard to read. I couldn't tell whether he really meant to help us, or was just telling us what we wanted to hear. You could never tell about interagency turf wars.

I turned back to Busby. "We've got some assets up at SouthCom," I said. "If we need to, we can send them down."

Joulwan had a P-3 surveillance plane up in Panama that could fly down and perform a high-altitude aerial stakeout over Bogota, transmitting SIGINT and imagery.

"If you don't have anything else," I said to the ambassador, "we'll get our guys briefed and start moving."

5

I SENT FOUR MEN NORTH TO MEDELLIN. Gary and Jack Alvarez went to the police headquarters. Tony Mafnas and Joe Vega went to establish a sniper/observer position at *La Catedral* prison, which overlooked all of the Medellin valley. They weren't up there to shoot anyone, but with their laptop computer, satellite phone, and long-range scopes and lenses, they could receive SIGINT on Escobar's location and zero in visually on any location in the valley below. On the grounds of his private prison, Escobar built rustic little individual cottages. The one where Mafnas and Vega set up was actually picturesque, with a little wooden railed balcony where they put up their observation gear. Compared to missions where we'd slept in rat-infested barrios and snake-riddled jungles, we joked that they were living high on the hog.

The next morning, I went with Ambassador Busby to meet *El Presidente*. Cesar Gaviria worked out of a kind of presidential palace, an elaborate office building in the heart of downtown Bogota. But his office was not at all opulent. Instead, it was simple and elegant, with a burnished conference table and some framed original landscapes on the walls. Busby made the introductions in Spanish, and my first impression of the Colombian president was that he was a man laboring under a heavy burden. His would-be murderer was on the loose again, now threatening not only his personal future, but that of the country he meant to lead.

We gathered around the conference table and I began to brief the president in my crappy Spanish, muddling along, mangling the syntax. Embarrassed, I said to Gaviria, "*Con su permiso, quiero hablar ingles.*"

"Certainly," said Gaviria, who spoke perfect English.

Relieved, I went on to explain the composition of our element and how our people were positioned. Then I concluded. "*Senor Presidente*, the United States is offering a $2 million reward for Escobar. We are prepared to train your people, and support them with all the intelligence we can gather on Escobar's whereabouts. We will stay as long as we have to."

"Thank you very much, Colonel," Gaviria said. "We need your support. I think you understand the importance of finding Escobar. This is in the best interests of both our countries."

While I was meeting with Gaviria, Gary and Jack Alvarez met with two senior Colombian military officers, including Lieutenant Colonel Lino Pinzon who would be in charge of the "Search Bloc," the military component tasked with hunting Escobar.

Gary and Pinzon immediately despised each other.

Pinzon, with his salt-and-pepper crew cut, was considered a bit of a Casanova and had a reputation as a careerist who saw other people as stepping stones to the next rank. He was exactly the kind of leader Gary couldn't stand. At their first meeting, Gary sized Pinzon up as unserious about the mission—at best afraid of failure, at worst on the take. And it quickly became clear Pinzon resented Gary's good-ol'-boy, take-charge manner. Clearly, Pinzon wanted to be deferred to. And Gary wasn't interested in deferring to a man he considered no better than a bureaucrat.

For credibility's sake and to avoid offending our hosts, Gary introduced Jack Alvarez as "Colonel Santos." Delta was working with a very aggressive ambassador who expected us to convince the Colombians to undertake a task that to them meant certain death. We could not force them to act, and so had to rely on persuasion, and on the Colombians' confidence that we were a highly trained force. Jack Alvarez was one of the world's elite warriors. But none of the Latin American countries had a professional NCO corps. If the Colombians thought Alvarez was an enlisted man, they would likely have dismissed his advice as that of an untrained grunt.

Back at the embassy, I got comms set up in the CIA station. With my radio operator and intel analyst, I could receive SIGINT reports from NSA, and human intel from Bill Wagner and Joe Toft. From there, I also had radio comms with Gary, SouthCom, and the guys up at the observer position. The next morning, I called SouthCom to update Joulwan on what we'd done to that point.

Joulwan's operations officer got on the phone and immediately went on the offensive. "What are those guys doing up there at *La Catedral*?"

"Just observing," I said.

"Are they armed?" the J-3 demanded.

"Yes, they're armed."

"Do they have rules of engagement? Are they allowed to engage targets?"

"No. It's purely a defensive position."

"Who else is up there with them?"

"There are a couple of Colombian soldiers up there for force protection."

"Okay. Don't do anything until we get back to you."

Oh, good, I thought as the line clicked dead in my ear. *Now I can go back to watching soaps and eating bon-bons.*

Three hours later the J-3 called back. "Your observers up at *La Catedral*? Just make sure they understand they're in an observer role. They're not up there to engage any cartel people unless it's in self-defense."

"We understand the rules, sir," I said.

That annoyed the crap out of me. First, I felt like the folks at South-Com didn't trust Delta, that they were convinced we were down there freelancing, gunning for Escobar ourselves. Second, I felt Joulwan didn't trust Morris Busby, thought he was too aggressive. I knew SouthCom was concerned about the legal and public relations issues associated with Americans getting involved in ground ops. The South American media— particularly those on Escobar's payroll—could certainly be counted on to call the use of any U.S. firepower an American invasion of Colombia, whether we were there to liberate them from under Escobar's boot heel or not.

Still, I thought SouthCom's reluctance was very strange: usually it was the other way around, with the generals ready to launch, but frustrated by foot-dragging diplomats.

I brushed my irritation aside, and all of us began working the intel really hard. Escobar liked to use a cordless phone, not radios. From the embassy, SouthCom, and from the air, analysts monitored all cordless calls, listening for the drug lord's voice. We relied very heavily on a couple of analysts who had listened to him again and again on tape, until they could recognize his voice instantly. And on the second day, Pablo Escobar made a phone call.

6

AN INTEL AIRCRAFT INTERCEPTED THE CALL and immediately transmitted coordinates to Mafnas, who trained cameras on the target and then fired imagery to Gary, who called Pinzon. It was a hot lead, Gary told the Colombian commander. He should order the Search Bloc to strike.

But Pinzon seemed bored by it all. "We get leads all the time," he told Gary. This one would be another dry hole like the rest. Hours passed as Pinzon sat on his hands. When he finally ordered his men to move, it was only because Gaviria called and intervened. Even then, Pinzon's response wasn't so much a strike as a slow-motion farce that crawled loudly up the hill where the cordless call carrying Escobar's voice had come from. A deaf drug lord could've heard them coming. And surprise: When the Search Bloc found Escobar's hideout, Escobar was gone.

Gary was livid. He called me to vent his frustration. "I don't think this guy has any intention of going after Escobar. I'm not sure whether he is scared or on the payroll."

The next day, new phone calls generated a new fix and a new opportunity for a strike. Instantly, Gary asked Pinzon to start prepping for a raid. Pinzon initially agreed, but again showed no signs of action.

Again Gary called me. "This mission ain't gonna go."

"Why not?" I said.

"When it looked like Pinzon wasn't moving again, I went to his house. He answered the door in his pajamas."

From that day on, we hung Pinzon with a new nickname: "Pajamas." And after that, there was more discussion about whether he was on the take. In the end, we gave him the benefit of the doubt and decided he was more likely a coward.

On the third day, we brought the P-3 down from SouthCom to do some pinpoint geo-locating. So the citizens of Medellin wouldn't spot it, we directed the aircraft commander to orbit above ten thousand feet. But at that altitude, the geo-locating gear wasn't returning precise coordinates, so Busby decided we should bring the bird lower. Somebody saw it and the next day, a Miami paper helpfully ran a headline that went something like "U.S. spy planes flying over Medellin."

SouthCom went nuts. The J-3 called me, machine-gunning questions: "What were you thinking?" "What was the purpose of lowering the altitude?" and my personal favorite, "Who authorized you to direct that aircraft to fly so low?"

"Ambassador Busby," I said, playing my trump card.

"Well, the P-3 is outta there. We're ordering it back to Panama."

"You'll have to talk to the ambassador about that."

At that moment, I was grateful Busby was the kind of man he was. Between Pinzon, the reluctant Search Bloc and SouthCom's constant mothering, I already felt like a pinball, and the mission was only three days old.

Busby prevailed. We were able to keep the P-3 as long as it stayed high. During the first week, the SIGINT kept rolling in. Several times we tried to get the Colombians to launch assaults, but they wouldn't. We couldn't blame them entirely. Many had seen friends and family members die on Escobar's orders.

About halfway through week two, the SIGINT dropped off completely. Human intel also dried up. Escobar either went underground or fled. We decided we'd better concentrate on turning the timid Search Bloc into a more formidable force.

7

BOTH GARY HARRELL AND LUIS PINZON rotated out of the operation. Gary was a squadron commander with other soldiers back at Fort Bragg so I let him return to his primary duties. Pinzon was replaced by Colonel Hugo Martinez, a Colombian colonel who originally founded the Search Bloc to hunt Escobar down after the drug lord in 1989 ordered the murder of Martinez's friend, Waldemar Franklin, chief of the Antioquia police.[4] After a bloody war between the Search Bloc and the cartel that ended with Escobar's farcical imprisonment in *La Catedral*, Martinez accepted a diplomatic appointment in Spain. Now, stoically, he said yes to an invitation to replace the useless Pinzon.

Among the Americans involved in the drug war to this point, Martinez had a reputation as a man with integrity and resolve. It was widely known that Escobar once offered Martinez $6 million to stand down the Search Bloc. Martinez turned it down.[5] When I met with him the second week we were there, I found him to be cool and aloof. But it was also clear he was prepared to pursue Escobar to the end even if it meant his own death. That was a likely possibility: In his earlier war with the Search Bloc, Escobar's *sicarios* more than once came close to killing Martinez, and his son, Hugo, Jr.

With Busby's support, we decided to start a vigorous training program for both the police and the military. I sent some trainers down to Tola Maida, a Colombian army camp in the lowlands south of Bogota, and I went down to join them. In contrast to Bogota's cool, mountainous terrain and hilly city streets that reminded me of San Francisco, Tola Maida was steamy and tropical, like being back in Panama. The camp itself was a compound of simple stucco and wood-frame buildings laid out in rows tucked in among jungle foliage. Open *bohios*, or pavilions, dotted the camp. And while the American Navy paints its structures gray and the Marine Corp paints them gold, the Colombians painted everything in the tropical parrot colors of a Cheeva bus. Not the buildings, but pretty much everything else—the security bar on the camp entrance, the *bohio* posts, even the rocks.

The Colombian soldiers' normal training routine called for lots of drills, but nothing realistic. We quickly learned they were not good marksmen. Ammo being expensive, they probably shot only about twenty rounds per year. Also, their idea of room clearing was to stand outside a building and empty their magazines through the windows. They had no concept of an organized assault, of covering each other, of shooting only the bad guys and letting the good guys live. And there was no such thing as a helicopter assault.

I called down more operators from Bragg. Using sixteen trainers, including aviators, we put about a hundred men through a three-week mini assault course that included marksmanship, CQB (close quarters combat), sniper/observer ops, explosives, communications, emergency medical treatment, and integrated assault. The Colombians soaked it up, increasing every day in skill and confidence. Three weeks later, we held an exercise, a live-fire night helo assault. Busby and Colonel Martinez came down to watch and went away impressed.

After that, we set up for the long haul, beefing up our surveillance capabilities and increasing our numbers in both Bogota and Medellin. The hunters were in place. Now we would go after the hound.

8

FOR THE REST OF 1992, I bounced back and forth between Bogota and Bragg, going south about every eight weeks. I kept about a dozen people in Colombia equally split between the Embassy, and the police and Army quarters in Medellin.

In the U.S., in early 1993, news reports began to trickle out about a strange cult that had barricaded itself in a compound in Waco, Texas. They called themselves the Branch Davidians, and were led by a nut named Vernon Howell, a high school drop-out who renamed himself David Koresh and convinced about a hundred men, women, and children that he was the Christ. Word was the Branch Davidians were some kind of doomsday cult and that Koresh taught his followers that they would all someday die in a violent clash with "unbelievers." After significantly sized shipments of weapons and weapon-building components began arriving with regularity at the cult's Waco compound, the Bureau of Alcohol, Tobacco, and Firearms launched an investigation.

Because it was a domestic matter, Delta followed the case like everyone else—by watching the news. Details began to emerge: Koresh had joined the Branch Davidians, a small sect that began in the 1930s, in 1984. After a dispute with the cult's leader, he was driven from the 78-acre Waco compound at gunpoint, but later returned to seize control of the cult in a shootout.

Koresh and his followers then settled into a weird blend of apocalyptic theology and survivalism, stockpiling food and weapons in preparation for their fiery last stand. Cult members lived a spartan, military lifestyle that included physical training, strict food rationing, and monklike conditions in which men and women—even married ones—lived separately and pledged themselves to celibacy. Except for Koresh, who had sexual access to all the women, designating numerous "wives" among them, including girls as young as twelve. Koresh dealt out harsh discipline to the children and preached long, scary sermons that lasted late into the night.

Eventually, ATF acquired a house near the Waco compound; an agent even infiltrated the Davidians' worship services. By late February, based on intel and shipments to the compound, the bureau was convinced the cult was preparing to build an arsenal of automatic weapons. Also, former cult members alleged child abuse and molestation, and there was growing concern about whether Koresh would initiate a mass suicide, taking the children with him. It had happened before. In 1978, People's Temple leader Jim Jones had induced 913 of his followers to drink poisoned Kool-Aid.

On the night of Sunday, February 28, I heard on the news that a hundred ATF agents launched a surprise raid on the compound. What was supposed to be a simple infiltration action to subdue the cult and take Koresh and his leadership into custody erupted into a firefight that lasted nearly an hour. The instant ATF agents entered the compound, the Branch Davidians attacked with a hail of small-arms fire, shooting through doors, walls and windows. After a 45-minute firefight, four ATF agents and six cult members lay dead.

The raid touched off the longest law enforcement standoff in American history. The FBI joined ATF, and the siege on the compound spun out for weeks.

Delta was directed to send technical support to help the FBI. I sent three Delta operators to the scene, where their role was to provide cameras and audio devices and advice on how to use them. The U.S. Constitution prohibited them from getting involved in the actual operation. Then, after about six weeks, the Justice Department decided that America's standoff with David Koresh had gone on long enough.

9

I HAD WORKED A LOT with the FBI's hostage rescue team, and particularly with an HRT commander, Dick Rogers, a man I considered to be one of the finest FBI agents I'd ever met. He was serious and technically proficient, going through all the same training and exercises his guys did. And unlike some federal agents, Dick was very supportive of the military.

He called me one day in April. "You up to speed on Waco?"

I said that I was. "Our guys are still down there in a support role."

"I've got to go up to Justice for a meeting with Janet Reno and William Sessions over this thing," he said. "We've put together a plan on how to take down Koresh's compound and they want a briefing. I want to swing by Fort Hood first and pick up Pete Schoomaker, then come up to Bragg and get you."

William Sessions was the FBI director. Janet Reno was the brand new American president's brand new attorney general: Both she and Bill Clinton had been in office less than four months. Dick's idea was that Pete, as the former Delta commander, and I, as the current commander, could certify to Reno and Sessions the soundness of any hostage rescue plan. We trained with the FBI, knew their capabilities. Dick wanted credible, outside voices who could speak to the merits of the operation.

"I've got to get clearance to do this," I told him. "Let me call you back."

I called Garrison and told him what the FBI wanted. A few hours and several Pentagon generals later, the request came back approved. The next morning, I drove to Pope AFB, hopped on a King Air with Dick and Pete, and headed for D.C.

On the way up, Dick laid out the FBI's assault plan. "We're going to use CEVs to drop CS into the main building." Agents would drive up next to the building in Combat Engineering Vehicles, a configuration of an M-60 tank, punch holes in the roof and begin injecting CS, a form of tear gas.

"If Koresh and his people don't start surrendering after that," Dick went on, "we're going to use a bulldozer to take off the front of the building, then go in and get them."

Dick told us he was very concerned with the possible effects of the CS tear gas on the Branch Davidian children. There would be an expert at Justice who would address that issue during the meeting with Sessions and Reno.

Although Pete and I agreed to help, we wanted firm limits on our involvement. "We need to be sure it's understood that Pete and I are here in an advisory capacity only," I said. I was concerned that any whiff of military entanglement in this operation could be perceived by the press and public as a violation of *posse comitatus*, the constitutional prohibition on using U.S. troops for any kind of domestic law enforcement.

"Absolutely," Dick said. "Also, your involvement will be kept strictly confidential. Sessions and Reno have already agreed to that."

We flew into Davidson Army Airfield at Fort Belvoire, were picked up by the FBI, and driven into D.C. to the Department of Justice. Sessions's office was on an upper floor, his name engraved on a large bronze plaque on the door. The office was large with a row of windows overlooking Constitution Avenue.

Dick Rogers introduced us to Reno, Sessions, and Sessions's deputy, a man who was starched, pressed, and pomaded to within an inch of his life.

Bureaucrat, I thought. *Capital B.*

Reno had invited Web Hubbell, Clinton's large and jowly deputy attorney general. He sat off a bit from the group, looking on from under the windows.

Along with Pete and me and the tear gas expert, Dick Rogers had also invited Danny Colson, the first commander of the FBI's hostage rescue team, who was known as a big SWAT guy.

The tear gas expert went first, explaining that the deployment of CS causes some people to panic—the children likely would, he noted—but that others would take measures to try to cope with the discomfort. The CS would induce a burning sensation in the eyes, tearing, and severe irritation of the skin and mucous membranes. Recovery would be fairly rapid, though, and the agent didn't cause permanent injury.

Janet Reno turned to me. "Have you had any experience with CS?"

"Yes, quite a bit," I said. "The fact is, CS is pretty bad, but people can usually find ways to work through it."

Next, Dick and Danny laid out their plan—the CEV, the CS insertion, the plan to arrest the Branch Davidians as they surrendered. The plan was to pump the tear gas into the far left and far right sides of the building in hopes of forcing people to exit near the center-front. Reno took it all in, friendly and clearly in the listening mode. She did ask a couple of tactical questions, such as how the FBI was organized to receive those who gave themselves up. As she spoke, I thought I detected a tremor in one of her hands.

Sessions, on the other hand, was very formal with all of us, even with Rogers and Colson, his own men. He didn't ask too many questions, but he asked good ones. Why, for example, did the FBI feel compelled to launch this assault now? Why not wait the Branch Davidians out?

Dick Rogers gave three good answers. "First, we have evidence that the children are being abused. Second, the people in there can hold out indefinitely, which exacerbates the problems with child abuse." Finally, he noted that his agents had been deployed at Waco for nearly two months. "They have perishable skills they have to maintain. If we don't go now, we'll need to withdraw and go into a period of retraining."

Reno turned to Pete and me. "What do you guys think of this plan?"

Pete's answer was very direct: "Listen, this is a law enforcement operation, not a military operation. We can't grade your paper."

Delta was confident in the HRT, Pete went on. "But we don't do law enforcement, and we are not able to give you a judgment."

Reno looked at me. "Would you like to add anything, Colonel?"

"Well, I can tell you that if this was a military operation, we would hit the place from every side, all at once, and it would all be over in seconds," I said. "Our tactics would be very different. That's why it's so difficult for us to evaluate a law enforcement concept."

From beneath the window, Web Hubbell swiveled his huge, round head in my direction. It reminded me of the turret on a tank.

"I've only got one question," he said. "Is this legal?"

I thought, *This guy's the deputy attorney general and he's asking me if this is legal?*

"Sir," I said, "that's a determination you're going to have to make."

Of course, the following year, Hubbell, a Clinton buddy from Arkansas, would plead guilty to mail fraud and tax evasion and admit to stealing almost $400,000 from his clients and partners in Little Rock's Rose Law Firm. So I guess the question of whether something was legal was a relative thing for him.

Reno stood, indicating that she'd heard all she needed to. "Okay, thank you very much for coming up. I need to talk to the president, and we'll let you know what decision he makes."

10

BACK AT BRAGG, I typed up a memo documenting the details of the meeting. Classifying it *Secret*, I sent it to Bill Garrison and Carl Stiner. Then on April 19, I was in my office preparing to depart for training in Kuwait when CNN broke the news that the FBI raid on the Branch Davidian compound had begun. Some of what I was seeing was replays and some was live footage. The FBI deployed one hundred-seventy men, plus the CEVs, each equipped with a long boom for punching through the building roof and inserting the CS. As news cameras panned back and forth across the scene, I could see four Bradley APCs and an M1A1 Abrams tank. I later found out that Dick Rogers directed the operation from inside the tank.

At first, the operation unfolded just as Dick had laid it out. But at around 2 p.m. Texas time, the wheels started to come off. On the television screen, I could see smoke, and listened as reporters noted multiple fires breaking out on the Branch Davidian property. As I watched, flames engulfed the compound and eighty people burned up inside.

The outcome shocked me. I knew there were risks, but I didn't think the FBI's op would go that poorly. I knew instantly that the incident would erupt into a huge scandal with Dick and his men directly in the crosshairs of Congress.

I did not realize, however, that I would wind up there, too.

It only took three or four days before Congress called Janet Reno on the carpet. I knew she was going to testify, so I turned on C-SPAN to watch. Reno told the panel that before authorizing FBI's assault, she consulted with both the current and former commanders of Delta Force, Colonel Jerry Boykin and Colonel Pete Schoomaker.

And she left it at that. She did not go on to say that Pete and I declined to give our opinion on the plan she authorized, nor that we stated we would have conducted a very different operation. And so her testimony left the impression that we concurred with the plan.

Some folks call that a "lie of omission." Where I come from, they just call it a lie.

The next year, 1994, Congress hauled me in to testify. I gave them the details of our meeting with Reno and Sessions, and they had my memo on the meeting. My testimony brushed away any doubts in Congress: Delta had not rendered a judgment on the FBI's plan.

Still, the conspiracy mongers crawled out of the woodwork, concocting nutball theories: Delta murdered the Branch Davidians...Ten Delta operators were driving Bradleys at Waco...President Clinton ordered a Delta attack on Waco then covered it up. Even reputable news organizations repeated a CIA agent's false story that Delta deployed to Waco "ready for war."

Then some media took the *partial* story of our meeting with Reno, the CIA agent's bogus story, and the truth that we did have three observers there, and cobbled together more crap about government conspiracies.

Because Delta is a secretive organization, some people assume it also considers itself above the law. Not true. Delta's stealth nature is by design. It enables it to perform its mission, not violate the Constitution. Before Congress and the Branch Davidians' families, Pete and I told the truth about Delta's involvement at Waco. Conspiracy theories may sell newspapers and magazines, but they also ruin the reputations of good men trying to do good work. *Secret* doesn't always mean *dark*.

BATTLE OF THE BLACK SEA

Mogadishu, Somalia
1993

1

FOUR MONTHS AFTER THE BRANCH DAVIDIAN compound went up in flames, a Boeing 737 spit me out at a rundown airport on the ragged edge of Mogadishu, Somalia. After months of watching Mohamed Farrah Aidid starve and murder his own people, President Clinton finally ordered in Task Force Ranger to capture the warlord and bring him to justice. Now, I stood on the smoldering tarmac near a shark-laced slice of the Indian Ocean, part of an advance team that included General Bill Garrison; Lieutenant Colonel Dave McKnight, commander of the 3rd Ranger Battalion; Delta surgeon Rob Marsh, and a team of communicators and logisticians.

A blanket overcast imprisoned the white Somali sun, holding the wet East African heat to the ground like the lid on a cauldron. A stench, something between rotting fish and burning trash, assaulted my senses.

The UN had taken over Mogadishu's commercial airport, but warring clans had long before reduced it nearly to rubble. Decrepit Russian transport aircraft leftover from the 1960s sat rusting on the tarmac. Jeeps buzzed across the airfield, darting between the relic planes. Their drivers laid on their horns, shouting in Arabic and broken English.

I looked toward what had once been the control tower and terminal and saw that part of the roof was missing. The hangar next to it was shot full of holes, and even from a distance I could see junk piled high and pigeons roosting in the rafters. That's where we would be setting up the JOC.

Tent cities stretched away from the tarmac down to a crushed shale beach, and nearly to the water's edge. These were support elements for UN participants who brought military forces to Mogadishu. I could see the flags of twenty nations, hanging limp on poles poking up into the humid air. Beyond the tents and a whole village of portable toilets, a fence and guarded gate separated the airfield from a street. On the other side lay

Mogadishu proper, where, I knew, thousands of living skeletons came from all over Somalia in search of food.

Less than a minute passed at the bottom of the 737 ladder as all these impressions flooded over me and gelled into a single thought.

This has got to be the worst place I've ever been.

I had seen poorer places. In El Salvador, I had watched ragged, legless beggars scoot around on carts; in Sudan, I had been with the Dinkas, a desperately poor people who raised scrawny cattle and owned nothing. And I had seen more decrepit paces: Trash heaped in the streets of Honduras, the rubble that once was Beirut, and in Khartoum, a dead donkey burning. But I had never seen hopelessness like this. A palpable oppression hovered over the rubble, the tent cities, and the low, smoky skyline. Whatever it was, it seemed to press in on me physically, as though jealous to give up territory.

As I waited for Garrison and the others to deplane, I flashed back to a conversation he and I had earlier that summer on a training range at Eglin AFB under a sweltering Florida sun. Standing with his arms folded across his chest and the trademark unlit stogie jutting from his mouth, he watched as elements of Delta, the Rangers, and the 160th SOAR finished up an exercise in preparation for what was then a possible deployment to Mogadishu.

"My spies in the Pentagon tell me Powell's not too shot in the ass with this thing," Garrison said.

Translation: Joints Chiefs chairman Colin Powell was not enthusiastic about our going into Somalia to hunt Mohamed Farrah Aidid.

"Why not?" I asked.

"Thinks it's mission creep," Garrison said. The term meant taking on new missions that were not part of the original concept.

Powell had a point. The 10th Mountain Division had been in Mogadishu since December 1992 to deliver humanitarian aid to Somalia, a country torn by civil war and drought. An estimated half million refugees had already fled to other parts of Africa. Hundreds of thousands more remained behind. U.S. forces landed in concert with nineteen other UN countries as part of Operation Restore Hope, a mission to provide secure distribution of food and relief supplies. In addition, U.S. and UN negotiators arranged peace talks between more than a dozen warring factions, including Aidid and his Habr Gidr clan. Tensions escalated as UN nations charged that Aidid was hindering peace talks. Then in June 1993, Habr Gidr militia ambushed and killed twenty-four Pakistani peacekeepers. A week later the UN issued a warrant for Aidid's arrest. Enter Task Force Ranger.

America was moving from a humanitarian mission to a direct combat role. So in that sense, Powell was right: Mogadishu was a damned-if-you-do, damned-if-don't enterprise. Human rights groups love to criticize the United States for not stepping in to squash genocidal conflicts in other nations. But when we do step in, they love to complain about how we're doing it wrong.

I respected Powell. He was an intelligent strategist, very astute. He understood Washington and the political scene better than any general officer I ever saw. And while he did serve the president, he was also his own man, someone who would provide the administration with his best military advice whether or not it was what they wanted to hear.

But standing there with Garrison, I wondered why Powell had not fought harder to make Task Force Ranger the "overwhelming force" that was a well known centerpiece of his war fighting philosophy. Instead, we would execute our operations with a force of only 450. Even at that, we'd have to peel off some combat troops for force protection—to stay back and guard our base of operations against the Sammies, as we came to call hostile Somalis. The Pentagon also denied us a Spectre gunship (saying it was too "provocative"), as well as a fleet of APCs.

Now, here we were.

I suspected our incursion into Mogadishu would not be a short-term mission. We had chased Noriega in Panama, and cornered him quickly— but in a country where we controlled the environment. In Colombia, though, a country where we didn't control the environment, Jack Alvarez and his team had been locked in the hunt for Pablo Escobar for over a year now—even though we had the support of the government there, our presence remained largely unknown. Mogadishu would be different in all those respects: Task Force Ranger would be operating in a country where racial differences would make it impossible for our elements to move freely in the streets, collecting human intelligence. We would be fighting with a force smaller than what our commander, Garrison, thought sufficient to do the job. And we would be operating from the knife edge of a hostile territory occupied by warring factions, and where most of the population was armed.

The next day, the troops and helos began to arrive from Fort Bragg. Since the 160th brought the only chaplain, I pressed him into service. We gathered everyone in the hangar—Rangers, Delta, SEALs, aviators, some "P.J.s," or parajumpers, Air Force medics whose specialty was parachuting into combat zones to tend the wounded.

Garrison and I addressed the troops briefly then the chaplain read Scripture and led us all in a prayer. Maintaining our tradition, we then sang *God Bless America*, and launched operations on an adrenaline high.

2

WE HAD BEEN IN-COUNTRY only for a few days when Aidid gave us the warlord version of the finger. After cleaning the pigeon crap out of the tumble-down terminal, we had set up our joint operations center in there. The JOC was equipped with three video screens for monitoring live battle feeds from the West-Cam Ball, a camera mounted on an OH-58 helo. The logisticians established sleeping and messing areas in the hangar next door. Garrison, meanwhile, moved into a small trailer provided by contractors, just big enough for his cot and a couple of chairs. One evening, he and I, along with Dave McKnight, gathered in there to talk about the next day's operations.

An older officer, Dave was a Special Forces expert and Vietnam vet who had transitioned into intelligence work. During the first Gulf war, he worked with CIA, and developed a deep understanding of both fields. Lean and ruddy, Dave burned through three packs of cigarettes a day, smoking them nearly end to end. Despite the atrocities he had seen in the darkest, most violent parts of the world, or maybe because of them, he always found a way to crack the tension with some nutty war story about jungle rot in 'Nam or farting all night in a two-man tent. Dave was always serious when it counted. When it didn't, he was spinning a tale.

"Intel is still sketchy," Garrison said from his seat on the cot. "First the Sammies tell us they saw Aidid in such and such a house, then they say they didn't. Makes it hard to hit him."

"The informants are scared," I said. I was going to add that Aidid's men had been known to literally cut out the tongues of traitors, when I heard a muffled thud from the direction of the airfield.

Dave and I locked eyes and said in unison: "Mortars!"

Instinctively, we hit the floor then both leapt to our feet and practically climbed over each other trying to get outside to see what was going on.

Another mortar round crashed into the tarmac, the concussion spraying concrete skyward. I couldn't see the falling rubble, but I could hear it showering down on the Black Hawks and Little Birds.

"Go, go, go!" I shouted.

Dave darted for cover beside an empty Conex and I followed, running low, my sidearm banging against my hip. The Somali night was coal-black, empty even of starlight. We flattened ourselves against the outer wall of the container and waited. The sulfur smell of spent ordnance hit me. I could hear the pounding of running feet and Ranger squad leaders barking out commands to their troops, "Stay down! Take cover!"

Then, silence.

The insidious thing about mortars is that you can't hear them coming. There is no whistle of incoming. There is no tracer fire or any telltale red glare as with small-arms fire or rockets. In a mortar attack, you know you're being shot at, but you can't tell when the next round will fall. Or whether it will fall on you.

The ground shook as another mortar slammed down. Orange light flashed at our 10 o'clock, and a hail of tile shards rained down on the pavement.

"I think that one landed right on the JOC," I told McKnight irritably. The JOC was no palace, but it was all we had.

We huddled against the side of the Conex for another three or four minutes waiting for the attack to end. I don't think you ever get to the point where things like that don't scare you. I think you get to the point where they don't scare you as much. This time though I was too pissed off to be scared. Here we were taking fire and there wasn't a thing we could do about it. Even if we had known where the Sammies were shooting from, we couldn't fire back. Aidid and his men were smart—or evil, I couldn't decide which. We knew from intel they'd pick a sandlot teaming with ten thousand refugees and start shooting from right in the middle of it. And they knew enough about Americans to know we wouldn't fire back into a defenseless crowd.

Two more explosions ripped the night, hitting the airfield out by the helicopters. Then quiet set in and, this time, spun out into an unbroken string of explosionless minutes. Finally, it appeared the Somalis were ready to turn in for the night. McKnight and I peeled ourselves off the Conex and jogged toward the JOC to inspect the damage.

The Sammies hadn't launched more than a half-dozen rounds. The blow to our operations center seemed like a lucky strike, with the shooters managing only to knock out a radio and blow over an antenna. From the flightline, a couple of the crew chiefs ran into the JOC and told us that a chopper mechanic had taken a piece of shrapnel in the arm. Somebody else came in and said that our hangar had been hit by shrapnel, but nobody was hurt. Damage wise, that was about it.

Still I had to admire the Somalis' guts. They used an American technique: Fire for effect. They had shown they knew who we were and why we were there, and that they weren't afraid of us. Fired right into our base, striking fear into a good portion of our troops, a couple of hundred young Rangers sitting in a vulnerable position, men who had never seen combat. The Sammies may have been terrible marksmen, but launching the attack was the kind of macho intimidation tactic that was probably the best thing they could have done. The incident formed in me a grudging respect.

As McKnight and I stood in the JOC, Garrison walked in, chewing his stogie. "McKnight, tell me where the last place was we saw this sombitch," he said mildly, referring to Aidid.

McKnight and Garrison walked over to a map of Mogadishu, and called over an analyst who immediately pointed to a house near the center of the city. "We haven't had a positive sighting in awhile, but that's the last place we know Aidid was for sure," he said. "That was a few days ago."

"Then that's our target," Garrison said. "I don't care if Aidid's there or not. Jerry, get the men ready. We're gonna let 'em know we're here."

An hour later, Garrison ordered the Ranger and Delta team leaders to assemble their men in front of the JOC. Now he stood before the task force on the open concrete, his arms crossed, cigar jutting from his mouth at a thoughtful angle.

"Now, some of you have never been mortared before," he said as casually as if the whole group had only fallen off a bicycle. "I just wanted to tell you that if one of them piddly-ass mortars lands in your pocket, it's probably going to hurt. If it doesn't land in your pocket, you don't have to worry about piddly-ass mortars."

I stood among the men, some as young as eighteen, and heard the intensity of their hush. Garrison let steel creep into his voice. "Now we're gonna go in there tonight and let 'em know we're here. And I have confidence in every one of you. So let's get it on and go do it."

It was as good as any Knute Rockne pre-game talk. Garrison motivated everybody, including me. When he finished, there was no loud cheer, but I could hear the low, approving rumble of young men ready to strike back. Most of the Delta operators were already battle hardened, but the Rangers had been stung, jarred into the reality that we weren't playing G.I. Joe. This was not an exercise. There was a real enemy out there, people who really wanted to kill them.

Two hours later, an assault force of eighteen heavily armed helicopters roared into the city and sixty very pissed off elite American soldiers hit the house where informants last spotted Aidid. The raid force captured several men, plus a large cache of Somali money, which we concluded was connected with Aidid's financial operation. The next day, we turned both the prisoners and the cash over to the UN.

In the larger picture, the raid didn't get us any closer to capturing the warlord. But from a morale standpoint, it served a vital purpose, particularly for the uninitiated young Rangers. They had been hit and it was important they hit back, that they not feel impotent in the face of Aidid's brazen strike.

Aidid had given us the finger. We gave him the finger right back.

3

THROUGHOUT SEPTEMBER, we gathered intel and launched five more strikes, all designed to capture elements of Aidid's infrastructure. Taking out a despot is a chess game. A dictator seizes control with a wave of violence and holds it with the threat of more. But iron fists leak. Exploit those leaks, mission by mission, systematically leveraging mistakes. Learn, profile, move closer, and even the most feared and cloistered man can be knocked down like rotten fruit.

Take Colombia, for example. Under the leadership of Hugo Martinez and with American intel support, the Search Bloc was systematically tearing the Medellin cartel apart. The body count was horrific: Pablo Escobar was fighting back savagely, ordering bombings and assassinations. Through the first six months of the hunt, more than sixty-five police officers were killed. But the Colombian government was winning the war of attrition, picking off major players in Escobar's power structure. Escobar's men began to turn on him, offering to provide information in return for concessions from the government, and the drug lord himself had gone to ground. Teams of Delta operators rotated through Medellin, assisting the Search Bloc as forward observers and advisors while being very careful not to get into the shooting end of the operations. Doing so earned them the Search Bloc's respect.

Then, a vigilante group calling themselves *Los Pepes* (an acronym for People Persecuted by Pablo Escobar) burst onto the scene in January 1993. The day after Escobar ordered a massive bookstore bombing that massacred innocent people in the streets of Bogota, his mother's *hacienda* burned to the ground. Then a pair of car bombs exploded outside Medellin apartment buildings where Escobar's family was staying. Soon after, the drug lord's mother and aunt were wounded in another bombing. While the Search Bloc confined its assaults to Escobar's known cartel associates, *Los Pepes* had no such manners: They went after the drug lord's family, his lawyers, his accountants, and his friends—and vowed in writing to do so every time Escobar injured innocent people.

Delta, Busby, and U.S. intelligence agencies suspected that the families of Fernando Galeano and Gerardo Moncada—the murdered men whose blood I thought I'd seen at *La Catedral*—were part of the force behind *Los Pepes*. Whoever it was, one thing was certain: Where Escobar had long had the advantage of fighting a government enemy that played by legal rules, now he was fighting a second enemy, and this one played by *his* rules: the rules of terror. Garrison and I agreed that if any evidence surfaced that the Colombian elements we were working with were involved, Delta was out of there.

And so, the noose was tightening around Escobar in Colombia. In Mogadishu, I was confident we'd get Aidid, too. It was only a matter of time.

Sunday, October 3, was my mother's birthday and I woke up wondering how I was going to manage to call her from this east African hellhole. By then we had already captured Osman Atto, Aidid's chief financial advisor, and he and I had our little meeting in the Conex where I told him he'd "underestimated our God."

After that, we published a list of targets: wanted men. These were Somalis we knew were either tied to Aidid, or whom we felt could provide us with useful intel. The idea was to stir the pot, to get Aidid's men wary and moving—or perhaps worried and ready to turn.

It worked. The CIA station chief came down to the airfield from UN headquarters to tell me a very worried Somali had come to visit American agents there.

"My name shouldn't have been on that list," the Somali complained to CIA. If the Americans would take his name off the list, he said, he would reveal the location of a secret meeting of many of Aidid's top lieutenants.

As the station chief briefed me, I listened, intent and skeptical. Top lieutenants? We'd heard that before and busted down courtyard gates only to frighten women and children. So far, the quality of intelligence in Mogadishu had succeeded as much in alienating the people we were trying to help as it had in getting us closer to Aidid.

Still, I listened. "Aidid's lieutenants are meeting to discuss strategy," the CIA liaison told me. "Today. In Bakara Market."

The place we least wanted to go. Located in the heart of downtown

Mogadishu, Bakara Market was like a sprawling, open-air farmer's market, rummage sale, and arms dealership all rolled into one. It was, and is, the largest and busiest market in Mogadishu. In better times, Bakara had been alive with men dickering over bags and barrels of maize, sorghum, and rice, with scampering children, and wives getting out of the house for a friendly visit or a snatch of gossip, their *hijabs* vibrant against their dark skin. Now, food was scarce, and trade had turned darker, with stalls and vendors selling everything from illicit drugs and foreign passports to RPGs and anti-aircraft guns. And it could all be had cheap—and no questions asked—with money changers deciding on the spot the going exchange rate of the Somali shilling against the dollar.

Aidid controlled Bakara, and vendors paid protection money to his thugs. People would do anything to prop up one end of the war between the clans. Some tribe members fought with guns; others fought with money and information. Businessmen not only profited from trading contraband, but used their gains to finance rival militias.

In Bakara, armed militia openly patrolled the streets on foot and in technicals. Women and children were armed and loyal to the Habr Gidr clan. The American policy was not to even drive *through* Bakara. Now we were talking about hitting Aidid there.

So the question was, is the CIA's informant reliable?

Danny McKnight sat across the battered table from me. "What do you think?" I asked him.

"Bakara?" he said. "I'd want to be sure."

"The informant has a good motive for turning," Garrison said. "He's trying to save his own ass."

"If he's telling the truth, there'll be a lot of targets at that meeting," I offered. "Might be too good to pass up."

Garrison sat back in his chair and considered the rafters. "All right," he said after a long pause. "If he'll I.D. the precise location of the meet, we'll hit it."

4

THAT AFTERNOON, Garrison, Dave McKnight, and I gathered in front of the JOC video monitors and watched a rickety sedan weave its way up Hawlwadig Road. In an adjoining room, an Arabic-speaking interpreter was in radio contact with the sedan's driver, our CIA informant. Hovering in the doorway between the two rooms, the CIA station chief relayed comms from the informant to the interpreter to us. According to our agreement, the driver was to park his car directly in front of the building where Aidid's lieutenants were to meet. As we watched the screen, the sedan crept slowly up the street away from the Olympic Hotel, then stopped.

"Is that it?" Garrison said.

"No, he passed it and stopped down at the corner," the station chief said. "It's back down at the other end of the street."

"Not good enough," I said. "Tell him to go back and park directly in front of the building. I don't want any confusion."

From the flightline, we could hear eighteen helos turning up, the Black Hawks' low thudding beat under the lighter hum of the Little Birds. Gary Harrell and Lieutenant Colonel Tom Matthews, a ruddy Irishman from Philly, were in the command-and-control bird. Among the Black Hawk pilots were two Special Ops veterans, Chief Warrant Officer Cliff Wolcott, piloting Super Six-One, and in Super Six-Four, Chief Warrant Officer Mike Durant. Mike had been with us in Panama, and we'd gotten to know each other better during the run-up to Mogadishu. I had known Cliff for several years, and thought of him as nothing short of a warrior. During Desert Storm, he flew SCUD-hunting missions deep into Iraq and was so coolheaded, he'd earned the nickname Elvis.

Between them, the helos carried an assault force of thirty Rangers under the command of Captain Mike Steele, a big ex-football player from the University of Georgia. In addition there were fifty Delta operators, four SEALs, and a couple of P.J.s. The entire assault force was under the command of Delta Captain Scotty Miller, a low-key, tactically savvy officer. The Rangers were to fast-rope into the streets from Black Hawks and set up a security perimeter while Delta and the SEALs stormed the target building and captured Aidid's men. This operation would be Scotty's first as an element commander. But only if the informant kept his word. If not, we'd scrub the mission.

On the monitors, I saw the informant turn around and drive back in the direction he had come, picking his way past merchants, and knots of women and children criss-crossing the street. He moved as slowly as if he were driving in his own funeral procession. From his point of view, he likely was. Finally, he stopped in front of a large two-story house on a corner opposite the Olympic.

Other than being a building with a lot of bedrooms, the Olympic bore little resemblance to the American idea of a hotel. Instead it was a virtual headquarters for the HG militia. An assault on the meeting venue would be like launching an attack across the street from an army base. Except that these guys kept their weapons locked and loaded.

Back in the JOC, I could see the informant step out onto Hawlwadig. A high wall surrounded the target building, forming the traditional Somali courtyard. The house had a perfectly flat roof where the residents could lounge in the sun chewing *khat*, or lie in wait for an ambush. A Somali man dressed in a loose shirt and slacks appeared at the wrought iron gate that formed the only entrance to the courtyard.

I turned to my operations officer and two of the communicators. "Okay, guys, that's the house." I stood briefly, and then knelt beside my seat and said a quick and silent prayer.

Lord, be with us on this mission. Protect these men, and give us success.

Then I stood and glanced at Garrison who with a nod, signaled that the op was a go.

I keyed my mike and issued the execute codeword.

"Irene."

5

AS THE AIRBORNE RAID FORCE LIFTED OFF, Danny McKnight led a ground convoy of trucks and Humvees off the airfield into the city. The convoy's mission was to transport any detainees back to base and, if the 160th couldn't land helos to extract the assault force, give the assault team a lift, too. Some Delta operators rode with Danny, including John "Mace" Macejunas, a muscular blond operator who had trained the Colombians at Tola Maida, and Master Sergeant Tim "Griz" Martin. An easygoing combat veteran of more than twenty years, Griz was a demolitions specialist who had this quirky, mischievous laugh he'd emit whenever he did an especially good job of blowing something up.

As the sound of the helos receded out over the beach, I focused on the West-Cam monitors. Any sign of Aidid's men leaving the target building and we'd immediately scrub the mission. Ten minutes later, the first Black Hawks came into view on the screen, unfurling thick ropes into the streets surrounding the target. I saw the Rangers begin their fast-rope insertion. In Super Six-One, Elvis took up a low orbit over the area of the target building. Then the Little Birds swooped in, discharged the Delta assaulters, and took off again.

Led by Delta Sergeant Matt Rierson, the assault team stormed the target building.

Suddenly, I heard one of the Ranger element leaders report that a Ranger had fallen from the fast rope and was in critical condition. I called Danny and asked if he could evacuate the Ranger.

Danny: "That's affirmative." Mace and Delta operator Chuck Esswein—with Ranger Sergeant Dominick Pilla manning an M-60—broke off in two Humvees to help.

Within minutes, Danny McKnight reported that he was on-station and taking heavy fire from the Olympic.

Twenty minutes later, Gary Harrell keyed up. "Target building is secure. We've rounded up twenty-three people."

"Roger," I said, then keyed up Danny. "They're ready to evacuate."

"Roger. We're moving up to the building now," Danny said.

This is moving like clockwork, I thought. Once the convoy onloaded the prisoners, the whole force would RTB in no more than fifteen minutes, twenty tops.

In the JOC, we watched Danny's element take up defensive positions around the convoy. Muzzles flashed as Rangers returned fire in the direction of the Olympic. I could also see four Delta operators moving carefully on the target building's flat roof, returning fire in several directions. We had expected a tougher fight in Bakara than on other ops, and we were getting it.

Then, cutting through the radio clutter, I heard Elvis say, "... Six-One going down."

His transmission was as calm as it was ominous. Instantly, the West-Cam pilot panned over and I saw Cliff Wolcott's Black Hawk, nose over and twist out of control. Hit by a ground-fired RPG, the helo did several complete pancake rotations, sickeningly slow. Then the Black Hawk simply slid out of the sky, snagged the roof edge of a building and keeled over into an alley.

I had seen helos go down before. And from the way Six-One piled in nose-first, I was almost certain Elvis was dead, and probably some in his crew. Still, for a moment, I was in absolute disbelief. Cliff Wolcott was such a leader, so full of life. One of those guys you picture riding invincibly off into the sunset, not dying in a dirty third world street. A piece of my insides went numb.

In the JOC, the immediate priority became getting rescue and force protection to the crash site. Already the West-Cam birds showed the streets filled with thousands of armed Somalis, some moving toward the crash site. We knew that if the Sammies got there first, they'd kill any survivors, and probably mutilate anyone who was already dead.

Garrison called Major General Tom Montgomery at UN headquarters and asked for immediate reinforcements. According to procedure, Mike Durant, in Super Six-Four, would replace Elvis's bird in the low orbit position.

As those contingencies were set in motion, things were unraveled quickly on the ground. The Somalis blocked the streets with heaps of junk metal and burning tires. As Mace and Esswein evacuated the fallen Ranger, Somali militia riddled them with withering fire. Pilla returned fire from the M-60 until a Somali round caught him in the forehead, killing him instantly.

Mike Steele rounded up his element and began moving through the streets to the crash, encountering heavy fire from every door and window they passed.

One West-Cam monitor showed the alley. I saw two men crawl out of the wreckage, stumbling and disoriented. Gunfire immediately pinned them against the wreckage. I saw Delta operator Dan Busch firing back. Somalis fell dead in the alley, but not before one of them shot Busch. He grabbed his belly and slumped into the street.

Near-constant muzzle flashes lit up the screens in the JOC. Scotty Miller called me and when he keyed his mike, I could hear the rattle and roar of gunfire.

"I have multiple wounded!" Scotty said, shouting to be heard. "We're going to need more ammo, medical supplies, and water!"

"Roger, we will get it to you ASAP."

Already, the number of wounded on the ground made it impossible for Scotty to execute a breakout on his own. Meanwhile, we had at least two dead brothers pinned inside Super Six-One. And no one was willing to leave those men behind.

Star Four-One, a Little Bird, came into view, landing in the cross street to the alley. Ducking incoming fire, the copilot ran into the alley. The pilot stayed with the helo and, with his sidearm, laid down covering fire, spraying bullets in a defensive arc at Somali assailants I couldn't see on the screens. I saw the copilot literally drag Busch back to the Little Bird. Another man from Wolcott's bird climbed aboard, and Star Four-One lifted off through a storm of Somali bullets.

Immediately, the CSAR Black Hawk, piloted by Dan Jollata, took up a hover over the alley. It had been eight minutes since Elvis crashed. As I watched the P.J.s scale down the ropes, an RPG streaked in from the left. Smoke bloomed from the helo's left side and the bird lurched sideways. The fast-ropes swayed with two P.J.s still hanging on them, now helpless mid-air targets.

My breath caught. We absolutely could not afford to lose another helo.

Nearly everyone we had was already tasked on some part of this mission. If another bird went down, there'd be no one left to send.

I could hear radio chatter, other pilots advising Jollata that he was hit badly and needed to put his bird down ASAP. But with his controls catastrophically mushy and smoke spewing from the top of his rotor, Jollata held his hover long enough for the P.J.s to reach the ground. Then, cool as ice, he nursed his bird back to base.

Danny McKnight's team finished loading Matt Rierson's assault team and the Somali detainees. After a brief discussion with Gary, I tasked the convoy to go over to the alley to pick up the Super Six-One survivors and the P.J.s.

"Ready for exfil and ready to move to the crash site," Danny transmitted.

Gary came back. "Roger. Go ahead and move."

The convoy rolled. It was like driving into a shredder.

Amid the dust and smoke and roadblocks, McKnight's lead vehicle quickly became lost in Mogadishu's narrow, unfamiliar streets. From overhead, a P-3 Orion spy plane reported it could see Mogadishu laid out like a grid-map. Trying to help direct the convoy, the Orion crew transmitted directions to Danny—"Turn left at the next intersection!" Still, Danny and his Rangers missed several turns only to run head on into more Somali fighters on each new street.

Scattered small arms fire now became a metal storm. RPGs seared in. One grenade blew three men out of the back of a Humvee, including Delta Master Sergeant Griz Martin, mangling the entire lower half of his body.

Every intersection bristled with crossfire, as hundreds of armed Somalis now pressed brazenly toward the limping convoy. Finally, Danny called to say his vehicles were shot up so bad he didn't think he could get to the crash. He was taking casualties as well and thought he needed to return to base to evacuate his wounded. I concurred and ordered Danny back to the airfield to try again after he refitted and rearmed.

Then, suddenly, our nightmare scenario materialized: the Somalis shot down Mike Durant's Blawk Hawk with an RPG.

6

I HEARD DURANT'S CALL ON THE RADIO: "Going in hard! Going down!"

One of the West-Cam birds quickly put a camera on the crash site, a ragged village about a mile and a half southwest of the main battle. I could see Somalis, many of them armed, already crowding into the area. Our CSAR element was already knee-deep in the first crash site, trying to extricate the bodies of Wolcott and his copilot, Bull Briley, from the wreckage. Danny's convoy had been decimated. Scotty Miller's men were holed up in defensive positions around the Six-One crash site. Who could we send? What did we have left? The Pentagon's skinflint commitment of forces was coming back to bite us in the ass.

I turned to Major Craig Nixon, the XO of the 3rd Ranger Battalion. Quiet and competent, Craig was a behind-the-scenes kind of guy. I had only known him since July.

"Start rounding up anyone you can get your hands on," I told him. "Grab any vehicles you can find and organize an element to go to the second crash site."

With the chaos in the streets and, it seemed, every breathing Somali ready to kill Americans, Craig didn't hesitate. "Roger that," he said and headed off, gathering every man who could fog a mirror to be part of his rescue team. By the end of the day, he would earn a Silver Star.

On the West-Cam monitors, I could see Super Six-Two, a Black Hawk, plus a pair of Little Birds circling Durant's crash site, trying to hold back the crowds. Three Delta snipers were aboard Six-Two: Sergeant First Class Randy Shughart, Master Sergeant Gary Gordon, and Sergeant First Class Brad Hallings. The Six-Two pilots circled low and reported that Durant and his copilot, Ray Franks, were alive. I heard Six-Two ask if they could insert two of the snipers into the second crash site. Shughart and Gordon were volunteering to go down there alone and try to hold off the advancing Somali mob.

Gary immediately denied the request, and I concurred. I keyed the mike and said to Gary: "Okay, listen, we've got a small Ranger element departing here in just a minute headed for the second crash site. Someone needs to vector him in."

The situation at the Six-Four crash site continued to deteriorate. From overhead, Shughart, Gordon, and Hallings picked off advancing Somalis with deadly accuracy. But instead of retreating, the Sammies kept coming.

The Six-Two pilots asked a second time to put the snipers in. Again, Gary and Tom said no. The third time, the pilots pleaded for approval. The desperation in their voices made the case, and I gave permission for my guys, Randy Shughart and Gary Gordon, to jump from a low hover and try to save the Super Six-Four crew.

7

AT JUST BEFORE 5 P.M., just yards away from the Six-One crash site, a Ranger element came under a hail of Somali fire hitting three soldiers inside a minute. Corporal Jamie Smith got the worst of it. A bullet pierced his thigh, traveled up his leg, and hit a femoral artery. Delta medic Kurt Schmid got to Smith almost immediately. In the hot-wash, Schmid said Smith was bleeding buckets. The medic had to tear open the entrance wound in Smith's leg, insert his hand, and feel his way up into Smith's pelvis to try and manually pinch off the bleeding. Every time Schmid tried it, Smith screamed in pain. But the Ranger had lost so much blood that Schmid couldn't risk giving him morphine. The drop in blood pressure might kill him.

Smith's chalk leader, Lieutenant Larry Perino, called for a medevac. Mike Steele relayed the request to Tom Matthews in the command-and-control bird. But the area was too hot to send in a helo.

At about 7 p.m., we sent a Black Hawk in to re-supply the troops pinned down around the Six-One crash site. They were running low on water and ammo, and it was going to take awhile to get the 10th Mountain Division ground convoy in to evacuate them. As soon as the Black Hawk roared in and took up a hover just south of the crash site, Somali gunfire exploded from every direction. Muzzle flash and RPG trails erupted all over the screens in the JOC. Dozens of rounds pierced the Black Hawk's skin, rotors, and gearbox as two Delta operators kicked out water, ammo, and IV bags, which fell to the ground below. The pilots held the bird steady until the re-supply was complete. Then, shot full of holes and leaking fluid, they were able to return to base. But that helo would not fly again.

About an hour after he left the base, Craig Nixon called me. Because of roadblocks and burning tires, he had to keep changing routes and hadn't been able to reach Durant's crash site. He eventually ran head-on into Danny McKnight's shot-up convoy and needed to help them get back. I agreed, and told Craig to bring them in. In half an hour, both elements limped back through the gates of the airfield. Craig refueled and rearmed and headed out again for a second attempt to get to the second crash site. This time, John Macejunas joined him, determined to get to Shughart, Gordon, and the Six-Four crew before the Somalis did.

Jamie Smith's condition was deteriorating.

Gary called me in the JOC: "We've got two critically wounded who are going to die if we don't get them out."

"I don't think we can get a medevac in there without losing another helo and more people," I said.

Then Scotty Miller called me directly, an urgent pleading in his voice: "I've got to have a medevac in here. We've got a man who's going to die."

If I sent the medevac, there was a very high risk of getting everybody on that helicopter killed, plus the added risk of creating another rescue scenario when we already had two helos down and the rest shot to pieces. If I didn't send the medevac, Jamie Smith would almost certainly die.

It was the most agonizing decision I have ever had to make. When I keyed my mike, my heart felt like a stone.

"Scotty, we can't send another helo in there and get it shot down."

At about 8 p.m., I heard Steele come up on the command net. Jamie Smith was dead.

8

___

THE BATTLE HAD RAGED FOR NEARLY NINE HOURS. Just before midnight, we got the Malaysians, Pakistanis, and the 10th Mountain Division launched toward the crash sites. When I knew they were en route, I walked outside with Chaplain Michalke from the 160th. In the darkness, we walked over near some sandbags fortifying a Conex. With scattered bursts of small arms fire in the distance, we knelt down and prayed for the men pinned down in the city.

Back in the JOC, I watched on the West-Cam as the rescue convoy wound toward the Six-Four crash site. But when the convoy stalled again, frustrated by Somali roadblocks, Macejunas rallied a small force to go and find Durant and the others on foot. With Mogadishu a blistering hornet's nest, it was an incredibly brave act. But it's what Shughart and Gordon would've done for them, what they *had* done for Durant and his crew. I watched on a FLIR, a Forward Looking Infrared monitor, as Mace reached the second crash site. The FLIR showed "warm" objects—like people and engines—as white images against a black background.

Praying silently, I watched Mace's ghostly image moving among the remains of Super Six-Four, which appeared as a pale mass against a black field. I didn't know what to hope for. Knowing the Somalis had already overrun the site, I didn't think there was a chance in the world Mace would find our guys just sitting there alive and well. I was hoping he'd find some evidence of their escape—or, knowing what the Somalis did to the dead, at least find their bodies intact.

Mace keyed his mike: No signs of life, he reported. Also, no bodies.

For a moment, the JOC echoed with a hollow silence. In one way, Macejunas's report was a devastating blow. Still, it left us with a shred of hope that Durant and his crew, plus Shughart and Gordon, had been captured and were still alive, or that they had escaped.

I called Gary. "Tell Mace to blow the helo."

"Roger."

The FLIR bloomed white as Mace and his team torched Super Six-Four with thermite grenades, then slipped back through the city to link up with the convoy.

9

WE COULD HAVE LEFT THE CITY HOURS before we did. As soon as the Malaysian APCs and Humvees got into the perimeter there, we could have picked up our force, including our wounded, and left. By the time Elvis's helo crashed, Delta had already completed the mission, capturing members of the HG leadership and loading them for return to base. But after the first Black Hawk crashed, the entire Battle of the Black Sea became about getting our guys back. There was never a question, never a discussion. Briley and Wolcott were trapped inside Six-One, and nobody was willing to leave them.

On a West-Cam monitor, I could see one task force element fighting its way up the street leading to Elvis's crash site. Tracer rounds flashed back and forth across the screen and smoke exploded where RPGs hit. I had the camera pan down to another group in time to see them get out of their vehicles to heave aside a barricade of junk and burning tires the Somalis had erected to stop them.

Every man out there was fighting for a cause, in this case, liberating a people from Aidid and his death squads. But when you get down in the dirt and the bullets and the blood, you're fighting for your brothers, and you don't want to let them down. You know that if you're wounded or killed, the man next to you is going to bring you out, and take you home to your family, and he knows the same thing about you. Your brothers are not going to leave you to die or rot in some foreign hellhole. It is an unbreakable code. Knowing that makes you a more committed fighter.

Gary called me to say two elements had closed on Elvis's crash site. "They're going to work to get the bodies out."

An hour later, he called me back. "They can't get them out. They're going to have to pull the helo apart."

I glanced at the clock. It was going to be light soon. We would lose our night-vision advantage, the Somalis would have retrenched and reloaded, and the relative quiet of the city would erupt again into hellfire.

Garrison walked up and stood at my shoulder. "It's going to be light in an hour."

"Yeah, I know." I keyed up Gary. "It's only an hour until daylight. Relay that to the crash site. We need to get out of there by first light."

"Roger," Gary said.

I passed the same message to Scotty Miller. "Start your evacuation as soon as you get the bodies out of the crash. When you head out of there, go to the Pakistani soccer stadium."

About 30 minutes before daylight, Gary called to say they had Elvis and Bull out of Super Six-One.

From that moment, all our troops commenced the long, slow trek back to base that became known as the Mogadishu Mile.

10

JUST AFTER DAWN ON OCTOBER 4, I was standing in front of the JOC when a five-ton truck carrying casualties drove onto the airfield and pulled to a stop near the M.A.S.H. tent. The rising sun already burned against my face, lighting the truck in red fire. Walking across the tarmac to meet it was like walking to my own grave. But I knew I had to. As I neared, a Ranger got out of the cab. In the back of the truck I could see corpses, torn and bloody, stacked like firewood, some with their eyes fixed wide open. The first man I recognized was Delta operator Earl Fillmore, shot in the head.

On top of the dead lay the wounded, moaning and writhing, calling out in pain. I saw another one of my guys, Griz Martin, lying there, still alive, but only semi-conscious. As a pair of medics emerged from the M.A.S.H. tent carrying litters, the Ranger lowered the tailgate. A cascade of blood as wide as the truck spilled out like a waterfall. I heard my men's blood splashing down on the ground. My stomach rolled and tears closed my throat. The medics began separating the living from the dead.

I raised my eyes and looked across the fence that separated our base from Mogadishu. The sunrise now poured gold light over the city, turning a dark and hopeless place temporarily beautiful, like Christmas lights on a brothel. This ragged place had just chewed up and spit out elite fighters from the most powerful army in the history of the world. Men whose safety I prayed for, men whom God placed in my charge.

As I stood by that truck with their blood pooling around my boots, its coppery smell boring into my brain, I felt I had failed them. Worse, God had failed them—and in failing them had failed me. A hollow ringing rose inside me, the strange noise of catastrophic personal and professional failure.

Defeat hung over me like a poison fog. Leaving the truck, I walked over to an area where the Humvees were parked. They told the story of the battle: bullet-shattered windshields, spent cartridges, the doors and hoods peppered with bullet holes. One Humvee had been pierced by an RPG. The interior of every vehicle was covered with brown, caking blood. In a couple of spots, I saw brain matter.

The assessment pierced more holes in my spirits, sinking them lower. But I kept my head up for the sake of the guys. The sun crept higher, heating up the air. I walked back toward the hangar and began talking with the troops, trying to get an understanding of who was dead and who was missing. Sergeant Rick Whittaker, a sniper troop sergeant, was standing at the door of the hangar.

He was a big guy and I had to look up to talk to him. "Rick, are you missing any people?"

His eyes welled with tears. "Yes, I'm missing Gordy and Randy," he said. "They went into the second crash site and they're gone." He paused, his throat working, eyes pleading. "They're gone."

"Rick, we'll get them back," I said. I think we both knew that didn't necessarily mean alive.

Next, I saw Tom Matthews by the door to the JOC. He had just come back in from the mission. "How many of your guys did we lose, Tom?" I said.

"Two dead and four missing," he said tightly. I had never seen Tom Matthews upset. Never. Now his jaws were clenched tight and he shotgunned his words out quickly then closed his mouth again as if he didn't trust his voice not to shake. "We've got to find them."

"We will," I said. "We *will*."

Rob Marsh and his medical team were receiving the wounded in a makeshift holding area near the M.A.S.H. tent. Crossing the tarmac, I felt like I was walking toward a nightmare. Dozens of men lay on litters, some awake, some unconscious, bullet holes and shrapnel peppering their flesh. As I knelt and began talking and praying with them, one by one, I saw pain in their faces. Not physical pain, but the pain of losing brothers.

I knelt next to senior NCO Tom Corbett, an old friend and golf buddy of mine.

"How are you feeling, Tom?" Shrapnel had ripped him up pretty good.

"I'm going to be okay, but we've got to find these missing guys."

"We will, Tom. We'll find them."

Every man I spoke with was more concerned about our MIAs than about himself. As I talked with them, one part of my brain worked on the next mission phase: What's our next move? Mogadishu had been a time bomb before; now it was a blood-torn, angry hive. How do we get our guys back?

That afternoon, Garrison, Dave McKnight, and I got in a van and drove to the UN compound. We knew the commanders of some of the other African nations that were part of Restore Hope kept open lines of communication with Aidid. Since they weren't combatants, this fact was not a foul. Now we intended to use it to send the warlord a message.

The three of us found the headquarters of one of the African commanders. I cut directly to the chase: "If you have any way to pass information to Aidid, you tell him we want our people back," I said, leaning closer. "You tell him we will not leave Mogadishu until we have them. And tell him that the sooner we get our people back, the fewer of his people will be dead."

11

THE DAY AFTER THE BATTLE was a flurry of organization, casualty counts, medevacing and regrouping. Delta's doctor, Rob Marsh, was in the thick of it, blood up to his elbows, his trademark good humor bucking up the wounded.

By then, I knew the full impact of October 3. Against the odds we'd faced—thousands to ninety-nine—the Battle of the Black Sea was a victory on paper. We'd completed our mission. But at a horrific cost. Now my heart felt like a lead weight. We had seventy-six wounded, more than a dozen confirmed dead, and several still missing, including Shughart, Gordon, and the entire Super Six-Four crew. I had seen the bloody pile of bodies in the five-ton truck. Dan Busch was gone. Earl Fillmore was gone. I prayed for Griz Martin, who fought hard, Rob told me. Just when it seemed he had slipped away, Griz would somehow find another reserve, another measure of strength to cling to life. He didn't make it.

Up to that point, I had focused on what I needed to do as a leader, on showing strength, on comforting and encouraging my men. But now, head down, I stumbled to my trailer, sat on the edge of my bunk and sobbed. I bent forward, elbows on my knees, my face in my hands, tears falling on the floor. But as grief tore lose from my chest, it began transforming into something else: Anger.

Where were *You!* I prayed. *Why did You let these men down? Why did You abandon us?*

Minutes passed. And I realized I had stopped addressing God. I came to a conclusion that hollowed me out inside. If God was real, He would have heard my prayers. If God was real, He wouldn't have let these good men die.

For twenty-three years I have been living a lie, I thought. *There is no God.*

12

TOM MATTHEWS AND I were standing in the JOC when CNN broadcast the infamous footage of Somalis dragging two of our guys through the streets. They had ropes tied around the bodies. I could see on the TV screen, one man was nearly naked; the other still had most of a flight suit on. We thought maybe that was Ray Frank. The sight wrenched my gut and seemed to suck the air out of the room. Tom's eyes burned with pain. His features barely moved, but beneath them I could see the muscles of his face tensed with rage.

CNN played and replayed the images, and I thought of our guys' families watching the bodies being desecrated over and over again: Somalis poking them with rifles, hooting, and raising their arms in victory as though they were dragging a safari kill through the streets. That an American news company would glorify the desecration of Americans enraged me.

Please, God. Don't let their families see.

My crisis of faith had passed. At the moment I sat on my bunk and denied God, I heard the Holy Spirit speak to my heart, saying, *If there is no God, there is no hope.* I didn't like what had happened. I *hated* what had happened. But I could not justify praising Him for miracles then denying Him in tragedy. I had seen Him at work in the world, and in my own life, too many times for that.

As I sat on my bunk that night and prayed for understanding, I decided to simply open my Bible. Not really looking for anything in particular, I opened it to the book of Proverbs and gazed at a verse I had marked somewhere along the way: "Trust in the Lord with all your heart and lean not on your own understanding."

Okay, Lord, I prayed. *But this is tough.*

While we watched the CNN broadcast in the JOC, the rest of Task Force Ranger watched it in the hangar. We all wanted to go back in and exact revenge, but it wasn't the right thing to do, and Garrison and I said no to a retaliatory strike: Too many civilian casualties. But we did arrange for Mace to go out into the city undercover. This would be his fourth trip into Mogadishu—his third since hell broke loose. A local NGO (nongovernmental organization) had agreed to discreetly help us look for our men. Mace was going in with them.

The next day, Tom and I were in the JOC again when CNN broadcast new footage. It was a grainy interview with a single man, an American. My heart soared—at least one of our guys was alive!

This man's face was swollen, misshapen, and streaked with what looked like blood.

"No, I am not a Ranger," he said to an interviewer off-camera.

"You kill people innocent," the interviewer said.

"Innocent people being killed is not good," said the American.

I looked at Tom. "Who *is* that?"

Peering closely at the screen, he said, "That's Mike Durant."

But looking at his face on the television screen, I didn't even recognize him. I would later find out that in addition to the wounds he received in the crash—including a broken leg—the Somalis had struck him in the face with the severed arm of one of his crew chiefs, breaking his cheek and jawbone. They also shot him in the shoulder as he lay in a tiny, dark room tethered by a dog chain.

Watching the interview with Mike, conflicting emotions surged through me. Outrage at the pilot's condition. Hope that Shughart, Gordon, and the others were alive. And dread that my hope was more like wishful thinking. If the Somalis had more than one prisoner, I was pretty sure they would have put them on camera to gloat.

Our passion became finding Durant. CNN broadcast and rebroadcast his interview footage, and our intel people scoured the scant tape for clues to his location. Durant's brothers in the 160th desperately wanted Mike to know that we were still out here, that we were turning the city upside down looking for him, that America hadn't abandoned him. They knew Mike was tough, trained not to break in captivity. Still, seeing his condition on television, they wanted to give him the most important psychological advantage of all: hope.

Tom Matthews came to see me in the JOC. "Let's get a loudspeaker on one of the helos and let Mike know we're still trying to find him."

"Great idea," I said, and we immediately rounded up the Black Hawk techs, who rigged up the necessary equipment. For the next week, the 160th flew regularly over Mogadishu, broadcasting calls that echoed off the city facades.

"Mike Durant, we will not leave you."

"Mike Durant, we are with you always."

13

THE HORROR JUST KEPT ON COMING. On October 5, Tom and I got in a Humvee with Danny McKnight, and Mel Wick, my command sergeant major, and drove out to a lone green tent staked at the other end of the airfield. The field morgue. The Mortuary Affairs unit had set up down there, near the water, and were taking care of the dead. The four of us rumbled in silence across the tarmac and along a crushed shale path. A somber dread pressed in on us, more smothering and oppressive than anything the Somali sun could muster. We knew identifying our dead was our responsibility, but none of us looked forward to the task.

Mel and I had been together since Delta's founding, and understood each other. We had shared defeat and victory and all the peaks and potholes in between. This, though, was the lowest, most agonizing road we'd ever traveled. The toughest thing I had ever done in my life was to deny that medevac to Corporal Jamie Smith. Now there was a second toughest thing and as we stepped through the flap into the field morgue tent, I was thankful Mel was with me.

Inside, the tent sweltered, lit from the ceiling by hanging steel fixtures. To our right, I could see green body bags on the floor. I was struck by the sheer number of them, lined up in rows like huge, dark tally marks. Two staff sergeants from Mortuary Affairs bent over a body on a gurney.

"We're here to identify the bodies of those who were killed yesterday," I said.

"Yes, sir," said one of the sergeants. Then he stepped aside to show us the man they were working on. "Can you identify this man?"

I willed my face to be still. For a moment, I couldn't speak as grief gripped my throat. It was Griz Martin. His face was pale and ashen, but for a moment, in my mind's eye, I could see it full of life again. I could see that big smile he was known for, the one that showed every tooth in his head, and hear his mischievous laugh.

Then I could hear his wife crying. I refocused on Griz as he was now, lying on that table. "That's Master Sergeant Martin," I said aloud, steeling my voice.

The mortuary affairs sergeant wrote something on a clipboard. Then the two sergeants led the four of us in among the body bags, unzipping each one just enough to reveal the face of the man inside. Tom identified the men from the 160th, Danny I.D.'d the Rangers, and Mel and I named the men of Delta—Dan Busch, a relatively new operator and a devout Christian; and Earl Fillmore, a fireplug of a man who had been with us in Panama and Grenada, loved life, and volunteered for every tough assignment with a sparkle in his eye. Putting a name, a *personhood*, to their lifeless bodies was my job as their commander. It was a final gesture of respect. But the image of their pale, silent faces still burns in my brain.

Since that day, I have given my officers in Special Forces a talk in which I tell them never to waste training time, never to take short cuts that might result in disaster. "One day, each of you is probably going to have an experience that will stick with you for the rest of your life," I tell them. "One day, you will go in and open a body bag and look into the ashen face of one of your soldiers. At that point, you will ask yourself a question: Did I do everything I could to make sure this soldier accomplished his mission so that he could go home to his family alive?"

In the years since Somalia, I have asked myself those questions again and again. Heading into Mogadishu, did I take short cuts? No. Did I train my men right, prepare them properly for battle? Yes. Was there something else I could have done to make sure they came home alive? I don't know.

I look back on the deterioration of the situation and second-guess myself. It has been popular in the newspapers to speculate that we were arrogant, complacent, or both. That is the view of those who were not there. The fact is we never underestimated the Somalis. We constantly changed our operating patterns out of respect for their tactics.

Did I do everything I could have done? I'll never know. And that is the ugly question I keep locked away in a certain drawer of my heart like a loaded gun.

14

TWO DAYS AFTER what would become known as the Battle of the Black Sea, I walked up to find Matt Rierson standing with Gary outside the hangar near a Conex. Matt was the Delta sergeant who led the successful assault on the target building that was the whole reason for our October 3 operation. Many of the casualties had already been medevaced out, some to Germany, some straight home. Those of us who remained sweated under a merciless Somali sun that bore down on our heads as if it meant to burn the rest of us out of the country.

I propped one boot up on a sandbag, part of a bunker fortifying the Conex so we could use it as a shelter during mortar attacks. I looked at Matt and could see in his eyes that his heart was as broken as mine. Delta had lost so many: Shughart and Gordon. Griz. Dan Busch. Earl Fillmore. Brad Hallings was alive but had lost a leg. Matt and I briefly held each other's gaze and the thought we shared in that moment was, "What do we say? What *can* we say?"

I had just opened my mouth to speak when a massive explosion shook the ground. The world tilted sideways as I was knocked to the pavement.

I heard Gary, in agony: "My legs! My legs!"

I struggled to my feet and saw Matt lying on the concrete. His skull was split and his eyes were closed. I saw brain matter on the pavement. To his right, I saw Gary writhing on the ground, bright arterial blood pulsing out from beneath him, forming a rapidly spreading pool.

"Find Doc Marsh!" I yelled.

Boots pounded, people running toward us. Another explosion rocked the compound. Two soldiers grabbed me and yanked me over the sandbag bunker into the Conex. One of them accidentally stepped on my right boot, and searing pain shot up through my leg. Until then, I didn't know I'd been hit. The Conex echoed with the muffled thuds of two more mortar rounds.

Then, as suddenly as it had begun, the attack was over. I scrambled out of the bunker. Gary was still lying on the ground, now gritting his teeth against consuming pain. I saw one of the 160th pilots on the ground beside him. He had his hand buried in Gary's thigh up to his wrist, trying to pinch off whichever vessel was steadily pumping blood out onto the pavement.

"Find Doc Marsh!" I yelled again. "Find Rob Marsh!"

Medics ran up with a pair of litters and laid them on the ground. "Sir, we need you to get on here and let us take you for treatment," one of them said to me urgently.

As more medics encircled Gary, I stared at Matt. Only two days before he had risked himself to save others in one of the most lopsided battles in American history. He had lived through that. Only moments ago, I was looking at the life in his eyes. *How could he be gone?*

"I'm fine," I said numbly, waving the medics off. "I'll walk over."

But when I tried to walk, I lurched badly, new pain lancing through my calf and thigh. *Shrapnel*, I thought, realizing at the same time that my foot was in worse shape than I'd thought. I gave up and lay down on one of the litters. And when I looked over at the litter next to me, I was shocked to see the man lying on it was Rob Marsh.

His face had already gone grey. From his waist to his thighs, his fatigues were soaked in blood. I hadn't even known he was near when the mortars hit.

Not him, too, I thought. *Not him*. I wasn't sure how my faith would hold up if God let this African hellhole rob us of another single soul.

Medics hoisted the litters and rushed us over to the same M.A.S.H. tent where I had watched the Air Force medical teams sort out living from dead two days earlier. Inside, they placed me on a gurney and Rob right next to me, on a gurney to my left. A medical team worked furiously on him, cutting away his uniform, inserting IVs, attaching lines to monitor his blood pressure and pulse.

I reached over and grabbed Rob's hand. It was covered in blood. Blood soaked the gurney, dripped on the floor. "Hold on, Rob. You're gonna make it," I said.

Slowly, he turned his head and looked at me. His pupils had dilated to tiny dark holes. His face was vividly white.

A doctor explored the wound in Rob's belly. "Looks like the renal artery's been severed." The doctor barked instructions. Medics ran up holding more IV bags. Instruments flashed in the low-hanging light.

Squeezing Rob's hand, I began to pray silently, *Lord, spare this man's life.* The coppery smell of blood hung in the tent.

Don't let this man die, God. For his family's sake, spare him.

"His pressure's dropping," a nurse said. "Ninety over fifty."

The portable monitor hung on a pole between the gurneys. I could see the red numbers ticking lower, lower.

"*Fight*, Rob!" I stared at him intensely, still squeezing his hand. His eyes were closed now. "Don't give up."

God, spare this man. Save his life. I ask it in Jesus's name.

"Seventy over forty and falling. Pulse forty." The nurse looked at me. "Sir, let go of his hand."

"Hold on, Rob! You're going to make it."

"Fifty over thirty, falling rapidly. Pulse is thirty. *Sir*, please let go of his hand."

I ask you in the name of Jesus to save him. Do not let this man die.

The nurse reached down to pry my fingers away, but I hung on desperately, *willing* Rob to hold on. Somehow, I thought that if I didn't let go, if I just prayed hard enough, God wouldn't take this good man with all the rest.

"Pulse twenty, pressure's bottoming out!"

At that moment, Rob opened his eyes wide and stared into mine, his pupils only pinpoints. "Tell Barbara I love her," he whispered.

Then Rob Marsh's eyes rolled back in his head.

15

I WAS MEDEVACED TO THE UN COMPOUND and into surgery, where doctors removed shrapnel from my legs and foot. When I awoke in recovery, my first thought was Rob. Was he dead? I asked a nurse about him.

"He's been in surgery," she said. "He's still critical. They're going to medevac him to Germany." I asked her to take me down to see him. He lay sedated in a bed at the other end of the ward, his face still pale and gray. Sitting in a wheelchair beside his bed, I laid my hand on Rob's arm and prayed.

The next morning I asked to return to the airfield so I could be with the rest of the troops. I had to use crutches to get around, and spent most of that day on my bunk trying to recuperate. As I lay there, I began to pray. *God, I need You to give me something to help me accept what has happened here. And I really need to come to closure on why this turned out so badly.*

As I was praying, one of the communicators came to my bunk and handed me a fax. It came from a dear friend in Loveland, Colorado, Yale King. There was no message, only a Scripture verse, Isaiah 40:31: "For they that wait upon the Lord shall renew their strength. They shall mount up on wings of eagles, they shall run and not be weary and they shall walk and not faint."

I can't explain why Yale sent that fax halfway around the world when he did, but I felt it was exactly the message God wanted me to hear.

While trying to stay off my feet, I also wrote letters to each of the Delta families who lost sons, husbands, and fathers: Shughart, Gordon, Fillmore, Rierson, and Martin. I prayed and asked God to help me put into words how much each man meant to me personally, and to their Delta brothers. I explained their bravery, their commitment and their sacrifice. I paged through my Bible and tried to include Scripture I felt might comfort the families. As I penned each letter, I pictured each man in life and my heart broke again and again. Tears came, blurring the words as I wrote them.

16

ON OCTOBER 14, 1993, Aidid released Mike Durant. We got word one day in advance, which gave us time to prepare a little ceremony. After a thorough medical checkup at the UN compound, Durant would be coming to the airfield to board a C-141 for home.

The following day, a Black Hawk airlifted Durant and his medical team to the field. By then, the Pentagon had authorized reinforcements—another Ranger battalion and another Delta squadron—bringing our force strength to around six hundred. Under a blue sky, all of us formed two lines flanking the path from the Black Hawk to the Starlifter. Garrison, Tom Matthews and I stood at the end of the line, near the door of the big jet. Somebody got hold of a fifth of Jack Daniels, Durant's favorite, mixed it with water in a five-gallon jug, and poured a tiny shot of the weak brew for every person in Durant's receiving line.

The medical team lifted Durant's litter off the helo and carried him through our welcome committee. On cue, we all toasted him, downed our highballs, and broke into a chorus of "God Bless America." Then Durant got on the Starlifter and headed home.

By the time Durant flew out of Mogadishu, the Pentagon had supplied us with all the things we asked for before we went in. Now that these assets had rolled in, I wondered how many men would still be alive had we received what we'd asked for to begin with.

And the more I contemplated that question, the more my resentment grew.

I wasn't blame-shifting. I'm not suggesting our Bakara operation was perfect. Still, I recognize that we executed a completely successful mission. We were outnumbered by thousands, yet completed our mission and achieved an overwhelming victory. But even today I wonder if we could have achieved that at considerably less cost if the Clinton administration had listened to the commanders on the ground.

A couple of days after Durant left I was standing in the JOC when Garrison walked in from the back room. I could tell by his face he wasn't pleased with what he had to tell me. But his delivery was matter-of-fact, as was his style.

"Just got off the phone with the CINC," he said around his cigar. "We've been directed to start wrapping it up and redeploy."

Translation: Bill Clinton had caved.

"How quickly do they want us to leave?" I said.

"He didn't say, but he did tell us to cease operations. The only thing we're supposed to do at this point is force protection."

"You know this is going to hit everybody pretty hard. We haven't completed the mission here."

"Yeah, I know. I tried to explain to the CINC how we felt, but I think this is coming from above him."

Garrison and I both knew the men of Task Force Ranger would not want to appear to tuck tail and run. They had been bloodied but victorious in a battle that would now go down in history as a defeat. We knew the men would want to see the mission through, and make sure their brothers had not died for nothing.

Later that afternoon, I called a meeting of the element leaders, and Garrison delivered the news. Around the JOC, the reaction was the same: Resigned silence. I think everyone anticipated it, but they still resented it. Most of us knew the Clinton administration didn't have the stomach for anything other than an antiseptic war. Our view was just the opposite: If you're going to commit the military to combat, go all the way. Make the full commitment, and be prepared to accept the cost in human lives.

If the men doing the dying were prepared to accept it, then the men in air-conditioned meetings ought to accept it, too.

17

WE ARRIVED HOME ON OCTOBER 24TH, 1993. Ten days later, Rob Marsh walked into my office, leaning on a cane. The Task Force Delta medical team had medevaced him to the UN compound and then to Germany, where he'd undergone extensive surgeries. The doctors did a miraculous job on Rob: through them, God gave him a second chance at life.

Within weeks of our return, Aidid would attend new U.S.-brokered peace negotiations, and the UN would release every man Task Force Ranger captured. In June 1995, Aidid would declare himself President of Somalia, but continue to fight for control with rival clans. On August 2, 1996, he would die of gunshot wounds sustained a week earlier in a fight with competing factions. Word was, Osman Atto was involved in his death.

On December 2, 1993, my guys in Bogota called me on my secure telephone at Bragg. "Sir, we wanted to report to you that Pablo Escobar was killed this morning." It had been just under seventeen months after his escape from "prison."

Excitement surged through me. I needed some good news. "Tell me what happened," I said.

"You know the SIGINT equipment we provided to the Colombians? They were out running a patrol in Escobar's mother's neighborhood, when Hugo Martinez's son tracked a signal to Escobar's safe house. Hugo, Jr. drove by and *saw* Escobar standing by a window. *Saw* him!"

Our trainers back at Medellin had helped the Colombians launch a quick op. A Search Bloc strike team went in, busted down Escobar's door, chased him out onto a rooftop and killed him: one shot in the butt, and one in each temple.

I called Garrison. "They got Pablo this morning. It's been a long haul, but it was worth it."

"That's good news," Garrison said. "Congratulations on the good work."

"Well, thank you, but the Colombians did it," I said. "We helped them a lot, but they did it."

Afterward, there was a lot of talk about the headshots. As with Waco, shadowy Delta rumors surfaced again. Even today, people still want to know whether Delta snipers were in on the kill.

I can answer that: no.

The official report from the Colombians was that Escobar was caught in a cross-fire. But that's a fairly miraculous story given the straight-on nature of the headshot wounds. I'd say it's more likely the Colombians downed him with a shot in the ass, then walked up and put a *coup de grace* bullet in each side of his head. There you go, Pablo, payback for two decades of murder.

WAR CRIMINALS

Washington, D.C. and
the Balkans
1995—1999

1

THE FALLOUT FROM SOMALIA provoked Bill Clinton to retreat even further into his philosophy of bloodless war. Because he feared another Mogadishu, Clinton kept American troops from intervening in the Rwandan genocide that resulted in the massacre of as many as a million men, women, and children. America's commander-in-chief also decided the use of infantry was too dangerous, and as a result, U.S. forces would rely almost exclusively on air power during our activities in Bosnia-Herzegovina in 1995, and later in Kosovo.

Mogadishu produced fallout for me personally, even beyond the pain of losing so many good men. In June 1994, I joined the Joint Chiefs staff as director of the Special Operations Division under General John Shalikashvili, the JCS chairman. I hadn't been on the Beltway for more than two weeks when an anonymous letter arrived in the hands of every member of the Senate Armed Service Committee. The writer attacked me as incompetent. I had fostered a tense and unlivable atmosphere at Delta, the letter said, and my poor leadership was the reason so many men died in Somalia. The letter triggered an Inspector General investigation into the command climate at Delta.

For me, the aftermath of Mogadishu was already like an emotional grave, and now it was as if someone was standing up top, shoveling in the dirt.

To make matters even worse, the admiral I worked for on the joint staff hated me. Not just me, but Special Operations types in general: He thought we were aloof and insubordinate, and that we thought we were better than everybody else. That doubled my misery.

Meanwhile, Lynne and I moved into a town home in Alexandria, a bedroom community for the D.C./Northern Virginia military-government complex. April, Randy, and Aaron had grown up and left the nest. Just prior to our move up from Bragg, I read a book, *Tender Warrior*, by an author named Stu Weber. Living out its principles, one in particular, changed my life.

Weber wrote that if you are a Christian man, and there's a young man without a father living in your neighborhood, it's your responsibility to mentor him.

We hadn't been in Alexandria long when I noticed two kids, a little boy and a little girl, playing a couple of doors down. I often saw their mom, a petite, short-haired woman, but I never saw a dad. One day when the mom was out in the yard with the kids, I went over and introduced myself as the new neighbor.

Ashley Steele was a 39-year-old single mom who operated a daycare in her home to support Grant, 9, and Mimi, 8.

Well, I thought, *maybe this is my chance to mentor.*

One day a couple of months after Lynne and I got settled in, I asked Ashley if she would allow me to take Grant fishing. She said yes, and suddenly, I had a new little buddy. Grant and I went on several fishing trips then when hunting season rolled around, we took off for the woods. He was a quiet, contemplative boy who still spoke of his dad fairly frequently even though Ashley told me he hadn't seen him for years.

"My dad has a truck like that," he'd say, pointing out the window. I could tell Grant missed him. I hoped I could be a comfort to him, a friend.

2

THE IG INVESTIGATION triggered by the anonymous letter lasted from August 1994 until February 1995. When the final IG report came out, I was completely exonerated. The investigators found not only that the letter writer's views did not reflect the attitude of Delta, but also that the writer hadn't even been in Mogadishu. He had his facts all wrong.

In September, I was nominated for brigadier general. Two months later, I moved from the Pentagon to CIA, where I became deputy chief of the special activities division. In December, the Dayton Accords brought about an uneasy peace between Muslims and Orthodox Serbs in war-torn Bosnia-Herzegovina. Ambassador Richard Holbrooke and General Wesley Clark helped negotiate the settlement. Part of the agreement was that PIFWCs (People Indicted for War Crimes) would be turned over to a tribunal at The Hague, Holland, where they would stand trial. The warring factions themselves were supposed to turn in the PIFWCs (pronounced "piffwicks"). But a large group remained at large, operating in Bosnia-Herzegovina, Belgrade, Yugoslavia, and Macedonia.

Goran Jelisic, for example. During the war, the Serbian side systematically imprisoned, tortured and murdered Muslims, all under the euphemism "ethnic cleansing." Jelisic, a slim, sharp-featured man with a strange little mouth, took particular pleasure in cutting Muslim prisoners with broken glass and beating them with clubs and truncheons. He didn't care whether they were men or women, old or injured. And when he was finished torturing them, he forced them to kneel over a grate, then executed them with two shots to the back of the head. Jelisic once told detainees in a camp called Luka that before he could enjoy his morning coffee, he needed to execute twenty to thirty people. The little monster called himself the "Serb Adolf."

One of my jobs at CIA was coordinating the collection and analysis of intel on people like Jelisic so the CIA and military units keeping peace in the Balkans could go after them.

A year had passed since Mogadishu nearly ripped away my faith in God. I was still healing slowly, day by day. With the anonymous letter, IG investigation, and the unpleasant admiral behind me, I felt as if I was beginning to contribute again, doing what I did best: hunting bad guys. Things seemed to be looking up. That is until Christmastime.

Lynne took a trip home to see friends in Fayetteville, North Carolina. When she returned she told me she wanted a divorce.

After she informed me of her plans to leave, I lay across my bed, and plunged back into despair.

I had had a great military career, but at what cost? Lynne's leaving was my fault, I felt. I had failed as a husband. I'd been a part-time father. The years of separation, years of stress from the secrecy associated with my assignments—my going away and not being able to tell her where I was going or when I was coming back—for her all of that had finally come to a head.

As I stared up at the ceiling, I prayed what Isaiah prayed: *Lord, just take me. I am a total failure.*

3

—

LYNNE AND I KEPT OUR SEPARATION CIVIL. She moved to Fayetteville and I stayed in Alexandria. We didn't play tug-of-war with the kids, and April, Randy, and Aaron were tender with both of us and tried not to take sides. It seemed that since Mogadishu, I'd claw my way up out of that emotional grave, getting to where I could just stick my head out, then something would happen to send me tumbling back to the bottom again.

Now, on the brink of what I considered to be the lowest point of personal failure, I prayed to God for comfort. And the comforter He sent was only four feet tall.

I continued to take Grant hunting and fishing, but now Ashley's daughter, Mimi, took a shine to me. She began going with me to do simple things like grocery shopping. She was just charming and would ride along, chattering away about ten-year-old things. After a few weeks, when we'd run an errand, she'd reach up and put her little hand in my big one, and all the heavy baggage in my life was stripped away. I wasn't the failed husband, the part-time father, the suspect commander, the tough-guy manhunter. I was just Jerry—a guy who, it seemed, was at least still decent enough that a little girl would consider me her friend.

On a Sunday night in February 1996, I went to church to be baptized. Ashley, Grant, and Mimi were there. Standing in the baptismal pool, I looked out at the three of them sitting together on a pew and realized that I loved them all. Still, I kept my distance from Ashley, not wanting to create the appearance that Lynne and I had separated because of her. But as weeks passed, I found that I couldn't stop thinking about her. I called my mother.

"I know divorce is wrong," I told her over the phone. "But I think I have feelings for Ashley."

"Look, your wife has left you," my mother said. "It's not something you

wanted and she's not coming back. I think you have to follow your heart."
As always, she told me she'd be praying for me.

In early spring, I decided to ask Ashley out to dinner. I was as nervous
as a school boy. I was forty-nine years old and hadn't asked a girl for a first
date since I was seventeen.

So I was amazed when she said yes.

4

IN APRIL 1997, I drove down to Fayetteville to meet my attorney, Debra Radtke, who accompanied me to family court. The judge called me to the stand, reviewed the dates I had been married, and said, "Is it your desire that this marriage be terminated by divorce?"

My desire had never been divorce. But by now I knew for sure that Lynne wasn't coming back. "Yes," I said quietly.

I signed a set of papers and walked back to a table with Debra.

"That's it?" I said.

"That's it."

"You mean after all these years, that's all it takes?"

"Yes," she said.

I drove back to Alexandria wrestling with my emotions. It was hard for me to believe that so many years of your life could end with just five minutes in court.

5

WHEN I LEFT CIA IN JUNE 1997 FOR A JOB with the Army staff, I thought I had left Goran Jelisic behind. But two months after moving into my office at the Pentagon, Lieutenant General Tom Burnett, the Army operations director, called me into his office.

I had been promoted to brigadier general by then, but I wasn't in uniform. I had just come out of the gym and was still sweating from my workout when I showed up in his office.

"Today is Monday," Burnett said. "By Friday, you are to be in the Balkans to head up a new task force assigned to chase war criminals."

I had done this before—Noriega, Escobar, and others. But my mind flashed instantly to Mohamed Aidid. Would this be another Mogadishu? Given the way Bill Clinton cut and run from Somalia, I was not confident he'd have the stomach to actually go after these people if we located them.

"Yes, sir," I said, and got the rest of the brief.

Not long later, I boarded a plane for SHAPE (Supreme Headquarters Allied Powers Europe) in Mons, Belgium, for a meeting with General Wesley Clark. I had served with Clark in the Pentagon when he was on the joint staff, and I also worked with him after he relieved George Joulwan at SouthCom. I saw him as a deep thinker who had an idea a minute, and thought through most of them out loud. He was aggressive, and also politically astute. Now Clark was serving as NATO commander. As a broker of the Dayton Accords, he had the Balkan war criminals in his sights and wasn't about to let them walk free.

The story on the Balkans operation was that Clark had originally appointed a retired Marine Corps general to head up the PIFWC task force there. But with a multinational military coalition, plus CIA, that marine decided after several weeks of treading water, his status as a civilian was hurting the operation. He just wasn't perceived as having the firepower to get things done. So Clark asked for a general officer and when my name came up, he decided I was the right man for the job.

"It is essential to the implementation of the Dayton Accords that we bring these war criminals to justice," he told me after we'd settled into his office at SHAPE. "We have five nations who have agreed to work together on it—the U.S., the UK, France, Germany, and the Netherlands. Your job is to provide leadership to this task force. You work for me. You'll coordinate your activities with Rick Shinseki."

He meant General Rick Shinseki, commander of NATO forces in the Balkans, a careful, circumspect man who preferred high-percentage options. Born in Hawaii and of Japanese descent, Shinseki was the first Asian-American to ascend to four-star rank. In 2003, he would famously tell Congress "something in the order of several hundred thousand soldiers" would probably be required to manage post-war Iraq. Don Rumsfeld and Deputy Defense Secretary Paul Wolfowitz publicly disagreed.

The day after my meeting with Clark, I was in the Balkans, where I found... practically nothing. While the war criminal task force had a little headquarters way up in Stuttgart, Germany, no presence had been established in the Balkans themselves. Immediately, I directed my staff to set up command-and-control centers in Sarajevo and Tuzla, both in Bosnia-Herzegovina, and also a series of satellite centers scattered across the Balkans from which we would run our intel collection activities.

My job wasn't to go after the PIFWCs myself. It was my task to find them, then send in the hounds. I already had the CIA paramilitaries in-country. From the U.S., I brought in elements from DELTA and the SEALs, and from Britain, elements of the S.A.S. France, Germany, and the Netherlands also sent Special Ops personnel. The hunt was on.

We worked from a list of about twenty-five PIFWCs, but we had a top tier of most-wanted men, a dirty dozen on whom we concentrated our efforts. Goran Jelesic was on that list. By then, the Balkans had been parted out into "sectors" under the control of NATO peacekeeping countries, including the task force nations. SEAL operators located Jelisic in a north central region controlled by the Russians. Using video surveillance, they tracked his routines until they practically knew when the man was going to take a leak.

Clark, Shinseki, and I formed an interesting trio. On one end, you had

Clark up in Mons, who was very aggressive and wanted the task force to launch on anything reasonably credible. On the other, you had Shinseki down in Sarajevo, who was much more conservative, and also faced with the on-site daily details of dealing with the task force countries. Shinseki wanted to make sure every op was precisely planned and the intel was as good as it was ever going to get. They were both right. But guess who was caught in the middle?

One of our first targets was the Muslim-murdering Goran Jelisic. We had accurately pinpointed his location. The SEAL element knew Jelesic's movements down to a T. This time Clark and Shinseki agreed: the snatch operation was a go. The SEALs pulled up in a van outside Jelisic's apartment building. When he emerged as per his normal routine, four SEALs jumped out, grabbed Jelesic, threw him through the sliding door, and were back in the van rolling. Time elapsed: sixty-one seconds. Jelisic was supposed to be this serious bad guy, but he went down like a scarecrow.

The SEALs took him down to a landing zone south of the city and put him on a helo back to Tuzla where I was waiting for him. Soldiers escorted him down to an old ammo bunker the Slavs had used. Stark and dirty with concrete floors, the air inside the bunker was stale. Naked light bulbs hung from the ceiling. Interrogators seated Jelisic at an old wooden table the size of a school desk. A Slavic-speaking military translator stood nearby. Two guards stood outside the bunker door, and two inside, all fully armed.

I stood inside the bunker, off to the side, watching Jelisic in the chair, pale and shaking. His eyes darted back and forth like a trapped rodent.

This is the feared and terrible "Serb Adolf?"

The interrogator approached him, and Jelisic looked up, flinching as though expecting a bullet. "Are you Goran Jelisic?" the interrogator asked.

"*Da.*"

"What was your role in the internal civil war here in the Balkans?"

Jelisic, voice quaking, answered in Slavic and the translator said, "I helped to defend my homeland."

"Did you know we had you under observation?" the interrogator asked.

"*Nyet.*" He knew he was a target, he said, but living in the Russian sector, he became complacent because he did not believe the Russians had any intention of apprehending war criminals.

Then the ammo bunker door opened and in walked Rick Shinseki. Four stars glistened on the collar of his camouflage uniform, and on his hip he wore a 9 mm pistol. Already pale with fear, Jelisic now turned paper-white. His chin dipped and his shoulders hunched as he seemed to try to make himself smaller. I watched his eyes lock on Shinseki's sidearm. Jelisic seemed certain that the Japanese-American general had come to kill him.

Very deliberately, Shinseki closed the door behind him. Then he strode straight to the little table and looked down at Jelisic. The Serb kept his eyes on the pistol. For several moments, the general said nothing. Then: "Are you Goran Jelisic?"

Jelisic looked up and nodded, just barely, as though afraid any movement might provoke Shinseki to draw his weapon.

"I'm General Shinseki, commander of the Stabilization Force. You are now under the control of the Stabilization Force."

Again, Jelisic managed a timid nod. I thought I could see anticipation in his face, as though he was expecting Shinseki to say, "You have been found guilty and I am now going to put a bullet in your head."

Instead, the general stood stock still and stared at Jelisic until the prisoner looked away. Then Shinseki spun on his boot heel and walked out of the bunker. I left with him so I cannot report whether Jelisic at that point wet himself, but I would not be surprised.

6

BY MARCH 1998, Pete Schoomaker was a four-star general and had taken over as commander of SOCOM in Tampa. He flew out to see me in the Balkans and we sat down to talk in my office. "As soon as I can get you out of here, I want you to take over the Special Forces Command at Bragg. I'd like to get you over there by next month."

"I'd love to do that," I told my old friend. By then, we'd bagged seven of our PIFWC dirty dozen. I was ready to spend some time at home. On March 11, I flew back to the States to attend my son Aaron's graduation from Ranger school. Randy had joined the Army reserves. I was proud that both my boys continued the family tradition of military service. After the ceremony at Benning, I went back to D.C. to check on my apartment, and to see Ashley, Grant, and Mimi.

It was a quick-turn trip. When it was time to fly back to the Balkans, Ashley drove me to Reagan National Airport. Sitting in the car in the parking lot, I turned in my seat to face her. "Pete told me last week that I'm coming back to Bragg to take command of Special Forces," I said. "Now you can either agree to marry me before I go down there, and you can go with me to the change of command ceremony. Or I'll go down there by myself and do the ceremony, and you can marry me when I get back."

Ashley eyed me for a moment with skeptical good humor, waiting for me to crack. Finally, I smiled. She laughed out loud and without hesitating said, "I'll marry you before you go."

I gave her a big kiss. "Okay, today is Friday," I said. "In a few minutes, I'm going to get on that plane, and I'll be back in exactly two weeks, on Friday. We'll get married on Saturday. How's that?"

"That'll be fine," she said, still smiling.

"Okay," I said. "Everything else is up to you."

I kissed her, got out of the car, and hopped a plane back to the Balkans.

Two weeks later, Ashley and I were married in a church in Springfield, Virginia.

Three years later, as I was finishing up my tour in command of Special Forces, Ashley and I attended a going-away dinner in my honor. My officers put together a little dinner, maybe fifty or sixty people, in a banquet room at a nice restaurant called The Barn. When it came time for me to speak, I stood at my table and began by thanking all the folks who'd made my tour there a successful one. Then I guess a little bit of the devil got into me.

"You know, the best thing that's happened to me in the past few years was when I married Ashley," I said. "Y'all probably don't realize that she had exactly two weeks to prepare for a wedding, and that she did it all on her own because I was in the Balkans."

At this point, Ashley, seated beside me, smiled up at me, listening to my little speech. "You know," I went on, "I asked Ashley to marry me because I loved her."

Ashley smiled wider.

"But another factor for our getting married," I said, "was that I hadn't had sex in about four years."

The room just exploded with laughter. Ashley collapsed on the table, head in her hands. But I could see her shoulders shaking and when she raised her head, she was laughing, too.

CRUCIBLE

Washington, D.C.
2003–2004

1

WHEN HISTORY TICKED PAST MIDNIGHT on September 11, 2001, I was airborne over a nation on the verge of a terrible new era. I didn't know it, of course. Still in command of the JFK Special Warfare Center and School (SWC) at Bragg, I had just finished a military tactics tour of the battlefield at Little Big Horn, Montana. There in 1876, warriors overran and killed 263 soldiers and other Army personnel along with their commander, Lieutenant Colonel George A. Custer. I had gone on the tour with the commandants of the other major Army schools and a military historian who replayed for us Custer's Last Stand. When the tour was over, I took a redeye flight home. I arrived after dawn, kissed Ashley and crawled into bed—

"Jerry?" Ashley gently shook my shoulder.

I cracked an eyelid, and my foggy brain told me I hadn't been asleep long. "What time is it?"

"It's a little before nine o'clock. Listen, a plane just hit the World Trade Center."

"Commuter type?"

"No, an airliner. I thought you'd want to know."

That's going to be a mess, I thought sleepily. "Okay, thanks," I said. "I'll be up in a couple of hours."

Ashley left the room, snicking the door shut behind her. I drifted back to sleep—

"Jerry, wake up." Ashley's voice was urgent this time. "I just turned on the news. A plane just hit the Pentagon, and another plane crashed into the World Trade Center. They're saying it's a terrorist attack."

Instantly, I came wide awake and peered at my bedside clock: 9:40 a.m. Inside four minutes, I was in uniform and out the door, headed to my office. At Bragg, I took the stairs two at a time up to the Army Special Operations Headquarters. CNN was on up there, and events were unfolding quickly:

9-1-1 calls reveal Muslim hijackers aboard U.S. flights... Air Force One airborne... An unprecedented ground stop on all air traffic over the U.S.... The south tower of the World Trade Center collapses... United Flight 93 crashes in a Pennsylvania field...

Senior officers from around Bragg gathered with me at Special Ops headquarters and we triggered our emergency plan for securing the post and its various installations. Within thirty minutes, the place was shut down like a vault, bristling with roadblocks and gate guards, with snipers locked and loaded.

Then at 10:28 a.m., we watched CNN in stunned silence as the World Trade Center north tower crashed to earth.

In the days following the 9/11 attacks, it quickly became clear the Special Operations community would play a major role in going after Osama Bin Laden and his enablers, the Taliban. There was no question America would strike in Afghanistan. But as discussions progressed with the Pentagon and the Joint Chiefs, there was a lot of speculation as to whether we would bomb or invade. And if we invaded, would we send in conventional forces for maneuver warfare, or send in Special Operations units to work with indigenous rebels and oust the Taliban?

In the end, we did both, with Special Operations leading the way. That meant a huge new stream of people coming through the SWC as seemingly overnight, the need for engineers, medics, communicators, civil affairs, and other specialists trained in special warfare increased geometrically.

As a soldier with a thirty-year track record, I wanted to be part of whatever military response America launched. I wanted to be on the battlefield in Afghanistan, doing my part to strike back against this outrageous attack on my country. Still, in the months that followed, I reluctantly accepted that my role was to train and prepare young men and women to go to war.

Soon, though, I began to receive requests—from churches, civic groups, and other private organizations—to speak to civilian audiences, and I saw another role taking shape: to encourage Americans and help them understand this new war. The War on Terror was not a war over money or territory or politics. This was a war over worldviews. One worldview, based in Judeo-Christians beliefs, was that all men are created equal, endowed "by their Creator," as Thomas Jefferson wrote, with the right to be free. The other worldview, based in the teachings of the Q'uran, held that all people on earth were to be subject to Allah and to Sharia law. In this jihadist view, those who refused to bow would be murdered. I had fought murder and oppression on live battlefields all over the world. But since I couldn't go to Afghanistan, I figured this was my battlefield now, enlisting Americans to pray for our country.

In the beginning, I spoke mainly to Christians, at patriotic observances such as Veteran's Day and the Fourth of July. But other groups also invited me and I found myself speaking to mixed-faith groups, including Muslims. I couldn't accept all the invitations because of the clip of operations at the SWC. But I spoke when and where I could, always tailoring my message to the particular audience.

No matter where I spoke, though, the main message I brought my audiences was that America's biggest battle was right here at home against societal enemies, many of them triggered by the so-called Cultural Revolution of the 1960s. The "Revolution"—which depended heavily on a rejection of traditional morality—and often on an outright rejection of God—had broken its every promise. Instead of liberty and equality, it had delivered broken families, irresponsible fathers, impoverished mothers and children, rampant addiction, violence, disease, and death. I asked people to recognize that our country was now locked in a spiritual battle for its own soul.

"Fight with me!" I would say, urging Christian audiences to pray for justice, for the safety of our troops, and for our civilian and military leaders.

As it turned out, there were quite a few folks in influential places who decided that was some kind of war crime.

2

IN JULY 2003, I arrived on the Pentagon's E-Ring as deputy undersecretary of defense for intelligence. I thought it would be my final Army tour. My military career had offered me a way to make a difference, a way to do some good in the world. I had not served perfectly, but with God's help, I had served faithfully. Now appointed by Defense Secretary Don Rumsfeld as a member of the cabinet staff, I looked forward to pouring 100 percent into this last task, then moving on to new callings—teaching or speaking, probably. Maybe both.

I had been tucked into my breadbox office for just a few weeks when I had a visitor, David Martin of the CBS news magazine *60 Minutes*. He sat down across the desk from me. "General Boykin, my wife and I saw a tape of you speaking at an event in Daytona, Florida," he said. "I want you to know that it really motivated us to start going back to church."

I looked at Martin and saw sincerity in his eyes. "Thanks for sharing that, David," I said. "I'm glad to hear it."

"General, I'd like to know if you'd consider letting me do a *60 Minutes* piece on you, a profile focusing on your faith," David said.

I thought about that for a second. The idea of going on a national program to talk about my faith and how it informed my military service was appealing. On the other hand, I had managed to keep my mug out of the news for more than thirty years. It was an unwritten code in the Special Ops community: stay out of the limelight.

"You know, David, I really appreciate your interest, but I don't think I'm ready to do that," I said. "If you wanted to do a larger story about faith with me as just a part, I'd consider it. But I wouldn't want to do a story that's just about me."

"Okay, I can understand that. I appreciate that," he said. Then his face changed, taking on a shadow of worry. "I wanted to ask you one more thing, General. My producer, Mary, has cancer. Would you please pray for her?"

Instantly, I admired him. So many reporters in the Washington press corps seemed cutthroat, just out for the Big Story, and yet David showed this compassion.

"Absolutely," I said. "I'd be honored."

That was in September. The following month, I got a call from a very different reporter, Aram Roston of NBC News, the one who wanted to talk about what a "controversial character" I was.

"They've chosen you to go after these high-profile Islamic figures, and you have a track record of hating Islam," Roston said.

An ironic statement considering that the last operation I'd led was hunting down Goran Jelisic and his Muslim-murdering friends. The conversation deteriorated from there, as Roston, pretending to get my side of a story that in reality had already been written, tallied the "evidence" against me:

> "You've made a statement to a Somali warlord that your God was bigger than his."
>
> "You've made statements like, 'God put George Bush in the White House.'"
>
> "You've said that this is a Christian nation."

And perhaps what Roston considered his most damning evidence: "You're an evangelical."

The next night, I stood in the secretaries' office as NBC News carried its story with Tom Brokaw anchoring: "NBC News has learned that a highly decorated general has a history of outspoken and divisive views on religion, Islam in particular."

As I thought back over my career, about how and when I had lived out my faith in my military service, about where I had served and whom I had fought for and *with*, this characterization stunned me.

Then Lisa Myers broke her big story:

> He's a highly decorated officer, twice wounded in battle, a warrior's warrior. The former commander of Army Special Forces, Lieutenant General William Jerry Boykin has led or been part of almost every recent U.S. military operation from the ill-fated attempt to rescue

hostages in Iran to Grenada, Panama, Colombia, and Somalia...But [his] new assignment may be complicated by controversial views General Boykin, an evangelical Christian, has expressed in dozens of speeches and prayer breakfasts around the country.... NBC News military analyst Bill Arkin, who's been investigating Boykin for the *Los Angeles Times,* says the general casts the war on terror as a religious war.[1]

The next morning, the *Los Angeles Times* story hit. I walked into my office to find it included in the October 16 edition of *The Early Bird,* a compilation of the day's media stories published every morning by Pentagon public affairs. As I began to read, my heart sank:

The Pentagon has assigned the task of tracking down and eliminating Osama bin Laden, Saddam Hussein and other high-profile targets to an Army general who sees the war on terrorism as a clash between Judeo-Christian values and Satan.... [T]he former commander and 13-year veteran of the Army's top-secret Delta Force is also an outspoken evangelical Christian who appeared in dress uniform and polished jump boots before a religious group in Oregon in June to declare that radical Islamists hated the United States "because we're a Christian nation, because our foundation and our roots are Judeo-Christian...and the enemy is a guy named Satan."[2]

Right out of the gate, *Times* reporter Richard T. Cooper got it wrong. It was not my job to track down and eliminate terrorists, and I never saw the war on terror as a "clash" between my values and Satan. I saw it as a clash between God and Satan. And I was not the only one: Islamic jihadists saw it that way, too—except in reverse—with Allah as the true god and America as the "great Satan."

"Boykin's religious activities," Cooper wrote, "were first documented in detail by William M. Arkin, a former military intelligence analyst who writes on defense issues for *The Times* Opinion section." I kept reading:

Discussing the battle against a Muslim warlord in Somalia, Boykin told another audience, "I knew my God was bigger than his. I knew that my God was a real God and his was an idol."

"We in the army of God, in the house of God, kingdom of God have been raised for such a time as this," Boykin said last year.

On at least one occasion, in Sandy, Ore., in June, Boykin said of President Bush: "He's in the White House because God put him there."[3]

Statement after statement, ripped out of context. Now the first hint of anger started simmering in my veins. Yes, I thought the Somali warlord in question—Mohamed Farah Aidid's right-hand man Osman Atto—served an idol: money. Yes, I thought that we "in the house of God"—believing Christians—had been called to battle, but on our knees, as spiritual warriors as the Apostle Paul wrote, to "put on the whole armor of God...take up the shield of faith...and the sword of the Spirit, which is the word of God...with all prayer and supplication."

But juxtaposed with his discussion of a "Christian nation" and the terror war, Cooper made it appear that I was calling all Americans to fight in the "army of God." Meanwhile, he buried a fact that would later be lost as the media painted me a Muslim-hater. Way down in the story, Cooper whispered, "In his public remarks, Boykin has also said that radical Muslims who resort to terrorism are not representative of the Muslim faith."

Cooper's selective reporting and ordering of facts struck me as vintage drive-by journalism, and I was furious. But not as furious as when I read the words of the man behind Cooper's curtain, *Times* "military analyst" William Arkin. In the same edition of the *Times*, Arkin wrote an op-ed in which he revealed that he had been conducting "a monthlong journalistic investigation" of me.

The Times had been investigating me for a month, *and no one from the paper has bothered to call me to get my side of the story?*

At least NBC News had called. Aram Roston hadn't listened to me, but at least he'd gone through the motions. Sitting at my desk, I read on:

Boykin is...an intolerant extremist who has spoken openly about how his belief in Christianity has trumped Muslims and other non-Christians in battle. He has described himself as a warrior in the kingdom of God and invited others to join with him in fighting for the United States through repentance, prayer and the exercise of faith in God....

[W]hen Boykin publicly spews this intolerant message while wearing the uniform of the U.S. Army, he strongly suggests that this is an official and sanctioned view—and that the U.S. Army is indeed a Christian army. But that's only part of the problem. Boykin is also in a senior Pentagon policymaking position, and it's a serious mistake to allow a man who believes in a Christian "jihad" to hold such a job.

For one thing, Boykin has made it clear that he takes his orders not from his Army superiors but from God...[4]

I finished the piece and set *The Early Bird* aside in disgust. I didn't know whose life this clown Arkin had been investigating, but it wasn't mine.

3

LATER THAT MORNING, I had to stand in for Undersecretary Steve Cambone at Secretary Rumsfeld's regular morning meeting with Joint Chiefs Chairman General Dick Myers, Deputy Secretary of Defense Paul Wolfowitz, and the other undersecretaries and support staff.

I had attended many such meetings, but as I waited with the others in the outer office, my stomach churned. Everyone had heard the news. At least one person told me he thought I was getting a crappy deal, though that wasn't the word he used. From Rumsfeld, though, I didn't know what to expect. Would he announce during the meeting that he was removing me as deputy undersecretary pending an investigation?

I didn't think he would. But I wasn't sure he wouldn't.

"Okay folks," Rumsfeld said when we were assembled in his office. "Let's get started."

The Secretary always began that way, very casually. With his size, square jaw, and sheer depth of experience, he was a formidable man. But his manner in these meetings was like a friendly uncle. As always, he had a stack of papers in his hand. Sheet by sheet, he went through the information with us, stopping to ask questions and listen to feedback. Then he wrapped up in the usual way, going around the table, asking us each if we had anything else.

At that point, I realized that the previous night's newscast was not on the Secretary's agenda and I relaxed a little. That let me know that his assessment, initially at least, was that Bill Arkin's allegations were not of serious concern. Still, after we discussed other business, Rumsfeld dismissed his staff and said to me, "You stay here."

He also asked General Myers and Larry Di Rita, his acting public affairs officer, to stay. Rumsfeld then peered across the table at me. "I've got to get to a press conference in an hour. What am I supposed to say about the controversy that started last night about you?"

His attitude was offhand, almost amused. Suddenly, I felt even better.

I hadn't rehearsed an answer to his question, as I hadn't known he'd ask it. But given the opportunity, I really spoke my heart. "Well, Mr. Secretary, first of all, you need to understand that I never cast this war in religious terms. In fact, quite the contrary. I'm on the record, in print, as saying that this is *not* a war between Christianity and Islam. Secondly, I think you need to say that you haven't really heard what I've said. You can't make a statement on something you haven't heard."

"I agree," Myer said. "I think that's the approach you need to take, Mr. Secretary." Di Rita also agreed.

At that time, Rumsfeld was just off the successful campaign against the Taliban in Afghanistan, and still on fairly good terms with the press. Reporters considered him combative and difficult—as did others—but in a likeable, curmudgeonly way. He was quick and blunt and witty. Dick Myers always went to the press conference with him, and that morning, they left the Secretary's office together and headed to the press briefing room.

I went back to my office and tuned into the conference on the Pentagon channel on the same set where I'd watched the NBC broadcast the night before. Within moments, with only one side of the story told and zero response from me, the Washington press corps was calling for my head.

"Would it be helpful to characterize Boykin's statements as 'them against us good Christians'?" one reporter said. "Which is apparently what he is doing."

"Well, see, *apparently* works for you," Rumsfeld said. *"Apparently* doesn't work for me."

The reporter persisted: "But what he's saying seems to be contrary to that policy, appears—"

Again, Rumsfeld cut off speculation. "Okay: *'Appears'* . . . *'Seems to be.'* You do *'appears'* and *'seems to be.'* I don't."

I thought, *This is one tough guy.*

I didn't know why he was defending me the way he was, but I was glad for it. Still reeling from the unfair and untrue accusations leveled at me on national television the night before, I hadn't been certain what the Secretary's reaction would be. I wasn't sure how much the increasing concern in DoD for political correctness would affect his response. But I should have known better: Donald Rumsfeld was focused on the truth—and he didn't know what the truth was yet.

Another reporter piped up: "Why don't you just fire him and then get someone—"

The Secretary cut him off: "This is the most bloodthirsty crowd I have ever seen!"

Asked about my speaking to religious groups while in uniform, General Myers spoke up. "At first blush, it doesn't appear the rules have been broken. The only thing I would say is there is a very wide grey area on what the rules permit."

Myers mentioned a time when he himself had spoken at a Washington prayer breakfast while in uniform. Rumsfeld added that my wearing a military uniform did not erase my First Amendment right to free speech and freedom to practice my religion.

"We're a free people," he said. "That's the wonderful thing about our country."

But it was not wonderful for the free press. Several reporters continued to badger the Secretary into commenting on what they claimed I'd said. He didn't bite.

The lift I felt after Rumsfeld's press conference quickly crashed to earth. For the rest of the day, I couldn't walk by a Pentagon television where some talking head wasn't yapping about the nutball general bent on holy war. The same day, David Martin of *60 Minutes* came to see me again. "The stakes are higher now, General," David said. "Maybe we should think about doing that *60 Minutes* piece..."

I looked into his eyes and thought I saw the opportunity for a fair shake. Still, I didn't feel it had come to that. "David, I'm not ready to talk about this publicly yet," I said.

Looking back on what happened next, that might've been the wrong answer.

4

LATER THAT DAY, my office telephone rang. It was Tom O'Connell, assistant secretary of defense for special operations and low intensity conflicts.

"Hey Jerry, I was just listening to the radio on the way in," he said. "I understand you're being fired."

I sighed and looked out my window at the Potomac. "Tom, maybe you know something I don't, but I haven't been told that."

He didn't. It was more "truth" in media.

As the day progressed, two different people stopped me on the E-Ring to say they'd heard I was resigning.

"No, I'm not resigning," I said.

That afternoon, I met with Larry Di Rita in an empty office with some of the public affairs people. We talked a little about a statement I would release to the media. In it I would apologize for any misunderstanding, any offense I had given.

Then I suggested a second solution. "Larry, why don't I just call for an IG investigation, and see if that will bring some relief?"

"Secretary Rumsfeld is not asking for an investigation," Larry said.

"I know, but I think it might be a good idea. Just get things out in the open, see if I've done anything wrong."

"Okay, but I just want to be clear that the Secretary's not asking for this."

I said I was clear on that, and Larry said he'd call the IG.

When I finally trudged into my own living room that night, Ashley had the evening news on. The anchor was busily repeating the same thing I'd heard over and over all day, what I came to think of as The Big Three: One, my statement that God put Bush in the White House. Two, that I'd said my God was bigger than Atto's god. And three, that I said America's enemy wasn't Osama Bin Laden, but Satan.

And as they had all day, reporters and anchors regurgitated what NBC had reported—no questions asked. That these people, whose stock in trade is supposed to be "facts" would do so without doing even the most basic function of reporting—getting both sides of the story—hit me harder than the triple-A fire in Grenada. I'm not exaggerating. I would rather have taken another .50 cal round.

I couldn't stand to listen to another word. I kissed Ashley and retreated to our bedroom, closing the door behind me. Then I lay down across my bed and considered what was happening. This wasn't some unfortunate rumor in the workplace or a misunderstanding with a neighbor, or even a local news story. I was being portrayed as a lunatic and my humiliation was destined to go *global*.

Soon, I began praying aloud. I was past my usual habit of asking God *why?* Instead another question crept in: How long was this going to last? Suddenly, like a neon sign, the phrase *Psalms 13* flashed into my mind. I had not memorized Psalms 13 and didn't know what it said. But I sat up, grabbed my Bible off my nightstand, and laid it on my lap, letting it fall open to the middle of the book. Paging back a bit, I found Psalms 13.

How long, O Lord? Will you forget me forever?
How long will you hide your face from me?
How long must I take counsel in my soul
and have sorrow in my heart all the day?
How long shall my enemy be exalted over me?

I was astonished to see the prayer I'd just said aloud looking back at me from the pages of this ancient book. In my heart, I felt God was saying to me, "Look, you're not the first man to pray this prayer. I hear you. I'm with you. I have *called* you for this. I have *prepared* you for this. Now get up off that bed, put your armor on, and get back in this battle."

5

ON OCTOBER 18, my son, Aaron, called me at home. "Dad, did you hear what Nina Totenberg said?" Totenberg was a journalist with National Public Radio.

Phone in hand, I sighed. "No. What did she say?"

"She said she hoped you aren't long for this world."

"You're kidding. You mean, like she wants me dead?"

"That's what it sounded like to me."

That's what it sounded like to the host of *Inside Washington*, too. Totenberg made the remark on the program, one of those televised journalist roundtables, this one hosted by a man named Gordon Peterson. Colbert King, a *Washington Post* editorial writer, was there, as was syndicated columnist Charles Krauthammer.

Totenberg said, "Now they've got this guy who's head of the intelligence section in the Defense Department who's being quoted as telling various groups, while he's in uniform, that this is a Christian crusade against Muslims. I mean this is terrible, this is seriously bad stuff."[5]

Bad enough that she had her facts dead wrong. But then Totenberg said, "Well, I hope he's not long for this world because you can imagine—"

Several people spoke at once, interrupting her.

PETERSON: "You putting a hit out on this guy or what?"

KING: "Are you Reverend Pat Robertson?"

TOTENBERG: "No, no, no, no, no, no!"

PETERSON: "What is this, *The Sopranos*?"

TOTENBERG: "In his job, in his job, in his job, please, please, in his job."[6]

That might've been easier to believe if I hadn't found out what Totenberg said on the same program in 1995. After Senator Jesse Helms said he felt a disproportionate share of federal research funding went to AIDS research, Totenberg said, according to the *Boston Globe*, "I think [Helms] ought to be worried about what's going on in the Good Lord's mind, because if there is retributive justice, he'll get AIDS from a transfusion, or one of his grandchildren will."[7]

Apparently it's not okay for a taxpayer-supported general to suggest that spiritual forces are at work in the world, but it's okay for a taxpayer-supported journalist to do so—especially if it's God doing the killing.

Totenberg's *Inside Washington* attack was just part of the national blitzkrieg triggered by William Arkin's report. An editorial in *The Atlanta Journal-Constitution* claimed that "for a ranking military officer, [Boykin's] beliefs are surprisingly benighted."[8]

A letter writer to *The Los Angeles Times* said, "Boykin, for all of his apparent professional skill, shows the markers of a religious fanatic...Let the general retire and find a private pulpit somewhere to preach his intolerant brand of Christianity, and let the fight against terrorism be waged by officials who understand their role and who bother to read the Constitution."[9]

As Arkin's story burned up cable news and then spread to international and Islamic media, few people outside Fox News and conservative talk radio wondered whether an "analyst" who had foamed at the mouth on the editorial page could be trusted to supply objective information for Page One.

I began to wonder: Who is William Arkin?

The first thing I learned was that his qualifications as a "military analyst" seemed pretty thin. Arkin served in the Army for four years during the 1970s. Some bios listed him as a "former military intelligence analyst," but the specifics remained...unspecific. I also learned he is a pedigreed leftist, a former political director for Greenpeace who in 2002, barely a year after 9/11, gave a speech claiming President Bush had declared war on terror in order to "enhance the economic interests of the Enron class." But I had to wait until 2007 for Arkin to fully reveal himself.

That February, on his blog on the *Washington Post*'s Web site, Arkin whined about an NBC story in which some soldiers serving in Iraq expressed frustration with war protests and asked for the support of the American people:

> I'm all for everyone expressing their opinion, even those who wear the uniform of the United States Army. But I also hope that military commanders took the soldiers aside after the story and explained to them why it wasn't for them to disapprove of the American people...[10]

When I read that, I thought, *The soldiers are the American people.* Arkin continued:

> These soldiers should be grateful that the American public...[does] still offer their support to them, and their respect...Through every Abu Ghraib and Haditha, through every rape and murder, the American public has indulged those in uniform, accepting that the incidents were the product of bad apples or even of some administration or command order...[11]

Those behind Abu Ghraib and Haditha were investigated and punished, not indulged. Was Arkin hinting here that Abu Ghraib and Haditha were the American military standard?

> So, we pay the soldiers a decent wage, take care of their families, provide them with housing and medical care and vast social support systems and ship obscene amenities into the war zone for them, we support them in every possible way, and their attitude is that we should in addition roll over and play dead, defer to the military and the generals and let them fight their war, and give up our rights and responsibilities to speak up because they are above society?[12]

Then Arkin refers to the comments of soldiers who, in an NBC report, asked for the support of American citizens as:

> ...an ugly reminder of the price we pay for a mercenary—oops sorry, volunteer—force that thinks it is doing the dirty work...America needs to ponder what it is we really owe those in uniform.[13]

So this is the "military analyst" who engineered the *L.A. Times* hit piece. A man who apparently believes that the American military is riddled with rapists and murderers. Who divides the American people and American soldiers into "us" and "them." Who believes that American soldiers are mercenaries and that despite the Twin Towers, suicide bombers and video-taped beheadings, the terror war is about money.

After a seven-year investigation, I have concluded that William Arkin is an anti-military, leftwing conspiracy nut and a religious bigot. I did not call him to ask whether this is true.

6

AS THE POUNDING IN THE PRESS CONTINUED, the nasty e-mails started rolling in. One person wrote to tell me that I had insulted every Jew in the nation. He went on to say that I should leave the Army, since I clearly did not value soldiers of other faiths. An Arab group sent me a Koran and told me that I was an "intolerant extremist." Many people wrote to Secretary Rumsfeld, urging that I be disciplined or fired.

And as the bullets flew, the firepower of the folks doing the shooting increased. Senate Armed Services Committee Chairman John Warner and Democratic Senator Carl Levin wrote to Rumsfeld, urging him to launch an inspector general probe.

"Remarks by a senior military officer denigrating another religion could be exploited by America's enemies," they wrote, "and even endanger U.S. troops serving in Muslim nations." Had anyone noticed that I hadn't denigrated Islam, but had specifically said *on tape* that a radical wing of Islam was to blame—a wing that was to Islam as the Ku Klux Klan was to Christianity?

Congressmen Barney Frank and John Conyers circulated petitions calling for my ouster. Senators John Kerry and Joe Lieberman, both still vying for the Democratic presidential nomination, trashed me. "Our cause in the war on terror isn't helped when we have army officers like Lieutenant General William Boykin speaking in evangelical churches and claiming this as some sort of battle for the Christian religion," Kerry said. "That's wrong. That's un-American."

If I hadn't been under so much stress, I might have laughed out loud at that one. I guess Kerry felt it was more American to come back from Vietnam and testify to Congress about American war atrocities—testimony that was later shot full of holes.

On Sunday, October 21, national security advisor Condoleeza Rice was asked about me on a national news program. "I think the president is very clear here on what [the president] means here," she said. "This is not a war between religions. No one should describe it as such."

Rice had just put the first measure of distance between me and the Bush administration.

7

I WASN'T SLEEPING MUCH. Each new accusation, each new twist on the truth stacked up on my shoulders like another lead weight. But as I prayed—moaned and groaned to God, really—I sensed Him saying to me, *Lift up your head. Open your eyes and look at what's going on around you.*

When I got my eyes off myself long enough, I realized that I was getting calls and e-mails every day from friends who said, "We're behind you. We're praying for you." Similar calls and letters poured in from my family and church in North Carolina, and from people I had never met before in places all over the world. In the Pentagon, people would walk up to me in the halls and say, "I know you don't know who I am, but I want you to know that I'm praying for you."

I had congressmen calling me to offer private encouragement, including Robin Hayes of North Carolina. "I'm standing with you, Jerry," he told me. "All you need to do is call me."

Twenty-seven members of Congress, both Republicans and Democrats, signed a letter to President Bush saying, in effect, "You need to stand by this man."

Conservative commentators like Sean Hannity, Hugh Hewitt, and Ann Coulter stood with me.

In *WorldNetDaily*, Pat Buchanan wrote, "Lt. Gen. William G. 'Jerry' Boykin, the former Delta Force commander, seems to be exactly the kind of warrior America needs to lead us in battle against the kind of fanatics we face."[14]

But the mainstream media continued their shelling until finally Ashley got fed up. Desperate to let people know what I had really said and what I really stood for, she called Gary Bauer, a Christian activist. He immediately used his radio program and newsletter to urge conservatives to support me.

Then Ashley called Focus on the Family.

We didn't really know anyone there, but when she told the switchboard who she was, they quickly connected her to Focus president James Dobson. After Ashley explained our position, Dobson immediately took up my cause. First, he issued a press release: "Since when does a man not have the right to express his private religious views in the company of fellow believers? Does a man forfeit his freedom of speech when he becomes a military leader?" he wrote, adding that my remarks with regard to spiritual warfare were made to audiences comprised exclusively of Christians who clearly understood the meaning of my message.

The following week, Dobson devoted an entire radio broadcast to my situation. At the end, he urged listeners who wanted to express their support for me to call the White House and the Pentagon. Dobson also provided two telephone numbers, one of which, it turned out, connected callers directly to Don Rumsfeld's office.

Problem was, Dobson has *millions* of listeners. In the first couple of hours after the broadcast, thousands of callers swamped the Secretary's private line. Finally Rumsfeld's junior military aide, Steve Bucci, a Special Forces veteran and a man of strong faith, called Focus.

"First, the Secretary gets the message," Bucci told Focus. "Second, can you please call this thing off? It's kind of an emergency. We've got to be able to keep some lines open to the Secretary's office."

"Sorry," came the message from Dobson: "Once it's out there, I can't turn it off."

8

___

A WEEK LATER, the inspector general's office called me in for questioning. I wound my way from the E Ring to the C Ring, where two guys waited for me in a room with a conference table. Both were civilians and had that tightly wound, self-important "I'm an investigator" air about them—dark suits, white shirts, pagers on their belts. One was dark-haired and heavyset. The other was thin and wiry. The skinny one introduced himself as a lawyer.

We all sat down at the conference table. A microcassette recorder sat in the center of the table. The big guy reached forward to switch it on, and a quiet hiss spun up from the table. Then he read me my rights.

My *rights*. That immediately pissed me off. Not because they did it—I knew they had to, and expected it—but because I was being read my rights over unsubstantiated allegations reported in the media. As though I was a criminal suspect. My anger might have passed, but then the suits started *treating* me like a criminal suspect.

"We've looked at tapes of your speeches," the big guy said. "What do you mean the real enemy of this country is Satan? Who authorized you to wear your uniform while giving these speeches?"

Then Skinny chimed in: "Did you have your JAG review your planned speaking activities?" He meant the judge advocate general, or command attorney, at the JFK Special Warfare Center and School where I had served at the time of my talks.

The interrogation, as I quickly came to think of it, went on for two hours. The big guy kept worrying with the cassette recorder, checking it to be sure the tape was still documenting my evil deeds. I tried not to let my frustration show, but I'm not sure I did a very good job of it.

Finally, Skinny said, "That's all we have for now. We're going to go down to Bragg and speak to some people. We're also going to talk with people at those places where you spoke. We'll contact you when we're ready to talk to you again."

I was dismissed.

On October 28, I watched from the secretaries' office as President Bush held a Rose Garden news conference. He had just returned from a trip to Asia and Indonesia, and was set that night to meet with Muslim leaders at an Iftaar dinner, a breaking of the fast during the Islamic holy month of Ramadan. During the press conference, the president called on reporter Tom Hamburger.

"I wondered if you could tell us your reaction when you encountered Muslim leaders in Indonesia," Hamburger said. "I understand that some of them brought up specific comments made by General Boykin—"

"Yes, they did," the President said.

Hamburger continued: "I wondered if you would address those comments and whether you think that General Boykin ought to be disciplined or resign."

The President didn't answer that last question. Instead, he said three Muslim leaders he met with wanted to know why Americans think Muslims are terrorists.

"My answer was, it's not what Americans think," President Bush said. "Americans think terrorists are evil people who have hijacked a great religion. That's why Mr. Boykin's comments were—General Boykin's comments don't reflect the administration's comments. And by the way, there's an IG investigation going on inside the Defense Department now about that. He doesn't reflect my point of view, or the view of this administration."

I was crushed. How could my commander-in-chief say that to the whole world without first finding out the truth? And how could he spin the IG investigation to make it look like the administration was taking action against me? *I* was the one who requested the investigation.

"Our war is not against the Muslim faith . . . ," the President continued. "We welcome Muslims in our country. In America, we love the fact that we are a society in which people can pray openly—or not pray at all, for that matter."

I had defended that right for more than three decades. I had defended Muslims against their enemies and persecutors in two different countries. And I *never* said or implied that America was against the Muslim faith. Now the President of the United States was reinforcing the idea that I had.

That moment was the lowest of my Army career.

9

THE MEDIA FIRESTORM CONTINUED. On October 31, Bill Press of *WorldNetDaily* joined the ranks of columnists who decided it was acceptable to judge me without getting my side of the story. "A 30-year veteran, Boykin does, indeed, have an impressive resume...The problem is, he comes to his job as an intolerant, religious zealot...Gen. Boykin is the American echo of Osama bin Laden."[15]

Press wasn't alone. By month's end, the American news stories that came out following Arkin's attack were being reported this way: "Gen. Boykin ...has been quoted as saying the war against terrorists, such as those who killed and mutilated U.S. soldiers in Somalia in the name of religion, is a battle between good and evil with terrorists representing 'Satan.'"[16]

The media got a lot of mileage out of the whole "Satan" thing. As soon as you start mentioning Satan, people start calling you a crackpot. It's okay to talk about him at church or a Bible study. But let it come out in the public square that you believe there is a real devil, and people start to wonder whether you're a little odd. And if you take the next logical step—that if there really is a devil, his influence in the world is real—people will put an index finger to their temple and twirl it.

I thought about that a lot. *Am I crazy? Am I the problem?* The crisis caused me to examine my beliefs regarding the God spoken of in Scripture, the same God whom something like ninety percent of Americans say they also believe in. The same Bible that talks about God talks about Satan. Was the Bible some kind of salad bar, where we just pick out the things that make us feel warm and spiritual, and reject the rest?

Apparently, for Arkin and company, believing in God was one thing. But to have Him be *real* in my life as a soldier, and to talk about that publicly, was some kind of war crime.

10

SOON, THANKS TO ARKIN and his media acolytes, more than my career was at stake. The worldwide news stories brought me to the attention of radical Islamic organizations, and information about me started to appear on their Web sites. For example, Adam Pearlman, an American citizen who joined al-Qaeda and now goes alternately by the Islamic names of Adam Yahiye Gadahn or Abu Shhayb al-Amriki, began calling for my assassination.

Another Islamic Web site posted this ominous question: "Does the position of Deputy Undersecretary of Defense warrant a personal protection detail? The discernment at the time of this report is no."

I had faced down violent men before, but another development truly struck fear in my heart: Islamic sites began posting maps to my home, and listing the names of my wife, my son Aaron, and my friends.

In February, the IG investigators called me in for a second interview. We set up in a small conference room again, and the big guy switched on his pet tape recorder. In the three months since we'd last met, both men had received an attitude transplant. And not for the better. Where they had been grim before, now they were overtly skeptical—snide, even.

"Let's talk about this JAG thing again," Skinny said. "We can only find one written opinion from your JAG on your speaking engagements."

"I told you last time that he only issued a couple of written opinions."

"How many different JAGs did you have?"

"Well, see, that's part of the problem," I said. While I was at Special Warfare Center, I had three different JAGs. One left the Army and the guy who replaced him was deployed to Afghanistan. That paved the way for a third attorney—three different JAGs within just a couple of years.

"Hopefully, you talked to all three of them," I said.

"Yeah, we did. But they don't remember any of the details," Skinny said.

"The question is, how much information did you really give them about these speaking engagements?"

Again, they had pissed me off. As though I had been withholding some kind of dark secrets about my speaking on the Fourth of July and Memorial Day at *churches*. I wanted to laugh: The darkest secrets at these very public events were probably what kind of pig parts were in the hot dogs.

"I'm going to tell you again," I said slowly, enunciating each word. "In most cases, I didn't give them much information. That was my secretary's job. She gave the JAG the details, gave him the invitation—"

"That may be part of the problem here," Skinny interrupted. "You didn't give them sufficient information for them to give a legal opinion on what you were doing. Do you have any proof that you told the JAG what these events were about?"

Suddenly it became clear to me that in this room, the principle of *innocent until proven guilty* had been turned on its head. In this room, it was *You're guilty unless you prove you're not.*

I took a deep breath and let it out slowly. "As I have told you before, there were only a couple of times that I personally sat down and talked to the JAG."

Now they zeroed in on a specific event, the patriotic observance in Daytona Beach, Florida—the one where my talk had motivated David Martin and his wife to go back to church. "What made you think you could wear your uniform to this event?"

"It was a public event," I said.

"Do you have any evidence of that?"

"Why don't you call the pastors of the churches that put it on?"

"We have."

Then why are we having this conversation?

The big guy switched horses. "While you were down there, you visited a friend of yours from Special Forces."

"Yes, I did. He works for a company that does simulations and I was running a school that wanted to use simulations. It was a business meeting, scheduled in advance."

Another new horse: "On another trip, you spoke at a church and to a law enforcement group and claimed that was the reason you were there.

We have evidence that the law enforcement speech was an after-the-fact decision."

"There are plenty of people who will provide you with evidence that it was planned ahead of time."

The investigators openly traded disbelieving sneers.

Then Skinny said: "What made you think you could wear your uniform in the church down there?"

It was the third time they'd asked me that and it was the last straw. I stood up, put both hands on the conference table and leaned toward Laurel and Hardy. "I've worn this uniform for thirty-three years," I said, biting off the words. "It's who I am. It's *what* I am. A *soldier.* For you to tell me that we can go out across this country and recruit young men and women to wear this uniform, then send them to war in this uniform, *and send some of them home in body bags wearing this uniform,* but that I can't wear it here in the communities of this country to encourage Americans—that's just something I just can't come to grips with."

The investigators glanced at each other, as if uncertain of which button to push next. Seething with frustration, I stalked to the window. I knew by now that only divine intervention was going to make any difference in this investigation.

Lord, I need Your strength right now, I prayed. *Help me stay calm and speak the truth.*

I glanced back at the investigators. *And, by the way, Lord, a little self-control would also be nice, to help me keep from walking over there and knocking these two clowns out.*

11

ON MARCH 17, one of the investigators called my office. "We have your preliminary report. If you're going to be available, we'll bring it down to you."

"Bring it on down," I said. I knew this was in God's hands and I hoped for the best. But based on the way they had interrogated me, I was leery.

Twenty minutes later, Skinny walked into my office and handed me a thick sheaf of paper tucked into an official-looking gray folder. "These are preliminary findings and you will have the opportunity to rebut them," he said. "You have until April 2 to respond."

"Fine," I said.

He left.

I placed the folder on my desk and opened it. The first words I saw: "We find you in violation of…"

It went downhill from there. My eyes skipped from charge to charge to charge—five in all, including two criminal violations.

Criminal. Numbness spread through my bones.

On three occasions, they said, I had used government money to travel to personal speaking engagements. Also, they claimed I used my aide for personal business and made him travel with me at government expense. Both charges were issues of fraud. I wasn't certain what the legal consequences would be, but I knew I could be demoted, forced to resign my commission, court-martialed, and possibly jailed. Even short of imprisonment, any one of the other options would end my career in utter disgrace.

Clutching the report, I walked out of my office into the admin area.

"Cancel everything on my schedule," I told my secretary. "I've got to go home."

Mind racing, I hurried through the E-Ring corridor and out the Pentagon's River Entrance. I wanted to talk to Ashley. I wanted to pray. I wanted to ask God *where He was*. I burst outside onto the River Entrance landing meaning to head for the parking lot, but saw David Martin standing on the steps taping a segment for his evening broadcast.

Lord, please don't let him see me, I thought. *All I want to do is get out of here.*

I veered off at an angle and took the steps two at a time, hoping David wouldn't notice.

"General Boykin!"

Crap.

"General Boykin!"

Turning to face David, I tried not to look as desperate as I felt. As he walked quickly over to meet me, I saw that a tall, well-dressed woman was following him over.

"General, I'd like you to meet my producer, Mary, the one you've been praying for."

The woman walked up and held out her hand. "Hi, General Boykin," she said with a warm smile. "I'm Mary Walsh. I wanted to thank you for your prayers and tell you that I'm cancer-free. Now, I was wondering, would you pray for my brother? He has inoperable prostate cancer."

Guilt washed over me. I was so wrapped up in my own problems—my career, my reputation—that I forgot that there were plenty of folks with far bigger problems than mine. Life and death problems.

I snapped out of self-pity mode. I felt God speaking to me: *I've got you covered. This woman needs your prayers.*

I told Mary how happy I was that her cancer was gone and promised to pray for her brother. We chatted for a couple more minutes then I drove home. Holding the report, I headed up to my bedroom to pray. When I had first received it, all I wanted to do was get alone and wrestle with God over it—all day and all night if that's what it took to deal with my despair. Now, though, I thought of Mary, free of cancer. I thought of her brother, facing death.

Sitting on my bed, I held the report. God had been with Mary. He would be with her brother. He would be with me. I thought about my life, my career. I had never rolled over for anyone. Not for Noriega, Escobar, or Aidid. Not for war criminals. Not for terrorists. I wasn't going to start now. The Special Forces creed calls soldiers to rely on the "help and guid-ance of God." Also, it says, *never surrender.*

I looked down at the report. "Lord, I don't understand this," I said aloud, "but it's in Your hands."

Then I got up and went straight back to work.

12

THAT NIGHT, ASHLEY AND I WENT TO CHURCH. We sat on the back row during the Spanish language service and prayed together. Afterward, a woman stopped us in the narthex. "Sir, I don't know who you are and I don't know what you're going through, but I believe I'm supposed to tell you something," she said.

"You don't know who I am?" I said. With jihadists eight thousand miles away issuing death threats against me, that was hard to believe.

"I've seen you in church, but I work for the Department of Energy and I'm on the road a lot. In any case, I believe I am supposed to tell you that you're going to be exonerated."

Ashley and I looked at each other, astonished.

"You really don't know what I'm going through?" I said to the woman.

"Sir, I have no idea."

Still shaking our heads, Ashley and I walked out to the car. During the drive home, my cell phone rang.

"Jerry! Sorry to call you so late, buddy." It was a friend of mine whom I hadn't heard from in six months.

"That's okay," I said. "I'm on my way home from church."

"Me, too. Listen, at our prayer meeting tonight, my pastor told me to tell you something."

"What?"

"You're going to be exonerated."

I looked over at Ashley, eyes wide. "That's amazing," I said to my caller. "Someone in church just told me the same thing."

Fifteen minutes later, I pulled into our driveway on Fort Myer. When I walked in my front door, the phone was ringing.

I picked up the cordless handset. "Hello?"

"Jerry? It's Gordon." A dear friend for more than a decade.

"Hey, Gordon. What's up?"

"Brother, I've been praying and I believe I've got a message for you."

"Let me guess: I'm going to be exonerated."

"How in the world did you know that?"

"You're the third person to tell me that in the last twenty minutes."

13

THE NEXT DAY WAS A THURSDAY. By the time I got home from work, I had made a decision.

"I'm not going to rebut the charges," I told Ashley. We were standing in the kitchen.

"What?" she said, taken aback. "You *have* to rebut."

"I don't *have* to..." I had put the IG report in God's hands, I told her.

"Jerry, you owe it to everyone who has prayed for you and stood by you. You have to make sure the truth comes out."

That stopped me in my tracks, and I started thinking about it. Maybe she was right. We decided to ask our pastor, Wendell Cover, and he agreed: "You have to rebut this, Jerry," he told me. And for the same reason Ashley gave: "The people who supported you need to know the truth."

I decided to listen to the counsel of my pastor and my wife. And once I made the decision to rebut, I went about it as though preparing for battle. I called the people who had coordinated several of the events where I had spoken and got statements from everyone who had heard me give a disclaimer. I had churches send me materials showing that events where I spoke were open to the public. I received photographs of posters advertising events to entire communities. At one time, the investigators had accused me of taking money for speaking, so I obtained statements showing that I never once was paid. I got copies of invitations and letters proving that I'd been asked to appear in uniform. I got brochures of programs that clearly showed other speakers. Finally, I got a statement from my former secretary avowing that she was the one who submitted invitations to the JAG and received legal approval for every event where I'd spoken.

I submitted my rebuttal in April. Collectively, my evidence proved I had not been out pressing some personal anti-Islam agenda, but only speaking at patriotic, open events that also featured other invited guests—or speaking at churches to exclusively Christian audiences. I think the Constitution calls that freedom of association and religious exercise.

14

IN MAY 2004, news broke about prisoner abuse at a prison outside Baghdad called Abu Ghraib. It would become one of the most embarrassing episodes in the U.S. Army experience in Iraq: Using physical cruelty and sexual humiliation, a handful of poorly led and unsupervised soldiers brought worldwide scorn on the American military, overshadowing the heroism and dedication of the men and women serving in the war on terror.

Incredibly, critics began to speculate that I had ordered the abuse.

I was "the heart of a secret operation to 'Gitmoize' the Abu Ghraib prison," former Clinton advisor Sidney Blumenthal wrote in *Salon* magazine. "He had flown to Guantanamo, where he met Major General Geoffrey Miller, in charge of Camp X-Ray. Boykin ordered Miller to fly to Iraq and extend X-Ray methods to the prison system there, on Rumsfeld's orders."

The headline on Blumenthal's piece was "Smiting the Infidels." He, along with other writers wearing tinfoil hats, seemed to reason that since it was a well-known "fact" that I hated Muslims, the abuses at Abu Ghraib were my way of vicariously seeking revenge. The facts, however, were different. First, Geoff Miller is one of the most honorable men I've ever served with. If anyone *had* ordered him to do such a thing, he'd have seen to it they were court-martialed. Second, in sworn congressional testimony, Miller stated that he neither spoke to me before he went to Iraq nor after he returned. In fact, the decision to send him to Iraq occurred before I ever arrived at the Pentagon.

Still, the leftwing blabocracy spun the story that I had dispatched Miller to Iraq to teach Lynndie England how to hold a leash. The truth, apparently, was optional.

15

BY JUNE, I still hadn't heard anything from the IG about my rebuttal. But one evening, a friend who was, as they say, "in a position to know," called me at home.

"Your rebuttal was so powerful they had to start all over," he said.

"What do you mean?"

"They had to start a new investigation," he said. "They had to start over from square one."

Finally, in late June, Skinny, the lawyer from the IG's office, came down to see me. Though my source had given me reason for hope, my experience with Skinny said that bad things tended to happen when he appeared.

He sat down across from me. I thought I detected a self-satisfied look on his face. "We've been reviewing everything very carefully," Skinny began. "We're adding a new charge. You went to a men's conference in Toronto. You had a plane ticket bought for you and you didn't report it on your financial disclosure."

What? "I specifically talked to the JAG about that," I objected. My JAG had approved both the Toronto ticket and a follow-on flight.

"Oh, that's not the problem," Skinny said. "The problem is you didn't list it on your disclosure form."

That was the moment my fuse ran out. I had proven their charges wrong so now they were picking me apart to save face. This wasn't even an issue of reimbursement or using government travel money or concealing a gift. It was a typographical omission on a legal and approved action, a missing entry on a form that was of zero consequence.

I looked Skinny straight in the eye. "I want to see the inspector general."

"That's not going to be allowed," he said as though I had asked for an audience with the Pope. "No one sees the IG directly. That's just not done."

I pressed forward. "I think you are holding me to a standard of proof that does not apply to everyone. I want to see the IG. In person."

"It's not going to happen," Skinny said. He seemed determined not to be the first to look away.

I leaned across the desk and said very carefully, "I am sending you an e-mail with my request and I want it forwarded to the IG. Now, let me suggest that you take your paperwork and get out of my office."

Never surrender.

16

IN CHURCH ABOUT A WEEK LATER, a friend of mine, Victor Filaye, a Nigerian dentist, walked up to me. "I was praying for you this morning," he said. "God impressed upon me that I needed to pray for a Gamaliel for you."

Gamaliel was a man who lived during the time of Jesus's apostles and the early church. When the apostles were on trial for heresy and about to be railroaded to a guilty verdict, Gamaliel reasoned with their accusers.

"Thank you, Victor," I said.

The next morning, I was walking down the E-Ring corridor, when I glanced into the open door of an office. A man in there was in the middle of a conversation and as I passed, he happened to turn and look out.

"General Boykin?"

I stopped and turned around. The man had stepped out into the hall.

"Yes," I said.

"I'm Joe Schmitz, the Department of Defense inspector general."

That knocked me for a loop. Instantly, I wondered whether he knew I had asked to see him.

Schmitz smiled. "General, I just want to assure you that I have read every word of your rebuttal and that I will ensure you are treated fairly," he said.

I could hardly believe what I'd just heard. As I watched Schmitz walk away down the corridor, I thought: *That's Gamaliel.*

17

IN EARLY AUGUST, I was in Germany on NATO business when a Pentagon number rang on my cell phone. It was Larry Di Rita's deputy, a public affairs officer named Bryan Whitman.

"General, the IG's final report is in."

I was standing in a hotel room in Stuttgart. It had been nearly a year since I had been caricatured as the lunatic, holy-war general. Because of a "journalist" with an agenda, my name had become globally synonymous with "religious nut." Worse, in Middle Eastern countries, I had become a target, a wanted man.

"As soon as it's released to you," Whitman went on, "they'll release it to Senator Warner and the Armed Services committee, then probably to the press."

Senator Warner was one of the Democrats who asked the President to fire me. Still, as I held the phone, I felt strangely confident. *There are two possibilities*, I thought. *They either found nothing, or something insignificant.*

"Have you seen a copy of the report?" I asked.

"Yeah, I've got it right here."

"What does it say?"

"It says you sometimes didn't provide a disclaimer when you spoke..."

Meaning I hadn't said every time that my speech represented only my personal views and not those of the government.

"....You didn't clear your talks with public affairs, and you didn't list your airplane ticket to Toronto."

In an instant, the cloak of dread I'd been wearing for nearly a year dropped away and relief surged through me. These were minor infractions—the result of oversights despite my best efforts to follow the rules. In fact, Whitman said, the IG found that I had made "good faith" efforts to have my activities reviewed and approved by my legal counsel.

"Basically," Whitman told me, "they've exonerated you."

18

THAT DIDN'T MEAN THE PRESS GAVE ME A BREAK. After the Pentagon released the report, typical newspaper headlines said, "Report finds general broke rules" and "Wrist slap for general." (As though Skinny and the boys had given me the old wink and nod.) Among major newspapers, only the *Washington Times*, under the headline "General cleared in church speeches case," put the IG report in its proper context:

> The Pentagon inspector general did not substantiate complaints that Lt. Gen. William G. Boykin misused his Army uniform, violated travel regulations or used improper speech when he addressed 23 church groups on his views on faith and warfare. Investigators also found Gen. Boykin did not improperly accept speaking fees.... [T]here was no finding that Gen. Boykin in any way violated expense-account rules. In fact, the Pentagon encourages private groups to reimburse military personnel for speaking-engagement expenses.
>
> One official, who asked not to be named, said the disclaimer violation was nit-picking because the topic of his speeches was his faith, not Pentagon policy. And, the rule on getting after-hours speeches approved beforehand by public affairs is so obscure that officials could not remember the last time such a case arose.[17]

Another Pentagon source told the *Washington Post* that the report was a "complete exoneration."[18]

Back in Washington later in August, David Martin came to see me. "Now that this is behind you, would you do the *60 Minutes* piece?" he asked.

I said I would. And on September 11, 2004, Ashley and I appeared on the program. Mary Walsh, David's colleague who beat cancer, produced the piece. It was the first time I'd gotten to tell the world my side of the story, what I'd really said, and as importantly, what I'd really meant. And once I did, everything just stopped. The hammering, the badgering, the jeering in the editorial pages.

It all just stopped.

By then, of course, I'd had plenty of time to think about how unfair it had all seemed. I thought many times that if I could quickly exfiltrate into obscurity, I would have. Looking back over my life, there were many times when I wanted to give up. During Delta selection, when I fell into that freezing creek and lost the feeling in my feet, I really thought maybe I ought to just stop and build a fire and let them find me. After Mogadishu, my personal sense of loss and failure was so great that I considered quitting the Army. After my divorce, I just wanted to quit life altogether.

But I knew people were pulling for me, praying for me. And in those trials and others, God constantly reminded me of His presence. I had to get beyond not only my own weakness, but also my own strength and learn to rely on Him alone. It was God who sustained me through three decades of defending this country. It was God who gave me the courage to face death in order to rescue others.

It was God I had relied on when I nearly lost an arm in battle.

It was God I prayed to when my men went to war.

It was God I cried out to when they returned maimed and bleeding.

And when they didn't return at all.

When I stood at pulpits and podiums rallying Christians to pray and encouraging non-Christians to stand strong for America, I was honest about all that. I declared the truth of this country's Judeo-Christian heritage, a truth reflected in our founding documents and reaffirmed by the Supreme Court in 1991. I declared the truth that the jihadists want Christians and Americans dead. And I declared the truth of God's sovereignty over man's affairs in war and peace and even in the White House.

For that the media branded me "an intolerant extremist" and turned me into a global target.

So, yes, during my year of public humiliation, I reflected on the unfairness of it all. But then I thought about Bill Garrison, who has a homespun saying on fairness that reflects his Texas outlook on life: "If you think the world will treat you fairly because you're a nice person, then you probably think a bull won't charge you because you are a vegetarian."

That really summed it up for me. And as I thought more about the way things unfolded, I saw that some of my statements, when taken out of context, could easily have been misunderstood. Still, by and large, my audiences knew exactly what I was saying: that the battle of this age, the battle sparked on 9/11, is a spiritual war, a war of good against evil, a war of Islamic jihadists against all of us.

The left can scream all it wants that the war on terror is about oil or American imperialism or George W. Bush's personal amusement. That if we weren't such big, bad bullies, the poor third world jihadists wouldn't have attacked us, and the French would like us better.

But we are not the bad guys. Our motto is life and liberty. The jihadists' motto is convert or die. And no matter how much the PC crowd would like to deny it, the inalienable right to liberty that America is fighting for is part of the Judeo-Christian heritage that is the bedrock of our nation. As Thomas Jefferson wrote, the right to liberty comes from *outside* us, planted in our hearts by our Creator, making it not merely an American ideal, but a *human* ideal.

America is a melting-pot society. We speak many languages, and respect many cultures and religions. But every man, woman, and child deserves the freedom endowed by their Creator.

That's why America's cause is just. That's why we're the good guys. And that's why we will never surrender.

Notes

A Medal and a Body Bag

1. Col. Charlie A. Beckwith and Donald Knox, *Delta Force: The Army's Elite Counterterrorist Unit* (New York: Avon, 1983), 144.

Merry Christmas, Noriega

1. Kurt Muse and John Gilstrap, *Six Minutes to Freedom* (New York: Citadel Press, Kensington, 2006), 36–38.
2. Ibid, 39.
3. Ibid, 39.
4. Ibid, 104.
5. Ibid, 106.

Drug Lords and False Prophets

1. Mark Bowden, *Killing Pablo* (New York: Penguin Books, 2001), 118.
2. Ibid, 23.
3. Ibid, 80–81.
4. Ibid, 63.
5. Ibid, 69.

Crucible

1. "Journalists Rebuke Army General's Christian Views as 'Divisive.'" Media Research Center, online at http://www.mediaresearch.org/cyberalerts/2003/cyb20031017.asp#1.
2. Richard T. Cooper, "General Casts War in Religious Terms," *Los Angeles Times*, October 16, 2003.
3. Ibid.
4. William M. Arkin, "The Pentagon Unleashes a Holy Warrior," *Los Angeles Times*, October 16, 2003.
5. "Totenberg on Gen. Boykin: 'I Hope He's Not Long for This World.'" Media Research Center, online at http://www.mediaresearch.org/cyberalerts/2003/cyb20031020.asp#1.
6. Ibid.
7. Jeff Jacoby, "Hate speech of the left," *Boston Globe*, December 28, 2003, online at http://www.boston.com/news/globe/editorial_opinion/oped/articles/2003/12/28/hate_speech_of_the_left/.

8. Cynthia Tucker, "Put Boykin on inactive duty," *Atlanta Journal-Constitution*, October 26, 2003.

9. Jan C. Gabrielson, "Apology didn't diffuse the controversy," *Los Angeles Times*, October 22, 2003.

10. William M. Arkin, "The troops also need to support the American people," washingtonpost.com, online at http://blog.washingtonpost.com/earlywarning/2007/01/the_troops_also_need_to_support.html.

11. Ibid.

12. Ibid.

13. Ibid.

14. Patrick J. Buchanan, "A Christian warrior under fire," *WorldNetDaily*, October 27, 2003, online at http://www.worldnetdaily.com/news/article.asp?ARTICLE_ID=35281.

15. Bill Press, "Backward Christian Soldier," *WorldNetDaily*, October 31, 2003, online at http://www.worldnetdaily.com/news/article.asp?ARTICLE_ID=35362.

16. R. Jeffrey Smith and Josh White, "General's speeches broke rules; report says Boykin failed to obtain clearance," *Washington Post*, August 19, 2004.

17. Rowan Scarborough, "General cleared in church speeches case," *Washington Times*, August 20, 2004.

18. R. Jeffrey Smith and Josh White, "General's speeches broke rules; report says Boykin failed to obtain clearance," *Washington Post*, August 19, 2004.

Bibliography

The authors consulted the following sources in reconstructing and ensuring the accuracy of historical events recounted in this memoir.

Books

Beckwith, Col. Charlie A., and Donald Knox. *Delta Force: The Army's Elite Counterterrorist Unit*. New York: Avon Books, 1986.

Bowden, Mark. *Black Hawk Down*. New York: Penguin, 1999, 2000.

Bowden, Mark. *Guests of the Ayatollah*. New York: Grove Press, 2006.

Bowden, Mark. *Killing Pablo*. New York: Penguin, 2001.

Carney, Jr., Col. John T., and Benjamin F. Schemmer. *No Room for Error: The Covert Operations of America's Special Tactics Units from Iran to Afghanistan*. New York: Ballantine Books, 2002.

Landau, Alan M. and Frieda W.; Terry Griswold and D.M. Giangreco; and Hans Halberstadt. *U.S. Special Forces: Airborne Rangers, Delta, & U.S. Navy Seals*. Osceola, WI: MBI Publishing, 1999.

Muse Kurt, and John Gilstrap. *Six Minutes to Freedom*. New York: Citadel Press; Kensington, 2006.

Web Sites

Accounts of Special Operation at Panama and Grenada were researched at http://www.specialoperations.com.

The transcript of the NBC News broadcast on pp. 13–14 and 315–316, and the Nina Totenberg interview on page 324 were retrieved from the Media Research Center at www.mediaresearch.org.

The account of the Battle of Ia Drang Valley on page 33 is online at http://en.wikipedia.org/wiki/Battle_of_Ia_Drang.

The war crimes of Goran Jelisic recounted on page 297 are documented in "Jelisic Case: Summary of the Judgment" by International Criminal Tribunal for the Former Yugoslavia (ICTY), online at http://www.un.org/icty/brcko/judgement/jel-tresj9912e.htm. Jelisic was sentenced to forty years in prison for his crimes.

About the Authors

LTG (Ret.) William G. "Jerry" Boykin spent over 36 years in the U.S. Army. He served most of that time in Special Operations; including the Delta Force, Rangers, and Special Forces. He also served a tour at the Central Intelligence Agency and retired in June 2007 after serving his last four years in uniform as Deputy Undersecretary of Defense for Intelligence.

Lynn Vincent, coauthor of *New York Times* bestseller, *Same Kind of Different as Me*, is a U.S. Navy veteran and features editor at WORLD Magazine where she covers news, politics and current events. She lives in San Diego, California, with her husband and their two children.